Microsoft 365 Certified Fundamentals MS-900 Exam Guide

Expert tips and techniques to pass the MS-900 certification exam on the first attempt

Aaron Guilmette
Marcos Zanre
Yura Lee

BIRMINGHAM - MUMBAI

Microsoft 365 Certified Fundamentals MS-900 Exam Guide

Copyright © 2020 Packt Publishing

Commissioning Editor: Pavan Ramchandani
Acquisition Editor: Heramb Bhavsar
Content Development Editor: Aamir Ahmed
Senior Editor: Hayden Edwards
Technical Editor: Jane Dsouza
Copy Editor: Safis Editing
Project Coordinator: Manthan Patel
Proofreader: Safis Editing
Indexer: Pratik Shirodkar
Production Designer: Deepika Naik

First published: February 2020

Production reference: 1210220

Published by Packt Publishing Ltd.
Livery Place
35 Livery Street
Birmingham
B3 2PB, UK.

ISBN 978-1-83898-217-1

www.packt.com

Subscribe to our online digital library for full access to over 7,000 books and videos, as well as industry leading tools to help you plan your personal development and advance your career. For more information, please visit our website.

Why subscribe?

- Spend less time learning and more time coding with practical eBooks and Videos from over 4,000 industry professionals

- Improve your learning with Skill Plans built especially for you

- Get a free eBook or video every month

- Fully searchable for easy access to vital information

- Copy and paste, print, and bookmark content

Did you know that Packt offers eBook versions of every book published, with PDF and ePub files available? You can upgrade to the eBook version at www.packt.com and as a print book customer, you are entitled to a discount on the eBook copy. Get in touch with us at customercare@packtpub.com for more details.

At www.packt.com, you can also read a collection of free technical articles, sign up for a range of free newsletters, and receive exclusive discounts and offers on Packt books and eBooks.

Contributors

About the authors

Aaron Guilmette, a technical specialist at Microsoft, provides guidance and assistance to customers adopting the Microsoft 365 platform. He primarily focuses on collaborative technologies, including Microsoft Exchange and Teams, but also works with identity and scripting solutions.

He has been involved with technology since 1998 and has provided consulting services for customers in the commercial, educational, and government sectors internationally. Aaron has also worked in technical certification exams and instructional design for Microsoft and other organizations.

Aaron lives in Detroit, Michigan, with his five kids. When he's not busy solving technical problems, writing, or running kids to events, he's likely making a pizza.

I'd like to thank my children for putting up with me while I tackled this project, which isn't relatable to anyone except people in this field. Specifically, I'd like to thank:

> *Liberty, for corralling her brothers and sisters*
> *Hudson, for keeping me updated on The Mandalorian*
> *Glory, for cleaning up dinners so I could get back to writing*
> *Anderson, for filling in the gaps that Hudson skipped over*
> *Victory, for her general cuddliness*

I'd also like to give a special shout-out to tacos, pizza, and Coke Zero. Without you, this endeavor would likely not have succeeded.

Finally, I'd like to thank Microsoft for continuing to make products that empower all of us to do more—even if that means taking tests.

Marcos Zanre is a program manager for Microsoft Teams and has been working for Microsoft for 8 years (and counting), supporting strategic customers in their adoption of Microsoft Teams, following best practices and fostering industry scenarios, including empowering mobile workers and creating or migrating existing lines of business applications into Microsoft Teams. Before that, he worked for 6 years as a technical specialist for Microsoft 365, supporting the assessment, acquisition, and adoption of cloud services for commercial and government customers.

He is passionate about company collaboration, enterprise social networks, modern intranets, mobile productivity, low code/no-code solutions with the Power Platform, process automation, and mobile and web app development. Marcos lives in São Paulo, Brazil, with his wife, and he loves to play guitar and have barbecues with his friends and family.

Yura Lee is a technical specialist at Microsoft with an Office 365- and Azure-consulting background. Today, she focuses on guiding and assisting customers in understanding the full potential of Microsoft Teams. Yura works with the whole collaborative stack, including Exchange Online, SharePoint Online, Teams, Flow, and security components such as Intune and Microsoft Information Protection.

Yura lives in New Jersey with her family. In warmer weather, she and her boyfriend are most often exploring Italian restaurants and seeking out great IPAs in the greater tri-state area. In the winter, she's staying in, hosting dinners for her friends.

First, we want to thank our friends and family who suffered through this labor of love. Writing a book frequently means putting other things in life on the back burner, and without our support networks, this book would not have been possible.

We also want to acknowledge the staff and editorial team at Packt (specifically Heramb, Divij, Aamir, and Hayden) for both giving us an opportunity to write and shepherding us through this process.

The technical reviewers (Sara and Alan) are seldom thanked for nitpicking an author's work or splitting hairs in code samples, and this book will be no exception.

Yura and Marcos would like to specifically shout out Aaron Guillmette, for the support and opportunity. Thank you!

Finally, we would like to acknowledge our dedicated team of peers at Microsoft who develop amazing products, empowering all of us to be better at everything we do.

About the reviewers

Sara Jardim Barbosa is an MCSE, MCP and has cleared all Office 365 exams. She is currently working as a Microsoft 365 Administrator and has over 5 years of Microsoft 365 experience. In 2012, she was awarded the Microsoft MVP for her contributions to the Brazilian BPOS, Office 365, and SharePoint communities. Since then, she frequently speaks at Microsoft 365, Power Platform, and SharePoint conferences around the world.

Alan Nicholls is a technical specialist at Microsoft, supporting and guiding his customers through their transitions to not only Office 365 but Microsoft cloud telephony. He has an extensive background in the industry, from starting a phone company in 2005 to being a senior consultant, working with Exchange, Azure, Active Directory, storage system, networking, data center operations, and migration services. He has worked with government, automotive, manufacturing, legal, medical, and non-profit organizations, ensuring they have the best tools and solutions for their organization. Alan lives in southern Florida, where you can find him in his office/lab, under a hood in his garage, at the beach, or up in an airplane.

Packt is searching for authors like you

If you're interested in becoming an author for Packt, please visit `authors.packtpub.com` and apply today. We have worked with thousands of developers and tech professionals, just like you, to help them share their insight with the global tech community. You can make a general application, apply for a specific hot topic that we are recruiting an author for, or submit your own idea.

Table of Contents

Preface

Microsoft 365 is the premier collaboration and business productivity platform. It is made of up dozens of integrated **Software-as-a-Service (SaaS)** applications, including Exchange Online, SharePoint Online, and Microsoft Teams. Microsoft also offers a full range of cloud data center and development products, made available on the Azure platform. Together, the Microsoft 365 and Azure platforms are used by millions of users and businesses every day to enhance communications, build relationships, connect communities, and create new products.

This book, *Microsoft 365 Certified Fundamentals: Exam MS-900 Guide*, is designed to help you understand key cloud computing concepts and how those concepts are represented across the Microsoft 365 platform.

This book will focus on the following key areas:

- Cloud computing concepts
- Windows 10 services
- Messaging, collaboration, and communication services available in Microsoft 365
- Licensing
- Service-Level Agreement concepts

The MS-900 exam focuses on the basic concepts and interdependencies between these services. This book will help you understand the basics of identity and authentication in Azure Active Directory as well as ways to secure the identity platform. This book will also help you enumerate the core services of the Microsoft 365 platform and the competitive advantages and features over the on-premises counterparts of these products.

By the end of this book, you'll not only be equipped to pass the exam but also to confidently articulate the features that make the Microsoft 365 platform compelling for business collaboration.

Who this book is for

Microsoft 365 Certified Fundamentals: Exam MS-900 Guide is targeted at Microsoft 365 service administrators and cloud technologists who want to prove their knowledge by passing the MS-900 certification exam. The qualified exam candidate should be able to demonstrate foundational knowledge of cloud concepts and the Microsoft 365 suite. Mastering the concepts tested in this exam provides a solid stepping stone to other more advanced Microsoft certifications. You can learn more about this exam at `https://docs.microsoft.com/en-us/learn/certifications/exams/ms-900`.

What this book covers

`Chapter 1`, *Introduction to Cloud Computing*, begins by explaining the foundational cloud computing concepts and the benefits that customers can expect to take advantage of.

`Chapter 2`, *Cloud Deployment Models and Cloud Services*, expands the reader's knowledge into areas such as public versus private clouds and the differences between software-as-a-service and infrastructure-as-a-service.

`Chapter 3`, *Core Microsoft 365 Components*, explains the basics of what makes up the Microsoft 365 suite.

`Chapter 4`, *Comparing Core Services in Microsoft 365*, compares the cloud SaaS components against their on-premises counterparts.

`Chapter 5`, *Understanding the Concepts of Modern Management*, provides an introduction to deployment and management options for Windows 10.

`Chapter 6`, *Understanding Office 365 ProPlus*, introduces the Click-to-Run software deployment and servicing method for the Office application suite.

`Chapter 7`, *Understanding Collaboration and Mobility*, dives into how some of the Office 365 services work together as well as how the Enterprise Mobility + Security Suite can be used to protect an organization's assets.

`Chapter 8`, *Microsoft 365 Analytics*, discusses analytics and usage reporting across the Microsoft 365 suite.

`Chapter 9`, *Understanding Security and Compliance Concepts*, introduces core security concepts such as users, groups, attributes, permissions, roles, and auditing capability inside the Microsoft 365 suite.

Chapter 10, *Understanding Identity Protection and Management*, explores key features of the Enterprise Mobility + Security suite and how they can be used to manage and review access to Microsoft 365 resources.

Chapter 11, *Endpoint and Security Management*, provides an overview of security features that can be used across Active Directory and Azure Active Directory plans.

Chapter 12, *Service Trust Portal and Compliance Manager*, discusses tools Microsoft provides for helping customers track and organize compliance activities as well as for gathering supporting documentation.

Chapter 13, *Licensing Options in Microsoft 365*, introduces the licensing and acquisition process for Microsoft 365, as well as key selling points of the platform.

Chapter 14, *Planning, Predicting, and Comparing Pricing*, gives the reader tips on conducting a cost-benefit analysis of Microsoft 365 services versus traditional on-premises services.

Chapter 15, *Support Offerings for Microsoft 365 Services*, provides guidance on how to obtain support as well as the service-level agreements for Microsoft 365 services.

Chapter 16, *Service Life Cycle in Microsoft 365*, discusses the various release stages of products in the Microsoft 365 service and how they relate to support policies.

To get the most out of this book

The Microsoft 365 platform is best experienced with either a laptop or desktop computer running a modern operating system, such as Windows 10 or macOS X 10.12 or later. Additionally, modern browsers such as Microsoft Internet Explorer 11, Microsoft Edge, or a current version of Chrome, Safari, or Firefox are necessary for the Office 365 portal user interface to render properly. Older versions of Microsoft Internet Explorer may not work correctly.

An Office 365 tenant will also be required to follow along with some of the configuration examples. You can sign up for a trial tenant (no credit card required) at `https://www.microsoft.com/en-us/microsoft-365/business/compare-more-office-365-for-business-plans`. Some configuration options will require an Azure AD Premium subscription, which you can obtain as part of a Microsoft 365 trial or by activating an Azure AD Premium trial within the Azure portal (`https://portal.azure.com`) once you have obtained a trial Office 365 tenant.

Some examples may require various tools, such as the SharePoint Online Management Shell (`https://www.microsoft.com/en-us/download/details.aspx?id=35588`), the Microsoft Teams module (`https://www.powershellgallery.com/packages/MicrosoftTeams/1.0.3`), or the Office Deployment Tool (`https://www.microsoft.com/en-us/download/details.aspx?id=49117`).

Get in touch

Feedback from our readers is always welcome.

General feedback: If you have questions about any aspect of this book, mention the book title in the subject of your message and email us at `customercare@packtpub.com`.

Errata: Although we have taken every care to ensure the accuracy of our content, mistakes do happen. If you have found a mistake in this book, we would be grateful if you would report this to us. Please visit `www.packtpub.com/support/errata`, selecting your book, clicking on the Errata Submission Form link, and entering the details.

Piracy: If you come across any illegal copies of our works in any form on the Internet, we would be grateful if you would provide us with the location address or website name. Please contact us at `copyright@packt.com` with a link to the material.

If you are interested in becoming an author: If there is a topic that you have expertise in and you are interested in either writing or contributing to a book, please visit `authors.packtpub.com`.

Reviews

Please leave a review. Once you have read and used this book, why not leave a review on the site that you purchased it from? Potential readers can then see and use your unbiased opinion to make purchase decisions, we at Packt can understand what you think about our products, and our authors can see your feedback on their book. Thank you!

For more information about Packt, please visit `packt.com`.

Introduction to Cloud Computing

1

Microsoft 365 Certified Fundamentals: Exam MS-900 Guide is for individuals looking to understand and prove their foundational knowledge of the considerations and benefits of cloud services and cloud models. This exam goes into the details of Microsoft 365 as a **Software-as-a-Service (SaaS)** model, its implementation options, and its benefits. To cover all the topics of the MS-900 exam, this book will start by discussing cloud computing concepts. It is critical to understand that cloud computing is essential not only for everyday use but it also has potential on an enterprise-level for the following:

- Microsoft 365 and its core services
- Security and compliance
- Privacy and trust
- Support and pricing

This foundation will also set readers up for success in further certifications, should you choose to take more related technology exams. After going through this book, readers will be well positioned to not only pass this exam but, more importantly, also demonstrate basic knowledge of the Microsoft 365 platform.

First, we will start with cloud computing, such as how cloud computing is already part of your daily personal use. Then, we will expand to enterprise scenarios.

In this chapter, we will cover the following topics:

- What is cloud computing?
- Benefits of cloud computing
- Uses of cloud computing

On to the basics!

What is cloud computing?

Cloud computing is everywhere. You use it on a daily basis for personal use—we can explore this a little bit, but we will also discuss cloud computing on an enterprise level. By the end of this chapter, you'll be able to clearly explain the benefits of cloud computing and provide some real-life examples. Microsoft 365 is an example of cloud computing. But before we discuss all that, we should explain what cloud computing is first.

The concept of cloud computing has been evolving over decades to help everyone, from daily, personal use cases to those of businesses.

Originally, you could think of cloud computing as the shared computer infrastructures on college campuses. Students and faculty would use dumb terminals to connect to a mainframe or minicomputer, and each user would share the resources of a large system. In today's terms, though, **cloud computing** refers to using internet-connected devices to consume services provided elsewhere, typically in some sort of shared environment.

A few years ago, you might have used portable USB devices or an external hard drive to store or back up your documents, pictures, or music files. That way, you have your files with you if you are carrying that physical device. Devices with large storage capacities or small physical devices generally cost significant amounts of money, but they have fallen in price over the years.

Now, you may use a cloud storage space such as a OneDrive account for documents, images, and other files. You may be using a certain amount of storage at no cost, and perhaps you have the ability to purchase more at a small price. Cloud capabilities allow you to eliminate the need for physical storage items such as hard drives. As long as you are connected to the internet, you are able to access your data.

Let's switch gears to the enterprise level and see how cloud computing fits there. Cloud computing allows users to access applications and data quickly and efficiently using a service provider's data storage space and computing power. When a service provider builds out a network of computing devices, storage, or applications, a customer can pay to use these resources instead of having to build an infrastructure of their own. You could say that it is like the customer renting these resources from the service provider. Microsoft Azure is an example of **Infrastructure as a Service (IaaS)**, where customers can build entire computing environments using the service provider's hardware, software, network, and storage resources.

Once built, a user can access these resources from anywhere, using any supported internet-connected device. Cloud computing allows organizations to outsource operational tasks such as updating servers and maintaining storage to service providers.

Now that you have a solid idea of cloud computing, let's explore its benefits in the next section. Understanding the benefits of cloud computing will strengthen your core concepts for the exam and will help you answer MS-900 exam questions that may come up.

Benefits of cloud computing

You can see how cloud computing helps reduce costs in maintaining your own personal files and data, while also making it easier to access. Now imagine that on the enterprise level, where an **Information Technology (IT)** department has to support thousands of users and their data. IT departments have a lot more to worry about than just cost and accessibility. Companies use a lot of applications and data as integral parts of their operations.

In fact, important data assets such as **Personally Identifiable Information (PII)** in healthcare companies or **intellectual property (IP)** can make up a lot of an organization's data. Therefore, it is absolutely critical that all of the business' requirements are met. Cloud service providers build infrastructure to address these important needs and considerations.

Cloud computing provides a lot of benefits to an organization. It can be any of the following:

- Cost-effective
- Scalable
- Quick
- Reliable
- Secure
- Current

Let's take a look at each benefit in more detail.

Cost-effective

In many cases, cloud services can help save a lot of operating IT costs. Usually, businesses allocate a budget on a yearly or fiscal basis. This may or may not work out, depending on market changes or large unplanned increases or decreases in business volume. Since Microsoft is a subscription-based service, it is easy to predict how your business expenditure may increase or decrease based on the number of users for whom you need to purchase licenses.

Business expenditures typically fall into two categories: **Capital Expenditure** or **Capital Expense (CapEx)** and **Operational Expenditure** or **Operational Expense (OpEx)**. CapEx is an upfront cost, such as purchasing a server, a desktop computer, or a network switch. Capital expenditures are frequently physical items.

OpEx, by contrast, is ongoing or recurring costs, such as maintenance or subscription fees, or other operating costs, such as electricity. MS-900 will have questions about both types of expenditure, so make sure you are familiar with this vocabulary.

In terms of cloud services' cost-effectiveness, consider this: on-premises infrastructure requires purchasing and maintaining capital expenses such as hardware, building space, security systems, and a host of other items. To that, add other operational expenses, such as engineers, consultants, and project managers, that are necessary to support the infrastructure. Organizations frequently experience difficulty determining how much equipment to purchase, especially if their business model has large activity swings. An organization might have to purchase an incredibly expensive and powerful system to ensure they can meet a peak demand or load situation that might only occur once a month or once a quarter, resulting in a system that will likely sit underutilized much of the time.

If you want to fulfill a demanding need with a cloud services model, you can rent capacity from a provider as you need it. With a subscription such as Microsoft 365, if your organization brings on seasonal workers, depending on your license agreement with Microsoft, you may be able to increase or decrease the number of licenses as your headcount changes. You're only paying for what you need.

Scalable

Cloud service providers typically allow you to immediately increase or decrease resources or services depending on demand.

Let's look at some examples:

- You host a website and, based on your usage metrics, you know that the busy time is 9 AM-5 PM during weekdays. During the weekend, however, it is much less active. In this instance, you want to make sure you have enough servers to support your website visitors during the specific busy times. You also want to decrease the server capacity outside of the busy hours. With the scalability of cloud services, you can meet the demand quickly and flexibly while maintaining minimal cost during off-peak times.

- You own a retail sporting goods store. You have estimated that you will need 10 seasonal workers on the floor to help with shoppers' demands. All of your staff need basic email, so you choose to provide everyone with Microsoft 365 Firstline Worker licenses. But because it is colder than usual, your store is busier and now you need to hire more workers. You can simply add additional F1 licenses to provide the new hires with email.

In both of those examples, you can use the flexibility of cloud services to scale to meet your organization's demand.

Quick

Scalability is a key differentiator of cloud services, but it's not very useful if it can't fit your business's schedule. It's critical to be able to *quickly* scale up or down:

- Cloud services enable you to quickly scale up your demand for website hosting resources to meet your peak load times and also allow you to scale down when you don't need the capacity. This frees your organization from having to spend capital on server, storage, or networking equipment.
- As your organization needs an email for additional staff, you can quickly add licenses in the Microsoft 365 admin portal and have mailboxes available for them almost immediately.

The speed of the scalability is an important factor in evaluating cloud services for your organization.

Reliable

As a consumer, you expect services you access on the internet to be accessible when you want them. As a business customer, you demand reliability for your cloud services to ensure that your organization can continue to operate fully, whether that's internal operations, hosting e-commerce sites, or another public-facing service.

Resiliency, recoverability, and disaster recovery are high priorities in a cloud service provider's infrastructure design, which is why providers typically rely on a blend of highly available infrastructure designs. These architectures can include network load balancing, data replication, redundant hardware, multiple network paths, and data backups. In addition, service providers also publish Service-Level Agreements that outline their commitments and responsibilities in this regard (for more on Microsoft 365's Service Level Agreements, see `Chapter 16`, *Service Life Cycle in Microsoft 365*).

To read more about Office 365's Data Resiliency policies and procedures, please visit
`https://docs.microsoft.com/en-us/office365/securitycompliance/office-365-data-resiliency-overview.`

When looking for cloud services providers, ensure your service providers have committed to providing a level of availability that meets your business requirements.

Secure

Security in this context addresses multiple concerns, both physical and logical.

From a physical security perspective, cloud service providers equip their datacenter facilities with hardware such as cameras, gates, locks, and equipment cages. They'll also implement personnel and procedures, such as guards and identification verification, to ensure only people who require access are allowed in the facilities.

 You can learn more about the security measures Microsoft implements at its datacenter facilities at
`https://docs.microsoft.com/en-us/azure/security/fundamentals/physical-security.`

Just as importantly, computing service providers secure electronic data. To ensure the utmost security, providers implement multiple layers of logical security, including secure protocols and encryption to protect data that is both at rest (sitting on physical media) and in transit (as it is being transmitted between endpoints). These security measures help prevent unauthorized access to data. In the event of breaches of physical security, cryptographic technologies can be used to prevent attackers and thieves from being able to access the contents of stolen equipment.

 Microsoft uses multiple logical security layers to protect data on disks and other media, as well as data being transmitted between servers, datacenters, and end users. You can learn more about the security tools Microsoft uses in its environment at
`https://docs.microsoft.com/en-us/office365/securitycompliance/office-365-encryption-in-the-microsoft-cloud-overview.`

Current

Cloud services are evergreen, meaning they are constantly under development and improvement. Both security updates and feature updates are constantly developed and deployed. In more traditional on-premises approaches, you might be waiting for security updates to be deployed on monthly, quarterly, or even yearly rhythms. Rather than waiting for the release of a security or feature update, spending the resources deploying said update, and then testing it, cloud service customers can focus on other operations, knowing that their environment is being maintained as part of their provider's commitment.

Features or new tools are made available to customers automatically, rather than having to go through the process of reviewing, deploying, and potentially integrating features.

When using cloud computing services, organizations can spend more of their valuable resources driving or transforming the business, as opposed to *just keeping the lights on.*

We've gone through the six main benefits of cloud computing: cost-effectiveness, the ability to scale, speed, reliability, security, and always being current with the latest releases. In the next section, we'll look at using some use cases for cloud computing.

Uses of cloud computing

While we covered the benefits of cloud computing, you probably already started thinking of some use cases from your personal life, such as email or social media.

Let's start with a basic one from earlier: storing your personal files in a cloud storage service such as OneDrive. Some of these storage services are integrated and included with a purchase of a phone, while others may come with a subscription. Here, as mentioned before, you are not spending money on a physical space to store these files; you are paying (or have paid) someone else to hold them for you. The benefits to you include costs and security: you don't have to buy or configure any extra equipment, it is inexpensive, and you can leverage password or identity protection to keep your files safe.

Audio and video streaming services are another great use case for cloud services. Consumers gain access to millions of songs, movies, and television shows for a low monthly or yearly cost. When an artist releases new tracks or a new episode of the latest television program becomes available, the consumer's subscription allows them access with no additional cost, as long as they are connected to the internet.

This type of service highlights several benefits: the cloud streaming service is always current with the latest content, the service scales automatically to accommodate both the growing amount of media as well as the increased number of subscribers without any effort or increased investment from the consumer, and the services are available on demand. Spotify, Amazon Prime Music, and Apple iTunes are all examples of cloud media streaming services.

For cloud computing examples in enterprises, let's look at use cases for a cloud service such as Microsoft 365. Suppose an organization onboards 20 or 30 new employees at the same time. In the on-premises architecture world, this might mean having to procure additional storage for both business and business files as well as the capacity for email. As a cloud service solution, Microsoft 365 allows you to scale quickly and efficiently. IT administrators can provide these mailboxes and storage resources by simply assigning licenses. The organization doesn't need to go through a lengthy procurement cycle for datacenter equipment to help support the new employees, this is all handled by the service provider. Cloud services can be advantageous to businesses from the perspective of being able to deploy services and resources more quickly by leveraging the investments, capabilities, and expertise of vendors.

 You can see even more potential use cases and examples of cloud computing at
`https://azure.microsoft.com/en-us/overview/examples-of-cloud-computing/`.

We've covered three different examples of cloud computing, from relatable, everyday personal use to business scenarios. They reiterate the fact that cloud computing is everywhere. These use cases are helpful to really solidify your understanding of cloud computing.

Summary

In this chapter, we answered the question of what cloud computing is. Cloud computing allows you to access data, either your own or your work, from any device, including your phone, tablet, or computer. We looked at the benefits of storing information this way and linked these benefits to a variety of popular use cases. We've also very briefly covered the power of Microsoft 365 as a business-oriented cloud computing service. It's critical to have this foundational understanding of cloud computing as it will help you answer cloud-related questions that may come up in MS 900.

In the next chapter, let's continue exploring basic cloud concepts by discussing the different types of clouds, including public and private clouds. We'll also examine different types of cloud services available, such as SaaS and IaaS.

Questions

Use the following questions to test your knowledge of this chapter. You can find the answers in *Assessment Answers*.

1. Microsoft 365 is primarily an example of what kind of cloud computing?
    1. IaaS
    2. PaaS
    3. SaaS
    4. AaaS

2. Identify three of the benefits of cloud computing.
    1. Scalable
    2. Current
    3. Outdated
    4. Cost-effective
    5. Interactive
    6. Free

3. Identify two examples of capital expenditures.
    1. Microsoft 365 subscription
    2. Desktop computer
    3. Electricity
    4. Network cable

4. Identify two examples of operational expenses.
    1. Microsoft 365 subscription
    2. Desktop computer
    3. Storage maintenance fee
    4. Storage area network system

5. CapEx generally refers to:
    1. Capital expenditure
    2. Captain extra
    3. Capture extended
    4. Capital execution

6. When talking about cloud services, what does the term "scalable" mean?
    1. Able to build models.
    2. Able to add or reduce service capacity on demand.
    3. Able to resize organizational data structures.
    4. Services are deployed in a redundant manner.

7. Identify three components that can contribute to a cloud service's reliability.
    1. Redundant hardware
    2. Multiple network paths
    3. Data backups
    4. Hybrid technologies
    5. IaaS
    6. Identity-based security
    7. Identity as a Service

2
Cloud Deployment Models and Cloud Services

In Chapter 1, *Introduction to Cloud Computing*, we introduced cloud computing, along with some of its basic concepts and benefits, as well as real-life examples and use cases. Now, we'll go a bit deeper by starting to examine the different types of cloud deployment models and cloud services that are available.

We will cover three different deployment models: private, public, and hybrid. The goal is to understand the differences between the three, as well as the specific advantages of each. We will explore the three service model types and examine their differences and use cases. The goal here is to understand each of these model types and then be able to explain them at a high level. Specifically, we'll look at these industry-standard models and see that Microsoft has offerings that fit into each of those categories.

Then, we will discuss Microsoft 365 in depth and you'll be prepared to identify where Microsoft 365 fits into an organizational strategy from the perspective of both cloud deployment and cloud service models. Finally, you will also be given the opportunity to answer questions that may show up on the MS-900 exam.

In this chapter, we will explore the following topics:

- Cloud deployment models
- Cloud service scenarios

Cloud deployment models

When designing a technology strategy for their organization, business and technology architects need to choose where to invest their resources. Cloud deployment models answer the question *where will we place our resources?* Hardware, such as servers, storage appliances, and network devices, all have to physically exist *somewhere*. When choosing a deployment model, architects also need to think about other aspects, such as serviceability and supportability, physical and logical security, redundancy and disaster recovery capabilities, business continuity concerns, ease of use, and performance.

Customers need to decide where they are going to put their equipment, which in turn defines where they will be storing their business-critical or potentially sensitive information. There isn't a one-size-fits-all design. Fortunately, there are several options, and organizations can choose the deployment model that makes the most sense for their business. Organizations typically choose from three options:

- **Public cloud:** This means using infrastructure and services provided by an external vendor.
- **Private cloud:** This means building and maintaining infrastructure on their own.
- **Hybrid cloud:** This means utilizing a combination of public and private cloud solutions.

In this section, we will explore each of those models more closely and identify the advantages and disadvantages of each.

Public cloud

Organizations can choose to leverage a public cloud to help achieve their business goals. A public cloud means that a service provider is responsible for provisioning, supplying, and maintaining resources such as application servers, networking hardware, and storage. There are public cloud options for specialized purposes, such as manufacturing resource planning and general ledger accounting, as well as more general purposes, such as file storage or email.

With public cloud solutions, you don't typically own anything except the actual data. You will probably share resources with others in some form of a *multi-tenant* configuration. Multi-tenant configurations function much like an apartment or office building: everyone shares the same physical building, but each person or business has a small space allocated that they rent. To translate this to cloud computing services, the service provider's infrastructure is the building, and your business's configuration and data are the office spaces.

One of the primary benefits of a public cloud solution is that you are dividing the cost of the resources between all of the other organizations using the service. Because you are sharing resources with others, you're not responsible for the large capital expenditure required to procure equipment or software, nor are you responsible for deploying, troubleshooting, or updating the shared resources. Competition incentivizes service providers to provide redundancy and fault tolerance—features and capabilities that may cost organizations significantly were they to deploy and manage them themselves.

Public cloud solutions provide a lot of the benefits that we discussed in the previous chapter, including scalability, agility, and reliability. In public cloud deployments, the service provider takes on the risks and responsibilities of the system, and the customers pay a subscription fee that's typically proportional to their usage of the service. Service providers use their scale to obtain pricing benefits and discounts in purchasing and can invest in the expert, specialized talent required to support the platform. The subscribers are then able to focus more of their investment on their core business instead of investing in people to maintain infrastructure.

Looking back at the office building or apartment models, building maintenance is handled by the owner of the building as part of the lease; each business with office space has access to that specialized staff as opposed to having to hire and maintain their own building specialists. Public cloud solutions work in much the same way.

Microsoft's Azure and Office 365 platforms are examples of public cloud platforms.

 To read more about the public cloud, please visit https://azure. microsoft.com/en-us/overview/what-is-a-public-cloud/.

Some organizations, however, have certain requirements or internal policies that might not allow them to use public cloud services. In those cases, private clouds are an alternative.

Private cloud

A private cloud essentially means that users connect to a restricted or secured private internal network. When an organization deploys a private cloud to meet their business objectives, they are responsible for virtually everything, from the disks that are used in the servers to network cables, switches and routers, firewalls, servers, storage appliances, and applications to the support staff, maintenance agreements for software and hardware, and building contracts.

When building and deploying a private cloud solution, you have the ability to restrict access to this private internal network to only employees or business partners. This level of control is a draw for many organizations. One of the benefits beyond access control and overall ownership is the ability to support unique business needs, such as legacy applications or particular regulatory and compliance requirements. With a private cloud solution, you control the storage of all the sensitive data in a data center you manage and you can maintain physical access to it—something that isn't typically allowed with public cloud services. Private cloud deployments allow you to have much more control over your environment. You can implement an unlimited number of security procedures and protocols, and you can customize as much as you need, as long as your budget allows for it.

Some of those advantages, however, can also become drawbacks. For example, owning your hardware and software means you have the utmost physical control over it. It also means that you must secure the upfront financing and purchase the equipment and support contracts, which can influence your ability to deliver the finished product to your organization. Depending on your organization's timelines and objectives, you may need to budget time for internal procurement, external financing, delivery, installation, and configuration.

Outside of the physical procurement and deployment concerns, you also need to consider security requirements when building private cloud solutions. If your organization doesn't already have security access controls, protocols, and technology, you may need additional investment in remote access and networking technologies. If your private cloud will communicate externally with partners, vendors, or customers, you may also need to expand your network communications capacity with additional circuits, as well as staff or consulting resources to design and implement both the policies and technology.

Availability and redundancy are two additional key concerns for private cloud solutions that organizations must consider. If the private cloud is going to house business-critical data for supporting operations, you'll likely need to evaluate, purchase, and configure options for fault tolerance inside your data center, as well as geographically separated sites to ensure business operations continue in the event of localized outages or disasters.

Financial, healthcare, and public safety organizations have frequently decided to use private cloud solutions. They typically cite regulation and compliance requirements. Some municipalities and public sector organizations have data residency requirements (geographic requirements pertaining to the storage of data) that they feel can more easily be met with private cloud solutions.

To read more about private cloud architectures, please visit `https://azure.microsoft.com/en-us/overview/what-is-a-private-cloud/`.

Most organizations, however, don't exclusively use public *or* private cloud solutions. They rely on a combined approach, called a *hybrid cloud*.

Hybrid cloud

The hybrid cloud combines the ideas of both public cloud and private infrastructure. With hybrid cloud solutions, organizations link their private cloud infrastructure with that of the public cloud service providers. In this scenario, organizations can have data residing in either cloud and, in some cases, have the ability to shift data and services between environments.

Properly designed and implemented hybrid cloud environments can create a seamless experience for users.

A common use of the hybrid cloud is to store non-sensitive data in a public cloud service while storing business-critical or sensitive customers in a private cloud infrastructure. Being able to use both of those services together can provide an advantage for organizations and can allow them to use the benefits of both cloud models. It's a model that can be used to save costs on general services (such as email) while introducing an organization to cloud services. The sensitive or critical line of business apps with more strict requirements can be kept on-premises or in a private cloud infrastructure until such time as a cloud model can meet business requirements.

If configured appropriately, organizations can slowly transition on-premises or private cloud workloads to a public cloud service with little or no service interruption. Organizations can also start new projects in a cloud service or platform and leave their legacy private cloud or on-premises infrastructure in place rather than migrating, letting it retire, or decommissioning it when it is no longer valuable or useful.

While being able to bridge the public and private cloud models has some advantages, it does introduce complexity. Having applications, services, or data split between two locations can introduce confusion and can be a disadvantage for hybrid cloud customers. This complexity can affect both the user and administration experiences, so it's important to architect hybrid cloud solutions in a way that directs users and administrators to the correct resources.

Check out the following link for more information on hybrid clouds: https://azure.microsoft.com/en-us/overview/what-is-hybrid-cloud-computing/.

Microsoft Azure has hybrid cloud options as well, which you can read about at https://azure.microsoft.com/en-us/overview/hybrid-cloud/.

There are several examples of hybrid cloud solutions, such as when an organization is starting to use a cloud service such as Microsoft Teams for collaboration, but also continuing to store and manage documents using an on-premises SharePoint Server 2010 environment. In this scenario, users have to be aware of which data is stored in which service and how to navigate to each service, as there's no direct integration between them. Another example might be an organization that is slowly transitioning on-premises mailboxes to a service such as Microsoft Exchange Online. In this scenario, however, the experience has been designed to be seamless for end users. Whether they are using Microsoft Exchange Server on-premises or Exchange Online, their desktop client is able to locate the appropriate services behind the scenes.

Now that we've now discussed the three different cloud deployment models (public, private, and hybrid), we can move on to the different types of cloud service scenarios.

Cloud service scenarios

The *Cloud deployment models* section answered the question *where are we going to deploy our resources?* In this section, we'll address the question *what type of resources are we going to use?*

Cloud computing services generally come in four forms:

- **Infrastructure as a Service (Iaas)**
- **Platform as a Service (PaaS)**
- **Software as a Service (SaaS)**
- **Serverless**

Your computing needs will drive what type of services you choose. Frequently, solutions can be built from any or all three types of services. It's important to identify what parts the organization wants to own or manage, what type of development the organization wants to do, and where the different points of responsibility will be.

This section will help you understand the types of services available. Knowing the capabilities and of each will help you choose what is right for your business needs.

IaaS

All services (whether public or private cloud, hosted or on-premises) require a combination of computing power, network connectivity, storage resources, and applications. At its most basic level, you need a way to host the servers that run your apps, a way to connect your servers to each other, and the storage medium where your data resides.

Iaas is a model that allows you to configure those resources in the cloud. The following diagram depicts the core pieces that an IaaS offering typically provides—namely, the physical aspects of data center infrastructure:

(Source: `https://azure.microsoft.com/en-us/overview/what-is-iaas/`)

Every environment has IT infrastructure-networks, firewalls, data centers, servers, and buildings. An organization's IT department is typically responsible for most of this. When using traditional on-premises or private cloud deployment models, organizations typically have their own hardware, and provision real or virtual server infrastructure to help support their applications and services.

When using an IaaS platform, the IT staff are responsible for maintaining network connectivity to the IaaS service platform and the virtual infrastructure provisioned in the IaaS platform. The organization is no longer responsible for the physical hardware that hosts virtual machines or applications. In fact, with some IaaS service providers, even the operating system updates are handled by the IaaS platform.

Organizations might choose an IaaS scenario because they have custom-developed applications that they want to deploy without having to invest in their own equipment or because the application they want to use doesn't have a public cloud service offering available. Customers can use IaaS to build entire data centers, complete with virtualized servers and applications, and manage configuration settings at a very fine-grained level.

For more information on the fundamentals of IaaS, visit `https://azure.microsoft.com/en-us/overview/what-is-iaas/`.

IaaS is frequently used to provide disaster recovery or site resilience at a low cost since it doesn't require upfront investment to obtain equipment. Customers also frequently use IaaS environments for development and testing scenarios due to the ability to rapidly redeploy virtual infrastructure as necessary. Other popular uses for IaaS include the following:

- High-performance computer clusters or grid computing
- Website hosting
- File storage
- Big data analytics with custom tooling

Microsoft Azure Virtual Machines (`https://azure.microsoft.com/en-us/services/virtual-machines/`) is an example of an IaaS product. In some cases, however, organizations don't want or need to manage the underlying virtual hardware and networking. That's where PaaS can help.

PaaS

PaaS is a slightly abstracted environment for developing and deploying cloud-based applications. In a PaaS model, the cloud service provider will provide all things IaaS plus operating systems, middleware, and development or runtime tools that are necessary.

PaaS can be valuable to developers within an organization since the platform can provide services such as database management, development tools, scheduling, load balancing, and business analytics. Depending on the type of PaaS being used, developers may not need to be familiar with scaling or redundancy and availability concepts, as they might be managed by the service provider.

You can see in the following diagram how PaaS provides a superset of features to IaaS. PaaS offerings include everything from IaaS, and then typically add operating system management and automation, deployment, and development tools. The following diagram illustrates the features of PaaS:

https://azure.microsoft.com/en-us/overview/what-is-paas/

The application development life cycle includes stages of building, testing, and deploying. PaaS enables developers to shorten their release cycles by utilizing tools that have already been made available on the platform.

Some popular use cases for PaaS include the following:

- **Multi platform testing**
- **Analytics**
- **Sophisticated development tools**
- **Integrated Development Environment** (**IDE**) to support rapid build and deployment

 For more information on PaaS, visit https://azure.microsoft.com/en-us/overview/what-is-paas/.

Microsoft Azure Kubernetes Service (https://azure.microsoft.com/en-us/services/kubernetes-service/), Azure Cognitive Search (https://azure.microsoft.com/en-us/services/search/), Content Delivery Network (https://azure.microsoft.com/en-us/services/cdn/), and App Service (https://azure.microsoft.com/en-us/services/app-service/) are examples of some of Microsoft's PaaS offerings.

While IaaS and PaaS offer a lot of functionality, there are also scenarios where it doesn't make business sense to deploy and maintain infrastructure and applications. SaaS, another type of service, solves that problem by providing ready-to-use environments and services that organizations can start using immediately, with little or no configuration. Let's discuss SaaS.

SaaS

With both IaaS and PaaS offerings, organizations have a lot of fine-grained control over the building, configuration, and deployment of infrastructure and applications. With SaaS applications, all of those management pieces are further separated from administrators and users.

SaaS products are fully deployed applications that are updated and managed by the service provider. When using SaaS applications, administrators usually don't have as many configuration tools available to them. The boundaries of what they can manage are well defined by the service provider. SaaS builds on the services offered by the provider. In the following diagram, you can see how now even the delivery of applications is managed by the cloud service provider.

To know more about SaaS, visit `https://azure.microsoft.com/en-us/overview/what-is-saas/`.

Users need an active internet connection to access these SaaS applications.

In the previous chapter, we identified a few types of cloud services (such as OneDrive and Spotify). These are examples of SaaS applications. As a user of the system, there is no way to control the amount of storage or networking allocated, nor can you update the infrastructure. Users connect to those services using a web browser or application on their devices and can only consume or create within the boundaries that the application allows.

Microsoft 365 is another example of a SaaS application. When users connect to the internet to access email with Microsoft 365, the Exchange Online SaaS application is responding. Microsoft 365 exemplifies the cloud service benefits outlined in the previous chapter: only the exact amount of service required is purchased, and the service provider is responsible for the maintenance of the application and its underlying hardware components. As a subscriber, the fee covers the servers, storage, and networking needed to provide the service.

 For more information on SaaS, please visit `https://azure.microsoft.com/en-us/overview/what-is-saas/`.

While the Microsoft 365 suite is an example of SaaS, each of its constituent applications (Office Online, Power Automate, and Teams) is *also* an example of SaaS.

Finally, we'll tackle the newest entry in the cloud services scenarios: serverless computing.

Serverless

Serverless computing is a bit of a misnomer. After all, the code and applications your business requires still have to run on *something*. With serverless computing, developers are fully isolated from the concepts of hardware and operating system management. Instead, the platform itself handles the dynamic provisioning and allocation of resources.

With serverless computing, code can be directly deployed to runtime environments without the developer having to manage anything except their code. Similar to other cloud service models, such as IaaS or PaaS, serverless computing offers organizations pay-per-use capabilities in an extremely cost-efficient model.

With IaaS or PaaS, you may pay to have environments running, even though they might not be fully utilized. Serverless computing, on the other hand, can frequently be purchased at a per-execution level, meaning that if your application isn't processing, it's not accruing costs.

Microsoft Azure Functions (`https://azure.microsoft.com/en-us/services/functions/`) and Amazon Web Services Lambda (`https://aws.amazon.com/lambda/`) are two commercial examples of serverless computing.

Depending on business requirements, organizations may wish to leverage one or more of these cloud service scenarios.

Summary

In this chapter, we covered the three types of cloud deployments (public, private, and hybrid) as well as the four types of cloud service scenarios (IaaS, PaaS, SaaS, and serverless).

Knowing the difference between the private and public cloud, and the advantages of them both in a hybrid deployment, is critical to helping organizations identify the best possible solutions. Furthermore, understanding the capabilities of each of the four cloud service models is also critical. Mapping business requirements to IaaS, PaaS, SaaS, and serverless technologies can help organizations leverage each service appropriately and return the most value.

In the next chapter, we will start exploring Microsoft 365's core services, such as Exchange Online and Teams. We will go over its features and administrative and end user experiences.

Questions

Use the following questions to test your knowledge of this chapter. You can find the answers in *Assessment Answers*.

1. Identify the three types of cloud deployment models.
    1. Private cloud
    2. Functional cloud
    3. Hybrid cloud
    4. Hosted cloud
    5. Public cloud
    6. Serverless cloud

2. In which deployment model is the customer organization responsible for acquiring, provisioning, configuring, and maintaining equipment?
    1. Paas
    2. IaaS
    3. Private cloud
    4. Public cloud
    5. Serverless computing
    6. Functional computing

3. In which deployment model does the customer lease compute, networking, and storage resources?

    1. Public cloud

    2. Private cloud

    3. Network cloud

    4. Serverless cloud

4. Identify three cloud service scenarios.

    1. IaaS

    2. SaaS

    3. Serverless

    4. Network cloud

5. Identify three cloud service scenarios.

    1. SaaS

    2. Hybrid cloud

    3. PaaS

    4. Serverless

6. Azure Functions are an example of what type of cloud service?

    1. SaaS

    2. IaaS

    3. PaaS

    4. Serverless computing

7. Microsoft 365 is an example of what type of cloud service?

    1. SaaS

    2. Serverless computing

    3. PaaS

    4. IaaS

8. Virtual machines are an example of what type of cloud service?

    1. SaaS

    2. Serverless computing

    3. PaaS

    4. IaaS

9. OneDrive is an example of what type of cloud service?
    1. SaaS
    2. Serverless computing
    3. PaaS
    4. IaaS

10. What type of cloud deployment model uses a mix of private and public clouds?
    1. Serverless computing
    2. Hybrid cloud
    3. Relational cloud
    4. Containerized cloud

11. Identify two benefits of SaaS.
    1. The cloud solution provider is responsible for managing application and software updates.
    2. The customer connects over the internet.
    3. The customer is responsible for allocating hardware resources.
    4. The customer only pays for what they use.

12. Identify two popular uses of IaaS.
    1. Disaster recovery
    2. Serverless computing
    3. Multi-platform development
    4. High-performance compute clusters

3
Core Microsoft 365 Components

In `Chapter 2`, *Cloud Deployment Models and Cloud Services*, we covered high-level cloud computing concepts, deployment models, and the different categories of services available. MS-900 primarily focuses on Microsoft 365, which is one of Microsoft's SaaS cloud offerings. If that still seems unclear, it's a good idea to go back to the first two chapters to brush up.

The objective of this chapter is to understand the core technologies that make up Microsoft 365. In the exam, you might run into a variety of terms and product names, including *Exchange Online, SharePoint Online, Teams, Stream, Office 365 ProPlus, Forms, Flow* (now called *Power Automate*), or *Yammer*. All of those products are part of a broader suite called *Office 365*.

Added to that are products such as *Intune, Azure AD Premium*, and *Azure Information Protection*. Together, these products make up another suite: *Enterprise Mobility + Security,* or *EMS*.

Finally, there's *Windows 10 Enterprise*, the flagship desktop operating system.

These three products together (Windows 10, Office 365, and EMS) make up **Microsoft 365**.

In this chapter, you will deep dive into these technologies, and learn about five core service offerings that comprise Microsoft 365. You will need to know these well in order to pass the MS-900 exam.

In this chapter, we will cover these core services of Microsoft 365:

- Windows 10 Enterprise
- Exchange Online
- SharePoint Online
- Teams
- Office 365 ProPlus
- Enterprise Mobility + Security

By the end of this chapter, you will be able to articulate all of the core services that make up Microsoft 365. It's important to have a solid understanding of the product suite—not only for the exam, but also to understand the value proposition of the platform as whole. This chapter will help you navigate through the different technologies that make up Microsoft 365 and understand their benefits.

Understanding Windows 10 Enterprise

Windows 10 Enterprise is a core component of Microsoft 365. Windows 10 is Microsoft's latest **operating system (OS)**. There are several different editions, including Home, Education, and Enterprise (as well as a few more, depending on your organizational vertical or country). In this book, we will focus on the Enterprise edition, as that is the edition of the product included as part of Microsoft 365.

Windows 10 Enterprise is the most current OS and is designed to be the best fit for mid- to large-sized organizations. It brings three very important improvements for both the IT administrators and the end users:

- Management
- Productivity
- Security

Let's look a little deeper at each of these areas.

Management

With Windows 10 Enterprise, managing hundreds (or even thousands) of devices has become significantly easier. IT administrators have the flexibility to customize the OS and secure corporate identities and applications using Azure Active Directory. Devices running Windows 10 can be managed through Intune (part of the EMS suite) or Microsoft **System Center Configuration Manager (SCCM)**.

Intune is Microsoft's cloud-based mobile device and application management platform. We'll go deeper into Intune in `Chapter 7`, *Understanding Collaboration and Mobility*. SCCM (now a part of Microsoft Endpoint Configuration Manager) is an on-premise solution for managing devices such as servers, desktops, and mobile devices. Administrators can also use the platform to deploy software and updates as well as collect system and application inventory. SCCM can also manage the health of a device or an application by leveraging native telemetry data.

In the previous versions of Windows, major OS updates were released on a yearly or biannual basis. Windows 10 can be delivered as part of Microsoft 365 and now follows a subscription service model (Windows-as-a-Service). With the new servicing model, Microsoft releases more incremental feature updates twice a year. Windows 10 deployment and servicing will be covered as part of `Chapter 5`, *Understanding the Concepts of Modern Management*.

Productivity

Advanced technologies such as Microsoft's digital assistant Cortana and Focus Assist, Windows Ink, and Windows Mixed Reality help end users with their productivity. These built-in apps can help an end user keep track of their priorities and reduce any distractions that may come up throughout the day by integrating with your schedule and reviewing your Office 365 application usage data.

 For information on Cortana, please see `https://support.microsoft.com/ en-us/help/17214/cortana-what-is`. You can also learn about Focus Assist (formerly called Quiet Hours) at `https://support.microsoft.com/ en-us/help/4026996/windows-10-turn-focus-assist-on-or-off`.

Security

Security should be a priority for IT administrators. Windows 10 Enterprise's new security features, such as **Microsoft Defender Advanced Threat Protection (MDATP)**, **Windows Information Protection (WIP)**, and **Windows Hello for Business (WHFB)** are all technologies that can help secure an organization's data and mitigate risk. MDATP is a threat protection offering as part of Windows 10 Enterprise.

MDATP is built into Windows 10 Enterprise and uses embedded sensors to detect anomalous behavior. MDATP is a platform of technologies that protect computers, or endpoints, from cyber threats such as data breaches and makes additional security recommendations. MDATP can offer automated investigations and remediation suggestions to help IT admins reduce manual efforts and respond more quickly to emerging threats.

WIP uses security mechanisms to provide information protection services to curtail potentially sensitive or otherwise essential company data from leaving the environment.

Finally, WHFB helps with identity and access management by providing a two-factor authentication method for logging into devices. WHFB is able to leverage biometric data with unique device PINs to help secure devices and reduce some of the risks associated with credential phishing attacks.

While the exam won't focus much on configuring advanced security measures, it's a good idea to become familiar with the terminology and feature set.

 For more information on Windows 10 Enterprise Security, please visit https://docs.microsoft.com/en-us/windows/security/.

Since Windows 10 Enterprise leverages other technology from the Microsoft 365 suite, such as Intune, Office 365, and Azure Information Protection, it's important to understand how they all work together to provide a complete solution. These separate technologies not only appear in the MS-900 exam, they are imperative to your understanding of Microsoft 365.

In this section, we've discussed Windows 10 Enterprise and its management, productivity, and security features as part of the core Microsoft 365 technology. Next, we'll discuss Office 365 ProPlus.

Exploring Office 365 ProPlus

Many users' first experience of the power of business applications was with Microsoft Office. Originally launched in November 1990, Microsoft Office has become the premier productivity application suite for millions of users worldwide. The Microsoft Office experience has been reimagined and is a fully integrated part of the Microsoft 365 platform. Office 365 ProPlus includes all of the desktop applications you've become familiar with, including Word, Outlook, Excel, Access, PowerPoint, OneNote, and Publisher.

Traditionally, Office has been a static product, licensed on a per-device or per-user basis. With Microsoft 365, the Office application has been transformed into an evergreen product with continuous updates and feature developments, leveraging the best of the Microsoft cloud. Like other parts of the Microsoft 365 platform, Office 365 ProPlus is subscription-based software. Here is a screenshot of Microsoft Word, one of the business productivity applications of the Office 365 ProPlus subscription:

Office 365 ProPlus is natively integrated with other parts of the Microsoft 365 ecosystem, including OneDrive for Business, SharePoint Online, Azure Information Protection, and Exchange Online. We'll cover Office 365 ProPlus in depth in `Chapter 6`, *Understanding Office 365 ProPlus*.

Next, we'll look at Exchange Online.

Exploring Exchange Online

If you've used Outlook before, you might have some familiarity with Exchange Online. Exchange Online, an essential part of Office 365, is the cloud version of Exchange Server. Exchange Online is a messaging collaboration tool that allows you to email your colleagues and clients, organize tasks, schedule meetings, and view calendars, and manage contacts.

You can do all of this through a desktop application such as Outlook, using a web browser, or from a mobile device.

Exchange Online for users

Let's discuss some of the basic Exchange Online end user features!

Each user has an Exchange Online mailbox. This allows users to send and receive email. Users may be required to preserve or archive content, so administrators can enable a variety of mailbox archiving and retention policies.

When a user views their mailbox using Outlook on the web, they will have an experience similar to the following screenshot:

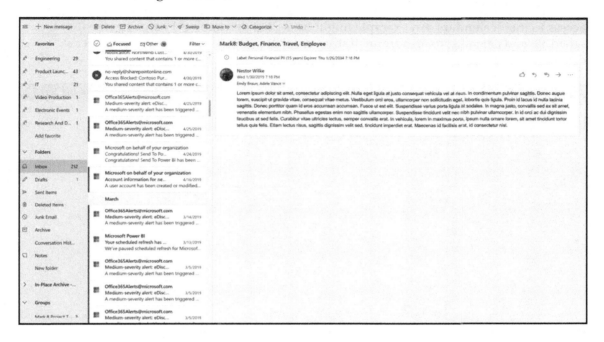

Users can schedule meetings, events, and appointments through Exchange Online's calendaring features. Each user can keep track of their own schedule as well as check for free/busy times for other coworkers or resources. Certain users may also opt to delegate access to their calendars. An example might be a CEO delegating the management of their schedule and calendar to an administrative assistant. Here is a screenshot of a user's calendar via monthly view:

Like other messaging platforms, Exchange Online allows users to attach files to messages. Frequently, organizations have multiple users that need to work together on projects or share a job role. For example, an organization may want to have a general email address such as *sales@contoso.com* that potential customers can use to contact sales staff. In this case, a shared mailbox might be useful. Exchange Online supports shared mailboxes (where multiple people can access one mailbox).

Exchange Online also has a feature called *Office 365 Groups*, which functions like both a shared mailbox and a distribution list. You can see an example of an Office 365 Group as it is displayed in Outlook in the following screenshot:

As previously mentioned, Outlook is available as a desktop client application as well as a browser-based application. Mobile clients are also available. You can learn more about the mobile clients for iOS and Android at `https://products.office.com/en-us/outlook-mobile-for-android-and-ios`.

Office 365 groups are used heavily throughout the Microsoft 365 system.

Now that you've become familiar with some of the features of the end user experience, let's take a look at how Exchange Online looks from an administrator's point of view.

Exchange Online for administrators

As an Exchange Online administrator, you will have access to the **Exchange Admin Center** (**EAC**). You can access the EAC from either the Microsoft 365 admin center (`https://admin.microsoft.com`) or by navigating directly to `https://outlook.office365.com/ecp`. There, you can configure mail flow rules, such as email forwarding or adding text and notifications to messages. Administrators also have the ability to configure message encryption settings to help secure confidential communications.

Administrators of a messaging system should be concerned with message hygiene configurations to manage spam and suspected malware. Exchange Online uses a mail protection gateway, **Exchange Online Protection** (**EOP**), to trap these threats. Message hygiene settings (including configuration options for spam, phishing, and malware filtering) are managed through the EAC.

Organizations may opt to configure an Exchange hybrid environment. Exchange Online hybrid allows user mailboxes to be moved between the on-premises and Office 365 environments. Building on your knowledge from `Chapter 2`, *Cloud Deployment Models and Cloud Services*, you can see that Exchange Online hybrid is an example of a hybrid cloud deployment model.

Exchange hybrid configuration settings are configured in the EAC, as shown here:

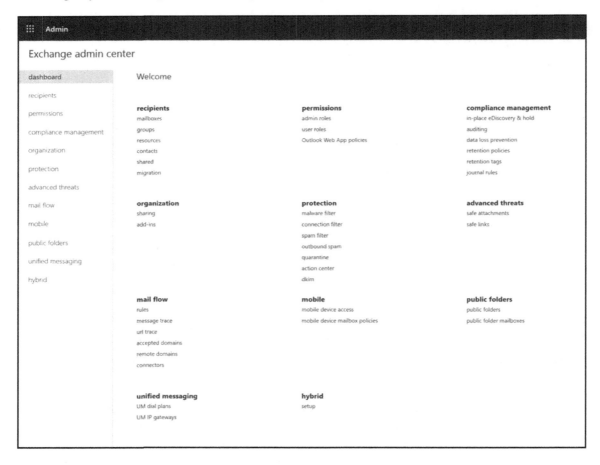

If your organization needs to meet regulatory compliance requirements, you'll probably configure those features in the Microsoft 365 compliance center (`https://compliance.microsoft.com`). This can be used to configure retention and data loss prevention policies as well as to conduct eDiscovery activities for content stored throughout the Microsoft 365 service (including content stored in Exchange Online, SharePoint Online, and Microsoft Teams). The compliance center also gives you access to alerting, logging, and auditing data:

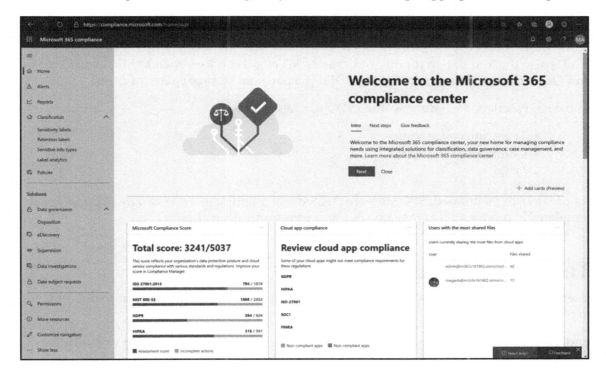

Accessing the compliance center requires a separate set of permissions. This enables organizations to separate and delegate administrative roles.

In this section, we covered Exchange Online's features. Further, we divided Exchange Online between the end user's experience and IT administrator configurations. It's important to familiarize yourself with both aspects, such as Outlook mobile for the end user and retention policies for the IT administrators. MS900 will contain questions regarding Exchange Online features but, more importantly, you should be able to demonstrate your knowledge of this core Microsoft 365 service.

Next, let's explore SharePoint Online.

Exploring SharePoint Online

SharePoint Online (SPO), another essential part of Office 365, is a web-based collaboration and communication platform. Many organizations use SPO as an intranet.

Content in SPO is organized into sites. There are a number of different templates available for creating sites that meet your organization's needs, such as team-based collaboration, wikis, and sophisticated search experiences. Organizations can create sites for groups of people that collaborate together often.

SPO is also the foundation for other Microsoft 365 cloud services, such as Microsoft Teams and **OneDrive for Business (ODFB)**. ODFB is a personal storage space for files.

In the next section, we'll discuss three SPO use cases:

- Team site collaboration
- Communication sites
- ODFB

As previously mentioned, SPO sites are created using templates. The two most popular site templates in modern SPO are **team sites** and **communication sites.**

Team site collaboration

Users can create documents, news posts, events, lists, and more, and then store the content in SPO.

End users can collaborate with other coworkers or even partners from other organizations securely using a SharePoint **team site**. Team sites allow you to create or upload files and then share them with your teammates easily. You can also use SharePoint team sites to manage lists, apps, and web pages. Here is an example of a team site landing page:

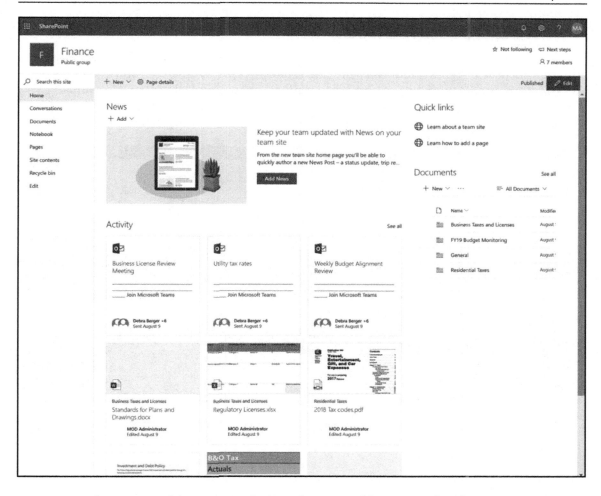

Team sites have several features, including document libraries and web components that can easily be customized. Team sites are primarily designed in such a way that everyone can contribute or update content.

 For more information on team sites, please visit https://support. office.com/en-us/article/What-is-a-SharePoint-team-site-75545757-36c3-46a7-beed-0aaa74f0401e.

There may be instances, however, where you don't want users to be able to contribute anything. In that case, a communication site might be a good fit.

Communication sites

Whereas team sites are designed for everyone to contribute, **communication sites** have a different focus. Communication sites are geared toward presenting the information. You can use a communications site to showcase content, images, links to other sites, and reports. You can see that the default communications site template allows you to format all this information in a modern layout, as you can see in the following screenshot:

 For more information on communication sites, please visit https://support.office.com/en-us/article/What-is-a-SharePoint-communication-site-94A33429-E580-45C3-A090-5512A8070732.

In some situations, though, neither a team site nor a communication site may be appropriate to store some types of data, such as personal files. Next, we'll look at using ODFB to address that need.

ODFB

ODFB is a personal storage space for end users. Here is a web view of an end user's ODFB landing page:

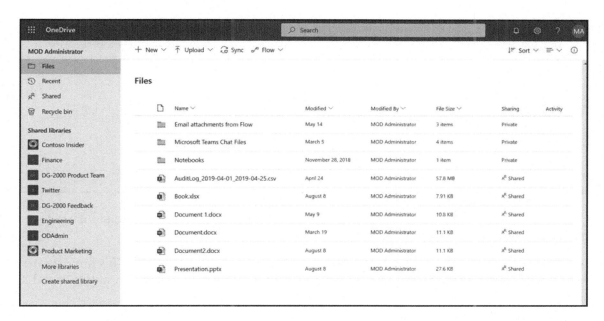

As we mentioned previously, ODFB is built on SPO. In fact, a user's ODFB storage space is actually their own SPO site. End users can deploy a client to their Windows or macOS devices that will allow them to synchronize a copy of their data from the service locally. This can be used to enable offline support.

Like Outlook, SharePoint and ODFB also have apps available for mobile devices that run on iOS or Android.

SPO for administrators

SPO also has a robust set of administration tools that allow you to manage site provisioning, search, sharing, and permissions. The current SharePoint admin center is shown in the following screenshot:

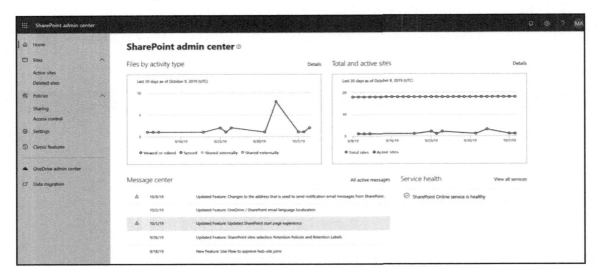

Compliance and eDiscovery tasks are managed inside the compliance center, similarly to other Office 365 suite applications.

As SPO provides the storage infrastructure for many Microsoft 365 services, it's important to become familiar with its concepts (especially around permissions, sharing, and external access).

SPO is also an integral part of Microsoft's collaboration hub, Teams, which we will cover next.

Introducing Microsoft Teams

Microsoft Teams, a relatively new service in Office 365, is the collaboration hub within your organization. It's based on Office 365 Groups, which, as you learned previously, incorporates Azure Active Directory, SPO, and Exchange Online features. Teams builds on the Office 365 Groups framework to allow users to chat, host and conduct meetings, share and collaborate on files, deploy bots and connectors to external services, and make calls. We can discuss the infrastructure later in this chapter, but it's important to first understand the basic capabilities of Microsoft Teams.

Let's take a look at some of the Teams features.

Chat

The first Teams feature we'll explore is Chat. Teams users can conduct both one-to-one (or peer-to-peer) chats and group chats. You can see a sample of the chat interface here:

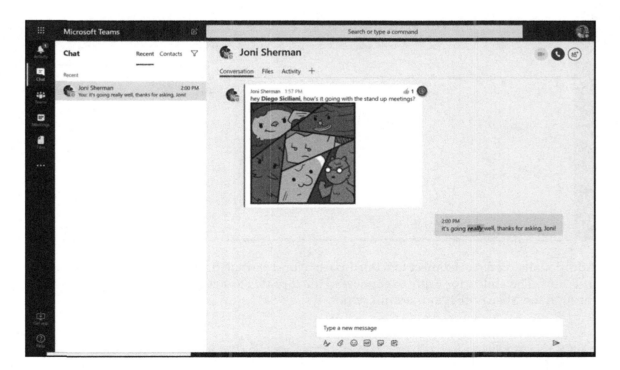

Teams users can communicate via rich text, with personal mentions, reactions (such as a like button), and popular social media animations such as GIFs, memes, and stickers. Users can also share files in the context of their chat. Files shared through Teams are first uploaded to the user's ODFB.

Files

The Files tab within Teams will direct you to all the files you can access, whether they've been shared in Teams or are located in ODFB:

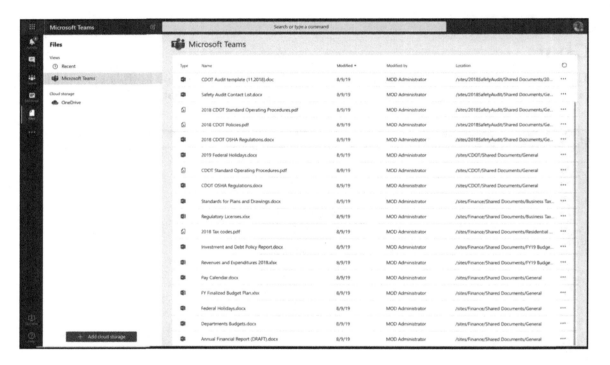

Additionally, you can connect to a third-party cloud storage provider and view those files in Teams. The ability for users to connect to third-party storage providers can be managed through the Microsoft Teams admin center.

Calls and meetings

Teams is also a full conferencing and calling platform. In addition to chatting, end users can make calls to both Teams users and those on traditional phone systems, as well as host meetings. Teams allow users to initiate PC-to-PC calls through the Teams client, dial out to phone numbers, and conduct impromptu meetings via the **Meet now** functionality. You can see an example of a Teams meeting here:

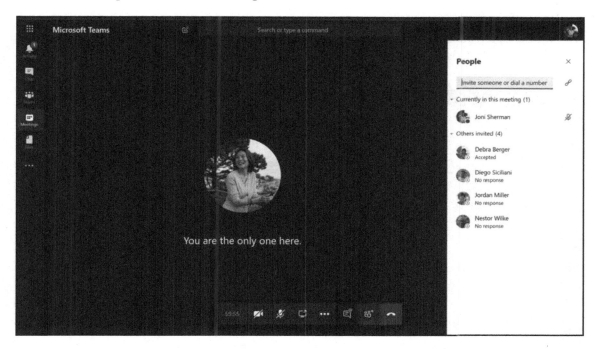

You can also bring Microsoft Teams into your meeting rooms. Users can leverage Teams Rooms to start sharing screens, present content, and collaborate with remote participants. Teams Rooms systems are audio and video conferencing devices capable of creating and hosting an end-to-end meeting experience.

Live Events

Microsoft Teams also allows users to produce streaming broadcast events called **Teams live events**. A live event is a one-to-many meeting. Organizations might choose to use these for town hall meeting-style broadcasts from management or during a product launch. Live events can host up to 10,000 attendees and can be recorded for later viewing.

Apps

Third-party apps can be critical to an organization's day-to-day operations. Hundreds of first- and third-party apps can be integrated right into the Teams client through the use of bots and connectors. For example, users can use connectors and webhooks to get data from social media sources such as Twitter to post directly to Teams conversation channels or incorporate data from their sales pipeline tools.

With these integrations, users are able to accomplish their work using these apps without leaving the Teams client. The following screenshot shows the Apps tab, which can be used to add and configure these tools:

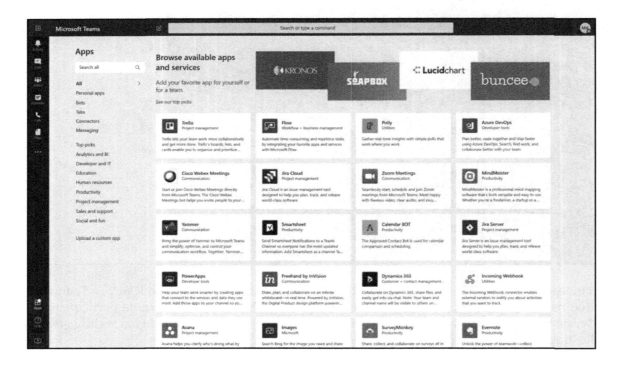

Multi-platform access

Microsoft Teams is available across all devices, including Windows 10, macOS, iOS, and Android. You can download the Teams client for those devices from https://products.office.com/en-us/microsoft-teams/download-app, as shown here:

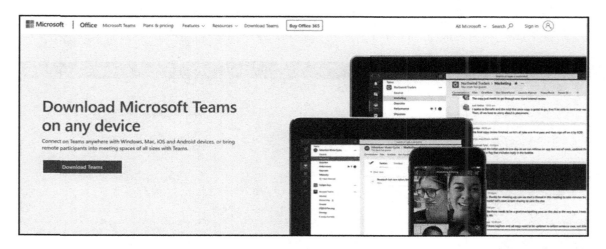

Microsoft also recently released a preview version of a client for Linux (`https://teams.microsoft.com/downloads#allDevicesSection`).

Teams for administrators

As Teams administrators, you'll need to think about a lot of settings to provide both the most productivity and security for your environment, including the following:

- Meeting room devices
- Meeting, messaging, and app policies
- Telephony options, such as phone numbers, audio conferencing licenses, call queues, and auto-attendants
- External and guest access policies

Additionally, you'll want to familiarize yourself with the different migration paths and coexistence modes, especially if you're integrating with or migrating from Skype for Business.

 Organizations that currently have deployed Skype for Business Online should start planning their Teams migration as soon as possible. Skype for Business Online will be retired on July 21, 2021. This announcement does not affect the Skype for Business on-premise server. For more information and the official announcement, please visit `https://support.microsoft.com/en-us/help/4511540/retirement-of-skype-for-business-online`.

The Teams admin center provides tools to manage all of those settings and more. You can get an idea of what the Teams admin center looks like from the following screenshot:

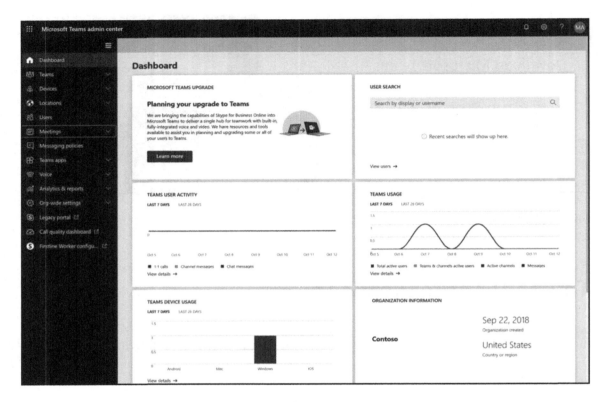

As you can see, Microsoft Teams brings together features of the entire Microsoft 365 ecosystem. It allows the user to communicate via chat, meetings, share, and integrate with other apps, all from a single tool.

Discovering EMS

EMS is Microsoft's security solution. It's an identity-driven, holistic approach to help address today's security threats. EMS licensing comes in two tiers: E3 and E5. Because identity is the crux of Microsoft 365's model, it's important to have a basic understanding of **Azure Active Directory (AAD)**.

If AAD is an unfamiliar term, please visit `https://docs.microsoft.com/en-us/azure/active-directory/fundamentals/active-directory-whatis`.

For the sake of the MS-900 exam, it's important to cover the basic elements of EMS:

- **AAD Premium:** AAD Premium 1 (part of EMS E3) allows you to use features such as **multi-factor authentication (MFA)**, dynamic groups for license and application assignment, and conditional access. MFA is a security protocol that prompts users to verify their credentials using a second method, such as biometrics or a one-time-use passcode. **Dynamic Group Management** allows administrators to determine group membership based on a user or a device's **Active Directory (AD)** properties and make licensing or assignment changes automatically. **Conditional Access** is an AAD tool that helps enforce company policy. For instance, company policy requires end users to sign in only from specific locations. Conditional Access can be configured so that when an end user is within that location boundary, access is granted. Otherwise, access is blocked. With AAD Premium 2 (part of EMS 35), organizations can enforce risk-based sign-in policies for MFA as well as use leaked credential detection to determine whether compromised user credentials are available on the dark web.

For more information on Dynamic Group Membership, please visit `https://blogs.technet.microsoft.com/pauljones/2017/08/28/dynamic-group-membership-in-azure-active-directory-part-1/`.

- **Microsoft Intune:** Microsoft Intune is a mobile management platform, encompassing both device (mobile device management, or MDM) and application (mobile application management, or MAM) capabilities. Intune allows you to manage a company-owned device remotely. MDM can be useful, for example, when a user loses their work phone. Once the loss has been reported, an administrator can go in and remotely wipe that device, preventing loss of data. Intune device management also allows administrators to determine if the device meets certain security controls (such as being up to date with device updates or having encryption enabled) and make access decisions based on that. MAM extends similar controls down to the managed applications, allowing administrators to require additional passwords and enforcing data storage controls. Intune is supported on Windows, macOS, iOS, and Android devices. Intune is managed from the AAD portal.

- **Azure Information Protection Premium: Azure Information Protection** (AIP) Premium 1, included with EMS E3, helps protect files by applying labels that allow or enforce specific actions according to company policy. AIP builds on technology from **Azure Rights Management** (ARM) to help define and apply these classification rules. A few common examples include using the protection of the rights to prevent message recipients from forwarding an email message or using the Reply All button, or applying watermarks to protected documents. While AIP Premium 1 requires users to manually apply protections to their content, AIP Premium 2 allows organizations to automate the classification and enforcement actions.

There are other important aspects of EMS as well, such as **Microsoft Cloud App Security** (**MCAS**) and Advanced Threat Analytics. Let's briefly walk through them. You can find more information on these at the end of the chapter in the *Further reading* section:

- **Microsoft Cloud App Security** (**MCAS**): MCAS is a **cloud access security broker** (**CASB**) solution that can be connected to Office 365 and other SaaS applications and provide sophisticated analytics. MCAS be used to detect shadow IT applications in your environment as well as evaluate risk factors.

- **Microsoft Advanced Threat Analytics** (**ATA**): This solution captures network authentication and authorization traffic and analyzes it for attack patterns and suspicious behavior.

- **Windows Server Client Access License Rights**: This usage right grants users the ability to access software deployed on-premises without additional license purchases.

It's important to understand the capabilities of the EMS suite, specifically features such as MFA and Conditional Access, for the MS-900 exam.

Summary

This chapter covered the core technologies that make up Microsoft 365. We learned about some of the advanced features of Windows 10 Enterprise and then covered four parts of the Office collaboration platform (Office 365 ProPlus, Exchange Online, SPO, and Teams). Finally, we discussed the breadth of capability in the EMS suite, Microsoft's holistic security platform.

After reading this chapter, you should be able to list the core Microsoft 365 services along with two or three of the key features of each. For example, you should be able to identify Microsoft Teams and that some of its key features are meetings, chat, and file sharing.

In the next chapter, we will talk more about the advantages of having to deploy these cloud-based services over traditionally managed on-premises software.

Further reading

The following links provide more information on the EMS feature set:

- **Multi-factor authentication:** https://docs.microsoft.com/en-us/azure/active-directory/authentication/concept-mfa-howitworks
- **Conditional Access:** https://docs.microsoft.com/en-us/azure/active-directory/conditional-access/overview
- **Microsoft Cloud App Security:** https://docs.microsoft.com/en-us/cloud-app-security/what-is-cloud-app-security
- **Microsoft Advanced Threat Analytics:** https://docs.microsoft.com/en-us/advanced-threat-analytics/what-is-ata
- **Windows Client Access License:** https://www.microsoft.com/en-us/licensing/product-licensing/client-access-license
- **EMS E5 capabilities and licensing:** https://www.microsoft.com/en-us/microsoft-365/enterprise-mobility-security/compare-plans-and-pricing

Questions

Use the following questions to test your knowledge of this chapter. You can find the answers in *Assessment Answers*.

1. Identify three core components of Microsoft 365.
    1. Enterprise Mobility + Security
    2. Windows 10 Enterprise edition
    3. Windows 10 Professional edition
    4. Office 365
    5. Windows Server 2019
    6. Windows 10 Home edition
    7. Azure Sentinel

2. Which Microsoft 365 feature utilizes biometrics?
    1. Windows Defender ATP
    2. Windows Hello for Business
    3. Windows Advanced Biometric Scanner
    4. Azure Information Protection
    5. Windows Information Protection

3. Exchange Online is primarily used for what?
    1. Creating and filling out online forms
    2. Composing spreadsheets
    3. Email and calendaring tasks
    4. Recording brief videos

4. The _____ can be used to configure **Data Loss Prevention (DLP)** policies.
    1. Microsoft 365 admin center
    2. SharePoint Online admin center
    3. Compliance center
    4. Matter center

5. Exchange Online hybrid is an example of what kind of cloud deployment model?
    1. Service cloud
    2. Hybrid cloud
    3. Private cloud
    4. Public cloud

6. Where would you perform an eDiscovery search for data stored in SharePoint Online?
    1. Microsoft 365 admin center
    2. SharePoint Online admin center
    3. Compliance center
    4. eDiscovery center

7. Audit logs for Microsoft 365 can be accessed from which location?
    1. Microsoft 365 admin center
    2. SharePoint Online admin center
    3. Compliance center
    4. Compliance manager

8. You need to perform an eDiscovery search for content in Exchange Online. What should you use?
   1. Microsoft 365 admin center
   2. SharePoint Online admin center
   3. Compliance center
   4. eDiscovery center

9. What are the two most popular site templates in modern SharePoint Online?
   1. Team site
   2. Hub site
   3. Collaboration site
   4. Communication site

10. OneDrive for Business is part of Exchange Online.
    1. True
    2. False

11. OneDrive for Business is part of SharePoint Online.
    1. True
    2. False

12. OneDrive for Business is part of Teams.
    1. True
    2. False

13. OneDrive for Business has native synchronization clients available for which of the following platforms?
    1. Android
    2. iOS
    3. Linux
    4. Windows
    5. macOS

14. What can you use to apply classification labels and actions to files?
    1. Label manager
    2. Azure Information Compliance
    3. Azure Information Protection
    4. Data Loss Prevention Manager

15. Microsoft Cloud App Security is an example of what type of product?
    1. Cloud app security proctor
    2. Cloud app security manager
    3. Cloud app security broker
    4. Cloud App security modeler

16. You need to prompt users to enter a value from a one-time pass token when they log on to Office 365 applications. Which type of technology should you use?
    1. Azure Information Protection
    2. MFA
    3. Private Identity Storage
    4. Federated Identity Manager

4
Comparing Core Services in Microsoft 365

In Chapter 3, *Core Microsoft 365 Components*, we covered the core technologies that make up Microsoft 365. Microsoft 365 consists of Windows 10 Enterprise, Office 365, and **Enterprise Mobility + Security (EMS)**.

In this chapter, we will begin by discussing the benefits of the cloud, specifically with reference to Windows 10 Enterprise management. Then we will address some high-level considerations when migrating from Exchange and SharePoint on-premise to their corresponding services in the Microsoft cloud. Finally, we will cover the benefits of Teams and Security in the cloud.

By the end of this chapter, you will be able to explain the difference between core services in Microsoft 365 and their on-premise counterparts. The topics we'll be examining are as follows:

- Understanding Windows 10 Enterprise management
- Evaluating Exchange Options
- Evaluating SharePoint
- Evaluating Teams
- Addressing security concerns

Understanding Windows 10 Enterprise management

In this section, we will go over, on a high level, what it takes for administrators to manage Windows devices and how that process changes for Windows 10 Enterprise. Microsoft 365 has new features that help ease the management of today's Windows 10 devices.

In this new, modern operating system, it's important to understand the new ways to manage devices. When making the transition from older Windows operating systems to Windows 10, an organization needs to make a decision on what tools to use to manage the devices, and whether those tools will exist in an on-premise or cloud deployment.

Let's begin by looking at traditional management strategies.

Traditional Windows operating system management

In the past, Microsoft would typically release a new operating system on several-year cycle. For example, Windows 2000 Professional was released in February 2000. Windows XP was released in October 2001, followed by Windows 7 in October 2009, Windows 8 in August 2012, and finally, the first edition of Windows 10 in July of 2015.

Notice there was an eight-year span from XP to 7 where no new desktop operating system was released. For many business and enterprise customers, desktop operating system updates were frequently tied to hardware refresh cycles. Compatibility testing, for example, could take months to complete. An operating system refresh also usually meant a significant amount of downtime for users.

Here's an example of the deployment life cycle in a legacy management scenario whenever an operating system was released:

- First, requirements gathering. Administrators had to make sure the existing hardware was capable of running the new operating system and applications. If not, this meant budgeting for hardware upgrades, potentially adding months to an upgrade cycle.
- Once the hardware requirements were satisfied, the next step was configuring a system to be representative of what would be deployed to users. The configuration would then be captured as an image: a point-in-time snapshot of the operating system, drivers, updates, applications, and settings that would get deployed on subsequent machines.
- As time went on, the image would become stale. Administrators would then have to re-create the baseline image, updating the operating system, drivers, and applications, and then recapturing it.

This process would normally get repeated for every brand and type of device: a unique image for each model of desktop or laptop device. Fortunately, there's a new approach with Windows 10 Enterprise management.

Modern Windows 10 Enterprise management

Now, let's talk about a more modern management platform.

Many large organizations already own a software deployment platform, such as **System Center Configuration Manager** (commonly referred to as Configuration Manager, **SCCM**, or just **CM**). It's typically used to manage devices such as desktops, laptops, and servers as well as applications and updates. Just like in the past, CM can be used to manage Windows 10 devices.

However, there's also an option to integrate the device management platform and Intune with CM. This configuration is called **co-management**. Co-management allows you to leverage both an existing CM deployment as well as Intune and gain benefits from both services. For example, you can deploy settings to co-managed Windows 10 devices from CM, while utilizing Conditional Access policies that leverage device compliance status.

Co-management brings several features to Windows 10 management, including the following:

- Conditional Access policies using device compliance
- Intune-based remote actions such as remote control, device restart, and factory reset
- Centralized visibility of device health
- The ability to link users, devices, and apps with **Azure Active Directory** (**AAD**)
- Modern, internet-based provisioning experience with Windows Autopilot

Let's have a look at some of the co-management features in more depth.

Conditional Access policies using device compliance

We've already touched on Conditional Access policies as a means to secure access to resources in the Microsoft 365 ecosystem. When you connect an existing CM deployment with Intune, you gain the ability to use device health and compliance as a condition. With Intune co-management, for example, you can determine whether devices are compliant with your current compliance policies, such as non-rooted or jailbroken devices or ensuring application updates are applied.

 For more information on Conditional Access policies with device compliance, see `https://docs.microsoft.com/en-us/configmgr/comanage/quickstart-conditional-access`.

Intune-based remote actions

Since the Microsoft 365 suite depends on access to the internet and the Microsoft cloud to deliver services, ensuring you have access to remote devices is key to ensuring user productivity and security. Co-management gives you the ability to perform a number of remote actions on managed devices, including the following:

- Deleting data on lost or stolen devices
- Restarting devices
- Renaming devices
- Gathering device inventory
- Performing immediate policy synchronization
- Performing remote control activities
- Removing factory-installed OEMs with Fresh Start reboot
- Performing a factory reset

To learn more about the Intune remote action benefits from a co-managed deployment, see `https://docs.microsoft.com/en-us/configmgr/comanage/quickstart-remote-actions`.

Centralized visibility of device health

Maintaining device health is critical to maintaining both user productivity and environment security. Since Intune is a cloud-based service, it can communicate with devices that are not on a corporate or organizational network. Intune bridges the gap between the client health monitoring tool CCMeval for the times when devices aren't on a managed network and enables auto-remediation for common health issues.

For more information regarding management and visibility of client health with a co-managed CM deployment, see `https://docs.microsoft.com/en-us/configmgr/comanage/quickstart-client-health`.

Ability to link users, devices, and apps with AAD

As we've discussed throughout this book, identity is the basis of security in Microsoft 365. It's the single most important entity and controls access to data, applications, and resources. With an Intune co-managed CM deployment and hybrid AAD joined devices, you get additional benefits:

- Automatic device licensing
- Self-service password reset
- Self-service BitLocker recovery
- Enterprise state roaming
- Device-based Conditional Access
- Windows Hello for Business
- Single sign-on to cloud-based resources

You can learn more about the hybrid AD benefits of co-management here: `https://docs.microsoft.com/en-us/configmgr/comanage/quickstart-hybrid-aad`.

Modern, internet-based provisioning experience with Windows Autopilot

Without on-premise infrastructure, you have the option to manage your Windows 10 devices remotely using Windows Autopilot. Windows Autopilot is a collection of technologies that provides administrators and end users alike with a modern experience when deploying, repurposing, or resetting devices.

Autopilot, together with Intune, creates a cloud management experience. One of the benefits of an Autopilot deployment is the ability to drop-ship new devices from manufacturers directly to field staff. When the remote worker receives the device, they simply have to boot it, connect to the internet, and enter their AAD identity. The Autopilot framework allows the laptop to identify that it belongs to a specific Microsoft 365 tenant and begin the AAD device join process. During this process, it downloads software and policies assigned to the user.

However, with co-management, this experience can be even better. Co-management allows administrators to ensure that all devices have the same end state, including Intune device enrollment (which provides the additional previously mentioned co-management features) as well as the CM client for any on-premise management activities. You don't have to maintain specific device images as you did with legacy deployment models since Autopilot leverages the **Original Equipment Manufacturer (OEM)**-optimized edition of Windows that is already pre-installed on the device. During the autopilot enrollment, devices are automatically upgraded to Windows 10 Enterprise and all of the Enterprise-based features are enabled.

Autopilot with CM also enables streamlined device upgrade processes from previous versions of Windows.

When deploying devices using Autopilot, the following steps are required:

- **Register devices:**
  - When purchasing devices from supported OEMs, the OEM performs the device registration. When purchasing from resellers, distributors, or partners that are members of the **Cloud Solution Partners (CSP)** program, they can also register the devices on behalf of the customer.
  - Existing devices running Windows 10 can be automatically enrolled if they are using a Mobile Device Management (**MDM**) service such as Intune.
  - Existing devices may also be manually enrolled by capturing the hardware ID and uploaded to the Windows Autopilot service.
- **Create device profiles:** Profile settings need to be set up to adjust experiences such as skipping the **End User License Agreement (EULA)** page, automatically setting up work or school accounts, or disabling local admin account creation.
- **Create user/group or device-based profiles and configure and customize the device using Intune:** This can help meet business needs such as installing certain group- or department-specific applications or configuring specific settings, as shown in the following screenshot:

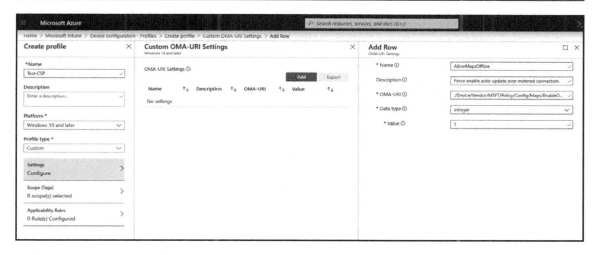

- **Boot the devices:** Connect to the internet and sign in using an Azure identity to complete the configuration.

In order to use all the modern co-management capabilities and features, CM must be updated to the current branch.

We have covered some of the differences between the legacy or traditional Windows management techniques and modern Windows management, including Intune and CM, as well as the benefits of shifting to modern operating system management.

Next, we'll begin looking at transitioning existing on-premise productivity applications such as Exchange and SharePoint to the Microsoft 365 platform.

Evaluating Exchange options

Many organizations have existing on-premise Exchange deployments and may be evaluating whether to upgrade to the next version of the on-premise edition or migrate to a cloud-based service such as Exchange Online. As it is with transitioning other services from traditional to cloud-based subscriptions, it's important to weigh the risks and benefits, such as cost, security, accessibility, mobility, growth, maintenance, and compliance.

Once an organization has decided to make the transition to Exchange Online, its next step is determining a migration strategy. Functionally, it's important to look at the following:

- How many user, shared, and resource mailboxes need to be migrated?
- What is the volume of data that must be migrated?
- How much bandwidth will be required?
- What services and features are you currently using, and what is the cloud-based equivalent?
- Is any data currently subject to litigation or retention policies, and does it need to be preserved?
- What mobility options need to be available?
- What is the least disruptive approach?
- Are there any features that won't be available or restrictions and limitations to work around?
- How will it be secured?
- Can any of the on-premise system be decommissioned?

Understanding the capabilities of Exchange Online and its migration paths is crucial for a successful transition.

From a feature perspective, it's important to note that organizations using Exchange Unified Messaging will need to select a new solution, whether that's moving towards an on-premise solution such as Skype for Business or a cloud solution such as Microsoft Teams with Phone System. Exchange Online still supports public folders and several types of shared and resource mailboxes. For organizations that synchronize their identity from an on-premise Active Directory, Microsoft recommends that at least one on-premise Exchange server is left to handle management tasks. You can learn more about its recommendation at https://docs.microsoft.com/en-us/exchange/decommission-on-premise-exchange.

Once the feature and capability questions have been answered, it's time to identify migration strategies. Exchange supports the following native migration paths:

- **Cutover:** All mailboxes will migrate over from on-premise to Office 365 over a few days. This also means that the mailboxes will be managed in Office 365. Cutover migrations support 2,000 mailboxes at a time, but are really recommended for less than 150 mailboxes.

- **Staged:** Batches of mailboxes will move from on-premise to Office 365.
- **Hybrid:** Mailboxes can either be on-premise or in Office 365 and can be moved between environments. Deploying a hybrid environment allows a single, feature-rich, and consistent end user experience. Hybrid deployments require at least one server running Exchange 2010 Service Pack 3 or later. For organizations that manage identity on-premise and synchronize it with AAD Connect, Exchange hybrid is the only supported method for managing mailboxes.
- **G Suite Migration:** Microsoft now provides a native G Suite migration tool if the source environment is the Google G Suite platform.
- **IMAP:** If your source environment is not Exchanged-based and doesn't rely on G Suite, you may consider using an IMAP-based migration. IMAP stands for Internet Message Access Protocol and is a standard interface used by a variety of third-party hosting platforms. Exchange also provides IMAP-based access to mailboxes, but it's far better to use a native Exchange migration. IMAP migrations frequently have limitations around contact and calendar folders, since those are typically extensions to the IMAP protocol and not part of the standard.
- **Third-party tools:** If your environment isn't compatible with performing a native Exchange-based migration or the built-in G Suite or IMAP-based migration methods don't meet your needs, there are a number of third-party products that can also be used to perform migrations.

The type of migration you can perform depends on several factors:

- Source environment (Exchange Server-based, non-Exchange based, or hosted)
- Number of users
- Type of data being migrated (user or resource mailboxes, email, calendars, contacts, personal archives)
- Types of email clients (current or legacy versions of Outlook, third-party mail clients, mobile devices)

Once the overall migration methods have been determined, you need to decide what steps must be completed to successfully complete a migration process. A high-level project plan might look like the following:

- Configuring the test or trial environment
- Configuring the production environment
- Configuring coexistence tools and methods

- Conducting test migrations and feature testing
- Testing third-party or on-premise application integrations
- Conducting pilot migrations and feature testing
- Establishing the migration schedule and logistical considerations

Part of the logistical considerations includes how to select users for migration, depending on their work role, business functions, or even internal political pressure. There may be considerations about how to configure environments for security and end user or data center components that need to be upgraded in order to facilitate a smooth transition experience.

As previously mentioned, Microsoft recommends using the native hybrid migration configuration whenever possible. It provides the best end user experience. Some examples of features provided by a hybrid migration are as follows:

- The ability to move mailboxes between cloud and on-premise environments
- Automatic updating of user devices without the need to reconfigure Outlook mail profiles
- Fully-functional address book
- Cross-premises permission delegation
- Fully functioning free/busy and calendaring features
- The ability to complete migrations when it is convenient for the business
- Little change for service desk/user provisioning practices

Other migration methods may require additional work, configuration, or coexistence software, and may not provide the best overall experience for users.

Now that we've discussed some of the considerations for migrating to Exchange Online, we'll look at migrating to SharePoint Online.

Evaluating SharePoint options

In addition to Exchange Server, many customers have also deployed SharePoint Server. SharePoint, as we discussed in the previous chapter, is a document management and collaboration platform.

When we discussed **SharePoint Online (SPO)** in the previous chapter, we discussed the two main types of site layouts: *team sites* and *communication sites*. These are considered modern site templates, whereas templates such as *enterprise wiki* and *development sites* are considered part of the classic site technology. The on-premise edition, SharePoint Server 2019, also has the concept of modern site layouts. Both on-premise and cloud SharePoint deployments can have a mix of SharePoint classic and modern sites. Microsoft 365's new products and services such as Teams and Planner utilize Office 365 Groups, which rely on modern site templates.

While both classic and modern sites support many of the same features, there are some important differences:

- User interface elements and layouts (classic versus modern, responsive layouts).
- Web parts are available.
- Site architecture concepts (classic site collection and site hierarchies versus modern hub site associations).
- Search experiences (refiners, search dictionaries, and so on).

The MS-900 exam (and this book) won't cover all of the differences between classic and modern site architectures but suffice it to say that modern groups and modern sites comprise Microsoft's identity, group, security, and collaboration strategy for a number of the cloud-based tools available in the Microsoft 365 platform.

Unlike Exchange Server, which has a direct migration path to Exchange Online through hybrid mailbox moves, SharePoint Server does not have the ability to do native site or document library migration to SPO. SharePoint *does* have hybrid and cross-premises capabilities, as shown here:

Feature	SPO and SharePoint Server without hybrid	SharePoint Server with hybrid
OneDrive for Business	OneDrive for Business is available in Office 365 for licensed users, but there is no link to it from SharePoint Server. If users have been configured with My Sites or OneDrive sites on-premise and have a license in Office 365, they will have two sites to manage separately.	OneDrive links in SharePoint Server direct users to OneDrive for Business in Office 365. No content migration is performed as part of hybrid; content migration must be performed separately.
Site following	The SPO followed sites listing tracks followed SPO sites. If you've deployed MySites, a second followed sites list in SharePoint Server tracks followed SharePoint Server sites.	Followed sites from both locations are consolidated in the SPO followed sites list. SharePoint Server links to the followed sites list redirect users to the SPO followed sites list.

Document following	If you've deployed MySites, the followed documents list in SharePoint Server tracks followed SharePoint Server documents.	There is no corresponding Hybrid document following feature. If you use hybrid OneDrive for Business, the SharePoint Server followed documents list will be hidden from users, though you can still favorite SharePoint Server documents if you have Delve enabled.
Profiles	Users have separate profiles in SPO and SharePoint Server.	Profiles continue to exist in both locations, but SharePoint Server links to users' redirected profiles in Office 365.
Extensible app launcher	Users see different app launchers in Office 365 and in SharePoint Server.	Their app launchers are still separate, but the SharePoint Server app launcher includes tiles from Office 365.
Hybrid self-service site creation	There are separate self-service site creation experiences in SharePoint Server and SPO.	The default SharePoint Server site creation page is redirected to the SPO Group Creation page, allowing users to create sites in SPO instead.
Search	There are separate search indexes and search centers for SharePoint Server and Office 365. Users must search from each individual to find relevant content.	Search results between the two locations are combined with either cloud hybrid search or federated search options.

SharePoint content migrations can be achieved using a number of mechanisms, depending on the type of content being migrated and the destination:

- On-premise file server shares can be migrated to SPO sites using the **SharePoint Migration Tool** (**SPMT**).
- On-premise user home directories can be migrated to OneDrive for Business using SPMT.
- On-premises SharePoint Server 2010 and 2013 sites and document libraries can be migrated to SPO using SPMT.
- Third-party tools to migrate on-premise or cloud-based content to SPO and OneDrive for Business.
- On-premise business workflows may be able to be migrated, or they may need to be recreated if particular workflow options or features are not available in SPO. Microsoft Power Automate (formerly Flow) can be used to recreate or extend many workflows.

In October 2019, Microsoft acquired the cloud-based *Mover*, a tool that can migrate workloads from a number of sources to SPO. For more information on the acquisition, please see http://www.mover.io.

While migrations to Exchange Online are purely administrator-driven, content migrations to SPO or OneDrive for Business may be either administrator or end user-driven (or a combination of both). Organizations should determine a strategy that covers the following areas:

- What SharePoint hybrid features will be configured (such as hybrid search, hybrid OneDrive, and hybrid user profiles)?
- Will sites and site collections be migrated?
- If sites and site collections are migrated, will they be migrated as-is or redeveloped with hub sites and modern site architecture?
- Will end user home directories or existing SharePoint MySites or OneDrive sites be migrated to OneDrive for Business?
- Are there any workflows that need to be evaluated and potentially recreated?
- Are there any legacy custom apps that could be redeveloped with Power Apps or Power Automate?
- Are there any dashboards or visualizations that may require features such as Gateways or Business Connectivity Services?

The process of configuring and migrating content to SPO, as well as configuring SharePoint hybrid options, is outside the scope of the MS-900 exam. However, it's important to be able to identify features of a SharePoint hybrid configuration and what migration options exist.

Now that you've seen what SharePoint migration options are available, let's examine Teams.

Evaluating Teams

Microsoft Teams is the collaboration hub that brings together many Office 365 services, integrating internal content, tools, and external data into a single interface. Unlike Exchange or SharePoint, Teams is cloud-only and doesn't have an on-premise counterpart. It's an all-new service that builds on familiar services such as Exchange, Skype, and SharePoint as well as new constructs and services such as Office 365 Groups and Planner.

In the previous chapter, we introduced Teams and its core features, such as chat, meetings, calls, connectors, bots, and file sharing. Microsoft Teams works with a core Office 365 architectural component, Office 365 Groups, and stores content in both Exchange Online and SPO. In the rest of this section, we'll look at how Teams, Exchange Online, and SPO work together to provide the optimal Teams experience.

The following diagram illustrates how Office 365 technologies come together with Teams:

Source: https://docs.microsoft.com/en-us/microsoftteams/teams-architecture-solutions-posters

An Office 365 Group is the security boundary for Microsoft Teams. When you create a team, you are creating an Office 365 group and attaching Teams features to it. The group dictates who has access to the Team, which in turn controls who can access documents and conversations or participate in meetings.

As the preceding diagram shows, a team is based on an Office 365 group, which in turn maps certain features and capabilities to other Office 365 services:

- Conversations and messages are stored in the Office 365 Group's connected mailbox.
- Channel files are stored in the Office 365 Group's connected SharePoint site.

A team can be public or private. If a team is public, anyone in the organization is able to search for and join it. Private teams aren't visible and users will need special permission or an invitation to join. In addition, a team (whether it's public or private) can be configured to have external members.

In order for Teams to function optimally, you need the following:

- Users should have mailboxes in Exchange Online. Teams is also supported when Exchange is configured in a hybrid with mailboxes on-premise, but cloud users still require a Teams license.
- Users must have a SharePoint license with OneDrive available for file sharing inside 1:1 chat to work.
- SPO resources must be available.
- Microsoft recommends that users be able to create Office 365 groups. Some organizations restrict this, so provisions must be made for another team or process to create the Office 365 group and then assign ownership to the correct end user.

There are a number of interdependencies for specific features, as detailed here: `https:// docs.microsoft.com/en-us/MicrosoftTeams/exchange-teams-interact`. While specific feature dependencies don't show up on MS-300, it's important to know that Microsoft recommends all users be configured with Exchange Online mailboxes and SharePoint Online licenses with OneDrive for Business sites to get the best Teams experience.

Now that you've seen how some of the core Microsoft 365 services compare to their on-premise versions, we'll shift towards cloud-only security controls and features that make the Microsoft 365 offering even more compelling.

Addressing security concerns

As organizations move to the cloud, one of the concerns they face is security. Fortunately, Microsoft has invested in developing a full range of security controls that can be configured and deployed. We've already discussed multi-factor authentication briefly. In this section, we'll learn about how additional security controls and features, such as Conditional Access, access reviews, and Cloud App Security can improve an organization's overall security posture.

Conditional Access

Conditional Access is a set of security rules used to describe conditions for granting or blocking access to managed data and resources. Common conditions include network location (on or off a corporately-managed network), geolocation to particular localities, using a managed or company-owned device, and group membership.

Using those types of conditions as factors for granting access can mean that a user can get access to a resource when meeting the parameters, or when introducing additional conditions (such as multi-factor authentication). Such scenarios might include allowing someone to access data only when they're on the network or to prompt for multi-factor authentication when they log in from an IP range located outside your current country. Maybe you want to grant someone access if they're remote, but you also want to restrict their access to web browser sessions only so they can't download content to an unmanaged device. Or possibly, if you detect someone logging in from two different IP addresses with very different geolocations in a short amount of time (for example, New York and then Ireland), you may wish to prompt for multi-factor authentication or deny them altogether.

 Detailed configurations for Conditional Access are beyond the scope of the MS-900 exam, but you should familiarize yourself with the concepts of using multiple conditions or controls to manage access to applications and services. You can learn more about common scenarios for Conditional Access at https://docs.microsoft.com/en-us/intune/protect/conditional-access-intune-common-ways-use.

Depending on your organization and the type of data it manages, there may be several different scenarios that you need to enable to ensure your organization's data is secure.

Access reviews

One of the more cumbersome parts of technical administration is the management of security controls such as group memberships. As people move throughout an organization, their roles change, and frequently, they'll gain access to new applications or tools to do their new role, but the access they had for their previous role won't get removed.

Access reviews and entitlement management are features of AAD Premium Plan 2 that allow organizations to implement a review process that can wait for administrator or reviewer input, but also take automated actions, such as removing a user's access to an application. You can implement one-time or recurring access reviews, and configure access reviews so that a group owner or designated reviewer can review the assignments and take actions. Access reviews also support self-service reviews, allowing users to attest that they still need access to a group or application.

Cloud App Security

Microsoft Cloud App Security is a **Cloud Access Security Broker (CASB)** with features including log collection, API connectors, and reverse proxy. As a CASB, it is able to provide visibility and control over any integrated applications. It's fully integrated with the Microsoft 365 stack and can plug into thousands of third-party applications as well.

Cloud App Security's features are broken into four main pillars. They are as follows:

- **Discover and manage the use of shadow IT (unapproved applications or services)**: Cloud App Security can identify the cloud apps and services used by an organization. Cloud App Security can provide analytics around usage patterns and the risk levels of more than 16,000 SaaS apps.

- **Protect sensitive information regardless of location**: By connecting business applications to Cloud App Security, you can discover sensitive data stored in non-Microsoft services and use built-in policies to apply controls such as data encryption across cloud apps.

- **Protect against cyber threats and anomalies**: Detect unusual behaviors across cloud apps to identify risky situations, ransomware, and potentially compromised. Cloud App Security allows you to define and customize risky behaviors using built-in templates and then automate remediation actions.

- **Assess the compliance of cloud apps**: Cloud App Security can assess your cloud apps for compliance. Cloud App Security can enforce your organizational policies targeting data leaks to non-compliant apps.

Cloud App Security's discovery features are included in AAD Premium Plan 1, and its enforcement and automation features are part of AAD Premium Plan 2.

The EMS Suite's features should very much be considered as a means to improve visibility and manageability across the security spectrum.

Summary

In this chapter, we compared the current state of Windows devices, Exchange, and SharePoint management with the capabilities that come with Microsoft 365, including modern management, co-management, and hybrid scenarios. In addition to comparing the features of Windows 10, Exchange, and SharePoint, we also looked at what makes Teams a unique, cloud-only application, and how to secure its infrastructure with the EMS Suite's features.

In the next chapter, we will learn about **Windows-as-a-Service (WaaS)** and its deployment and release models.

Questions

Use the following questions to test your knowledge of this chapter. You can find the answers in *Assessment Answers*.

1. CASB stands for:
    1. Cloud app service broker
    2. Cloud app security broker
    3. Cloud app service buffer
    4. Cloud app system buffer

2. Identify two pillars of Microsoft Cloud App Security:
    1. Block bulk email campaigns
    2. Trigger Access Reviews
    3. Discover and manage the use of shadow IT
    4. Assess compliance of cloud apps

3. You are the security administrator for your organization. You need to ensure that people accessing the system from outside your corporate network are using company-managed devices. Which tool should you use to meet the requirement?
    1. Access reviews
    2. Conditional Access
    3. Multi-factor authentication
    4. On-premises data gateway

4. You are the security administrator for your organization. You need to ensure that group memberships are periodically checked, and you want to delegate the management of this to group owners. Which tool should you use to meet the requirement?
    1. Conditional Access
    2. Access reviews
    3. Privileged Identity Management
    4. Privileged Authentication Management

5. System Center Configuration Manager can integrate with Intune using a feature called _____.
    1. System connection
    2. Co-location
    3. Co-management
    4. Hybrid management

6. Identify two features of an Exchange hybrid deployment:
    1. All mailboxes are either in-cloud or on-premise
    2. Requires third-party tools to complete migration
    3. Allows cross-premises calendaring and free/busy
    4. Move mailboxes easily between on-premise and cloud
    5. 10 additional free shared mailbox licenses

7. Which of these is NOT part of a SharePoint hybrid deployment?
    1. Migrating document library content
    2. Hybrid search
    3. Document following
    4. User Profile redirection

8. Microsoft Teams replaces what on-premise product?
    1. SQL Server
    2. Team Foundation Server
    3. It doesn't replace any product
    4. Windows for Workgroups

9. What are the three requirements for Microsoft Teams to function optimally?
    1. Exchange Online license
    2. Office 365 ProPlus license
    3. SharePoint Online License
    4. Microsoft Teams license

10. With Configuration Manager and Intune configured for co-management, which two Intune remote actions are available?
    1. User reset
    2. Factory reset
    3. Remote control
    4. Application reset

5
Understanding the Concepts of Modern Management

In Chapter 4, *Comparing Core Services in Microsoft 365*, we covered modern Windows 10 Enterprise management, Exchange Online, Exchange Server features, SharePoint Online, and SharePoint Server features, as well as hybrid and migration considerations. Then, we covered how Teams integrates with Office 365 Groups, Exchange Online, and SharePoint Online. Finally, we covered security features such as multi-factor authentication and Conditional Access to elevate protection on cloud services.

In this chapter, we will introduce the **Windows-as-a-Service (WaaS)** model and the Windows Deployment and Release model. Then, we will be navigating Microsoft 365 admin center for tasks such as managing licensing, monitoring service health, and creating and monitoring a service request.

The following topics will be covered in this chapter:

- Understanding the WaaS model
- Understanding the Windows Deployment and Release model
- Navigating the Microsoft 365 admin center
- Navigating the Microsoft 365 portal

Understanding the WaaS model

In Chapter 4, *Comparing Core Services in Microsoft 365*, we reviewed historically how Windows deployment and servicing has been managed. To summarize, Microsoft traditionally released operating system feature updates once every 2 to 4 years. Due to the large feature and capability changes, operating system upgrades would frequently require significant amounts of testing to ensure hardware and application compatibility. This tedious update and refresh cycle could consume organizations for months or years.

WaaS, is Microsoft's modern way to keep operating systems current and secure.

In today's landscape, the traditional model of releasing feature upgrades or enhancements would not be practical. Today, there are constant cyber-attack attempts and ever-developing threats, meaning organizations must be in a position to continuously adapt new defensive strategies. From a security perspective, organizations need to be able to respond faster to emerging threats. And, from a productivity and business view, organizations need to be able to adopt new technologies more quickly to help to attain a competitive advantage.

With the release of Windows 10, WaaS allows IT administrators to receive incremental updates that will help to reduce the time to deploy throughout an organization. WaaS provides organizations a methodology to deploy operating system updates and enhancements in a streamlined fashion, efficiently keeping devices current.

Feature and quality updates

With a new update model for Windows 10 comes new some terminology around the type of software that is delivered. First, there are **two types of updates**:

- **Feature updates:** Feature updates are bite-sized chunks released twice a year—once in March and then again in September. Any new feature releases such as improvements in a specific built-in application, visual refresh, or user experience enhancements in the operating system are deployed as feature updates.
- **Quality updates:** Quality updates denote the mandatory monthly release that contains both security and non-security maintenance fixes. These updates are cumulative, which means it contains the previous month's quality update. This cumulative nature means that no matter when you choose to deploy the WaaS model, you'll all of the quality updates to that point.

Let's get started with servicing tools in the next section.

Servicing tools

Next, there are **servicing tools**. Servicing tools are a mechanism that IT administrators can use to push updates. Microsoft provides four options for IT administrators to use:

- Windows Update
- Windows Update for Business

- Windows Server Update Service
- System Center Configuration Manager

They are explained as follows:

- **Windows Update:** Windows Update Standalone Installer is available for Windows 10 and uses the API to install packages onto a client device. Windows Update Standalone Installer requires manual feature update deferrals and cannot approve updates. It will support Delivery Optimization.

  Delivery Optimization is a peer-to-peer sharing mechanism in which devices on the same network can leverage its services to reduce pressure on the bandwidth. For more information on Delivery Optimization, please visit https://docs.microsoft.com/en-us/windows/deployment/update/waas-delivery-optimization.

- **Windows Update for Business (WUfB):** WUfB leverages Intune or Group Policy to control how and when Windows 10 devices are updated. WUfB has more controls than Windows Update Standalone, in that it allows for Group Policy configuration options and the ability to push feature and quality updates as well as non-Microsoft driver updates. WUfB also includes the ability to deliver updates for other Microsoft products. Microsoft's published recommendations for best experience with Windows Update are to make sure devices have at least 10 GB of free space and allow devices access to the Windows Update service.

- **Windows Server Update Service (WSUS):** WSUS requires an on-premises server such as Windows Server 2012 R2, Windows Server 2016, or Windows Server 2019. Like WUfB, WSUS allows the servicing of Windows and other Microsoft applications. However, one advantage of WSUS is that it provides a single place for an organization to service Windows with more flexible controls such as approving updates and choosing when to deliver them. WSUS requires some planning and on-premises resources to deploy.

  Refer to this page for more information and how to configure relevant Group Policy settings for managing updates through WSUS: https://docs.microsoft.com/en-us/windows/deployment/update/waas-manage-updates-wsus.

- **System Center Configuration Manager:** Of all of the servicing tools, System Center Configuration Manager provides IT administrators with the most control as they can control both quality and feature updates in addition to the other device, server, software management, and reporting capabilities. Configuration Manager can also leverage BranchCache and Peer Cache to distribute updates to remote clients more effectively. Configuration Manager also provides tools such as Desktop Analytics to provide insight around planning for and managing Windows 10 devices.

 For information on Desktop Analytics and its role in Windows 10 deployments, please visit `https://docs.microsoft.com/en-us/configmgr/desktop-analytics/ready-for-windows`.

Hardware compatibility has also traditionally been a barrier for upgrading operating systems. However, Windows 10 has the same minimum requirements as Windows 7. For organizations looking to upgrade from Windows 7 to Windows 10, their devices are most likely already supported and capable.

Now that you have an understanding of the feature and quality updates as well as updating methodologies, we'll move to the next section. Next, as an extension of this section, we will also introduce servicing channels and deployment rings to understand the deployment and release model.

Understanding the Windows Deployment and Release model

With the continual release of updates, IT administrators may have concerns about how to control these releases to an organization. Common questions include *"Can I get a preview of upcoming features?"* and *"How can I control which users or devices receive updates first?"*.

These issues are addressed with the concepts of the Windows deployment and release model, which uses the concepts of servicing channels and deployment rings to answer these questions.

Servicing channels

Servicing channels are a way to determine how often end users get feature and quality updates pushed to their Windows 10 devices. Servicing channels can be divided into the following three groups:

- **Windows Insider Program (WIP)**: The WIP is for those who are eager to get the latest updates. This may be a group of IT administrators or even end users who are willing to test features before they're made available to everyone. The WIP is on a monthly release cadence and requires registration. Once registered, updates can be managed through Group Policy Configuration Manager, Windows Update for Business, or another device management platform. Microsoft recommends you have at least a few devices enrolled in the Windows Insider Program.

- **Semi-Annual Channel (SAC)**: After common issues are fixed, private builds are then made public and available for deployment. Then, the latest build is available for the rest of the public. SAC versions are released twice a year, once in September/October and then again in March/April. IT administrators can defer or delay these new builds from the SAC up to 365 days. They can use this opportunity to first deploy the latest public builds to a pilot group of users and test before pushing it out to the rest of the organization. SAC builds have an 18-month life cycle. So, it's highly recommended that organizations stay within the time frame of support. The Semi-Annual Channel is recommended for enterprise customers running Windows 10 on their end user devices.

- **Long-Term Servicing Channel (LTSC)**: Devices that do not need as many feature updates and receive just quality updates can subscribe to the LTSC. It is designed for special or single-purposes devices, such as ATMs, medical equipment, and kiosks. LTSC editions do not have access to services and features such as Microsoft Edge, Store, Calendar, OneNote, and more. The core applications that aren't included aren't supported, even if you attempt to install them via side loading. LTSC is not the recommended nor preferred channel for enterprises.

 For more information on features, limitations, and recommendations regarding servicing channels, visit `https://docs.microsoft.com/en-us/ windows/deployment/update/waas-overview`.

Let's talk about deployment rings in the next section.

Deployment rings

While servicing channels determine the update cadence, *deployment rings* are the mechanism used to specify who will be receiving software from a particular servicing channel. Deployment rings can be used to configure pilot groups for new releases. A common best practice is to include a handful of users from every department in each deployment ring.

The following table illustrates a sample of an organization might structure servicing channels and deployment rings for their users:

Deployment ring	Servicing branch	Weeks after SAC release
Preview	Windows Insider	Pre-Semi-Annual Channel Release (monthly)
Ring 1 Pilot IT	Semi-Annual Channel	SAC + 0 Weeks
Ring 2 Pilot business users	Semi-Annual Channel	SAC + 4 weeks
Ring 3 Broad IT	Semi-Annual Channel	SAC + 6 weeks
Ring 4 10% Business users	Semi-Annual Channel	SAC + 8 weeks
Ring 5 90% of Business users	Semi-Annual Channel	SAC + 10 weeks until all devices deployed

In the preceding table, Windows Insiders get the earliest builds. Then, pilot IT users get it upon release. Once IT is satisfied that it is working, they begin releasing to pilot business users. Pilot business users are a representative cross-section of the organization who can test in conjunction with their daily application usage and workflow.

After pilot users have verified that it has been successful for them, the deployment can proceed through the rings until the rest of the computers are updated.

Now, we'll shift the focus from the desktop to the Microsoft 365 admin portal.

Navigating the Microsoft 365 admin center

After purchasing a Microsoft 365 subscription, the organization's staff will have access to the Microsoft 365 admin center. There are basic tasks IT administrators should know how to do. Roles are critical to consider within an organization as well, so this section will also contain a table of the roles available in the Microsoft 365 admen center, and a short description of each.

In this section, we will go over the Microsoft 365 roles available in the admin center and then cover some of the common tasks as an administrator such as checking billing and service health statuses.

Roles

There are a handful of essential administrator-related tasks in the **admin center**. Each task can be completed by users with certain administrative roles. For example, the Global Administrator role has access to everything within the Microsoft 365 admin center and can delegate additional roles. The most commonly delegated roles include the service administration roles, such as Exchange admin or Teams admin, though there are many others designed for specific groups such as helpdesk or billing users.

The following table is a complete list of roles available in the Microsoft 365 admin center:

Role	Description
Application Administrator	This role has full access to enterprise apps, app registrations, and app proxy settings.
Application Developer	This role can create app registrations and consent to app access on their own behalf.
Authentication Administrator	This role can require users to register or reregister authentication for non-password credentials, such as multi-factor authentication.
Azure Information Protection Administrator	This role manages labels for the Azure Information Protection policies, activates protection policies, and manages protection and classification templates.
Billing Administrator	This role makes purchases and manages subscriptions. Billing admins also can manage service requests and monitor service health.
Cloud Application Administrator	This role has full access to enterprise applications and application registrations. The role has the same permissions as the Application Administrator, except for being able to manage Application Proxy.
Cloud Device Administrator	This role enables, disables, and deletes devices in Azure AD and can read Windows 10 BitLocker keys. Cloud device administrators cannot manage any other properties of a device.
Compliance Administrator	This role manages compliance and data governance policies, audits, and regulatory requirements across the Microsoft 365 compliance center, Microsoft 365 admin center, Compliance Manager, Azure, Intune, and the Office 365 Security & Compliance Center.
Compliance Data Administrator	This role tracks data and audits in the Microsoft 365 compliance center, Azure, Intune, and the Microsoft 365 admin center. Compliance Data administrators can also track, assign, and verify compliance activities in the Compliance Manager.

Role	Description
Conditional Access Administrator	This role manages Azure Active Directory Conditional Access settings, but not Exchange ActiveSync Conditional Access policy (users must be a Global administrator to deploy the Exchange Activesync Conditional Access policy).
Customer Lockbox Access Administrator	Manages (approves or denies) Customer Lockbox requests, and can turn Customer Lockbox feature on or off.
Desktop Analytics Administrator	This role can access and manage Desktop management and Office Customization and Policy tools and services.
Device Administrator	Users with this role become local computer administrators on Windows 10 devices joined to Azure AD. This role *does not* grant rights to manage objects in the directory.
Directory Readers	Users can read all basic directory properties and information.
Directory Synchronization Accounts	This role is only for use with the AAD Connect service. It is not intended for any other purpose and should not be assigned to users.
Directory Writers	This is a legacy role designed for applications that do not support the modern Consent Framework for application role delegation. It should not be assigned to users.
Dynamics 365 Administrator	This role has full access to Microsoft Dynamics 365 Online. This role also grants permission to open and manage service requests and monitor service health.
Exchange Administrator / Exchange Service Administrator / Exchange Online Administrator	This role has full access to Exchange Online creates and manages mailboxes and groups. This
External Identity Provider Administrator	This role configures identity providers for use in the direct federation. Users in this role can manage the federation between Azure Active Directory and other external identity providers.
Global Administrator / Company Administrator	This role has unlimited access to all management features and most data in all admin centers. Only users with the Global administrator role can assign other administrator role delegations.
Global Reader	This has read-only access to all management features and settings in most admin centers. There are some limitations currently around the role. The Global reader role isn't supported in SharePoint or OneDrive admin centers or features such as Privileged Identity Management, Customer Lockbox, or Sensitivity Labels.
Group Administrator	This role creates groups and manages all group settings, such as naming and expiration policies, across admin centers.
Guest Inviter	This role manages Azure Active Directory B2B guest user invitations when the **Members can Invite** setting is configured as **No**.
Helpdesk Administrator	This role resets passwords and reauthenticates for all non-admins and some admin roles (Directory readers, Guest inviter, Helpdesk administrator, Message center reader, and Reports reader), manages service requests, and monitors service health. This role was previously called *Password Administrator*.

Role	Description
Intune Administrator / Intune Service Administrator	This role has full permissions within Microsoft Intune, as well as the ability to create and manage groups. This role is identified as *Intune Service Administrator* in the Microsoft Graph API, the Azure AD Graph API, and Azure AD PowerShell. This role is identified as *Intune Administrator* in the Azure portal.
Kaizala Administrator	This role has full access to all Kaizala management features and the ability to open and manage service requests.
License Administrator	This role assigns and removes licenses from users and edits usage location on user objects. This role cannot purchase, update, or renew subscriptions or billing.
Message Center Privacy Reader	This role has access to all messages in the Message center, including data privacy messages, and gets email notifications on privacy-related messages. Only users assigned the Global Administrator or Message Center Privacy Reader roles can read data privacy messages. This role cannot create or manage service requests.
Message Center Reader	This role reads and shares regular messages in the Message center, gets weekly email digests, and has read-only access to users, groups, domains, and subscriptions. This role cannot read data privacy messages in the Message center, nor can it create or manage service requests.
Office Apps Administrator	This role manages cloud-based policies for Office and self-service downloads. Users in this role can manage the *What's New* content that users see in their Office apps, as well as create and manage service requests and monitor service health.
Power BI Administrator	Users with this role have full permissions for the Power BI service, as well as the ability to create and manage support tickets and monitor service health.
Power Platform Administrator	This role has full access to all Power Platform apps, including Microsoft Dynamics 365, PowerApps, data loss prevention policies, and Microsoft Power Automate (formerly Microsoft Flow).
Privileged Authentication Administrator	Users with this role can set, reset, and manage non-password credentials for all users, including Global administrators, and can update passwords for all users. Users with this role can also force users to re-register against existing non-password credentials such as multi-factor access tokens and revoke the *remember MFA on the device* setting, prompting for multi-factor authentication on the next login of all users.
Privileged Role Administrator	This role manages role assignments in Azure Active Directory as well as Privileged Identity Management and Administrative Units. This role doesn't grant any specific user, group, or device management privileges, though members of this role can grant themselves any other role that does have those privileges.
Reports Reader	This role reads usage reporting data from the reports dashboard and Power BI adoption content pack. Reports Reader also grants the ability to read Azure sign-in reports and use the Microsoft Graph reporting API.

Role	Description
Search Administrator	This role has full access to Microsoft (activated through the Microsoft 365 admin center **Services & add-ins** page), assigns the Search Administrator and Search Editor roles, and manages editorial content. This role also grants permission to monitor service health and manage service requests.
Search Editor	This role can create, edit, and delete content for Microsoft Search, such as bookmarks, Q&A, and locations. This role does not permit managing service requests.
Security Administrator	This role grants permission to manage security-related features in Azure AD Identity Protection, Azure Security Center, Azure Information Protection, the Office 365 Security & Compliance Center, Cloud App Security, Intune, and the Microsoft 365 admin center. This role also can see service health.
Security Operator	This role grants permission to read security-related features in Azure AD Identity Protection, Azure Security Center, Azure Information Protection, the Office 365 Security & Compliance Center, Cloud App Security, Intune, and the Microsoft 365 admin center. This role also can see service health as well as respond to alerts in the Identity Protection portal.
Security Reader	This role grants permission to read security-related features in Azure AD Identity Protection, Azure Security Center, and Identity Protection center. Azure Information Protection, the Office 365 Security & Compliance Center, Cloud App Security, Intune, and the Microsoft 365 admin center. This role also can see service health. The only difference between this role and the Security Operator role is that the Security Reader role cannot manage alerts or respond to alerts.
Service Administrator / Service Support Administrator	This role creates and manages service requests for Azure, Microsoft 365, and Office 365 services. The role is also granted permission to monitor service health. This role is identified as a *Service Support Administrator* in the Microsoft Graph API, the Azure AD Graph API, and Azure AD PowerShell. It is identified as *Service Administrator* in the Azure portal, Microsoft 365 admin center, and Intune portal.
SharePoint Administrator	This role has full access to SharePoint Online and can manage Office 365 groups. It creates and manages service requests and can monitor service health.
Skype for Business Administrator	This role has full access to all Teams and Skype features Skype user attributes. The role can create and manage service requests and monitor service health.
Teams Communication Administrator	This role manages the voice and telephony features of Microsoft Teams, such as the ability to assign telephone numbers and manage voice and meeting policies. This role also grants access to the call analytics toolset.

Role	Description
Teams Communication Support Engineer	This role uses call troubleshooting tools in the Microsoft Teams and Skype for Business admin centers. Users can view full call record information for all participants. It cannot create or manage service requests.
Teams Communication Support Specialist	This role uses call troubleshooting tools in the Microsoft Teams and Skype for Business admin centers. It cannot create or manage service requests.
Teams Service Administrator	This role has full access to the Teams and Skype admin centers and can manage Office 365 groups. Creates and manages service requests and can monitor service health.
User Administrator	This role resets user passwords and creates and manages users and groups. It can create and manage service requests and monitors service health.

Most organizations do not use all of their specialized roles. However, they are available. A preview feature called *Custom Roles* allows organizations to create even more fine-grained control as well.

 For more information on the available roles, please visit `https://docs.microsoft.com/en-us/azure/active-directory/users-groups-roles/directory-assign-admin-roles`.

Next, we'll review some common tasks related to the Microsoft 365 admin center.

Common tasks

One of the most common tasks available as an administrator is to create and manage service requests and monitor service health. Another operational activity would include viewing the bill or the invoice details, licensing, and checking the Message center.

Let's review each of these common tasks!

Billing

As a Global Administrator or Billing Administrator, you can navigate to the Billing page to view your bill or invoice details. To access billing features, launch the Microsoft 365 admin center (`https://admin.microsoft.com`) and select **Billing** from the navigation menu. You may need to select **Show all** at the bottom to see all of the menu options.

The Billing menu has several options, as the following screenshot shows:

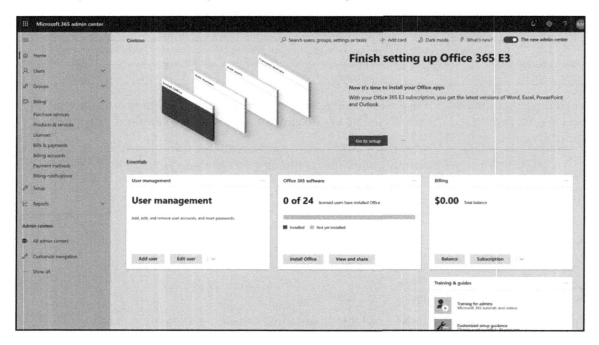

From these options, you can purchase new services, review aggregate license details, and manage invoices and payment methods.

Licensing

The licensing view shows general information on the SKUs and licenses available in the tenant, as well as aggregate usage details. Go to Licensing to view different product licenses available to the tenant. To view general license details, launch the Microsoft 365 admin center (`https://admin.microsoft.com`) and select **Billing** from the navigation menu, and then select **Licenses**. You may need to select **Show all** at the bottom to see all of the menu options.

Once the **Licenses** page is displayed, you will see a list of the services available in your tenant:

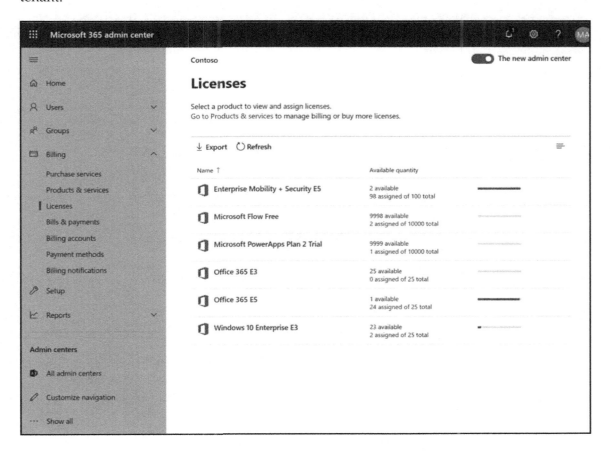

If a user is a member of one of the roles that can manage user licenses, they can also assign the licenses by following these steps:

1. Launch the Microsoft 365 admin center (`https://admin.microsoft.com`).
2. From the navigation menu on the left, select **Users | Active Users.**
3. Select one or more users, and then select **Manage product licenses**.
4. Use the toggles for each license to assign licenses or sublicense service plan features. Click **Add** or **Save** (depending on the type of modification being made), as the following screenshot indicates:

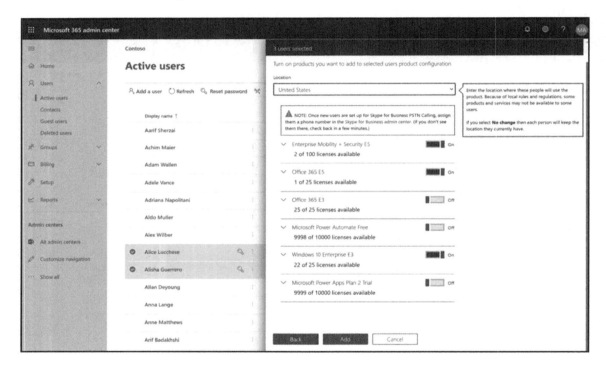

License changes are effective immediately, though some services may take a few minutes to provision or enable (such as mailbox creation or OneDrive for Business site creation).

Service health

Many roles support viewing the health status of the service. The service health dashboard can be accessed using the following process:

1. Launch the Microsoft 365 admin center (`https://admin.microsoft.com`).
2. From the navigation menu on the left, select **Health | Service health**:

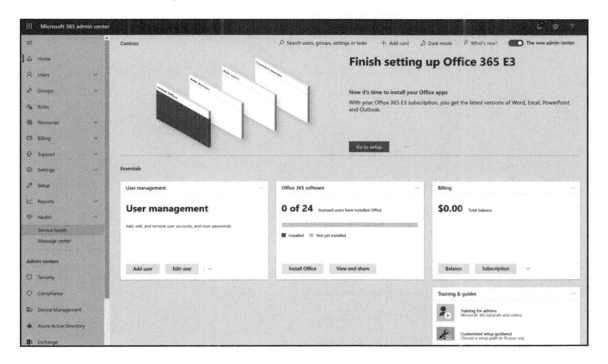

3. Select the **Incidents**, **Advisories**, or **History** tabs to filter and organize events, as displayed in the following screenshot:

For a list of status definitions, visit `https://docs.microsoft.com/en-us/office365/enterprise/view-service-health#status-definitions`.

Events, services, and notifications can be viewed, sorted, and filtered.

Message center

Microsoft makes its product announcements in several places, such as blogs, news articles, and events, and the Microsoft 365 Message center. Follow the steps given here to access the **Message center**:

1. Launch the Microsoft 365 admin center (`https://admin.microsoft.com`).
2. From the navigation menu on the left, select **Health** | **Message center**:

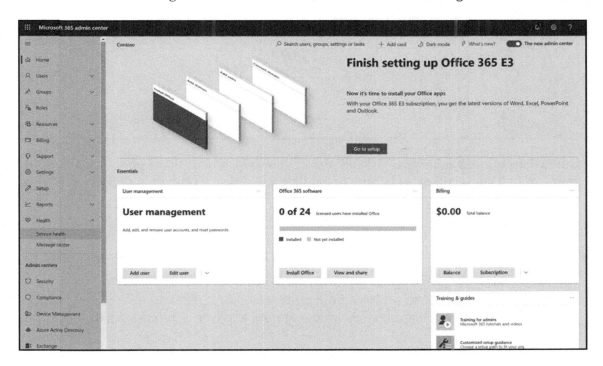

Administrators can filter by high importance, unread, and dismissed messages, as well as search and sort, as shown in the following screenshot of the **Message center** page:

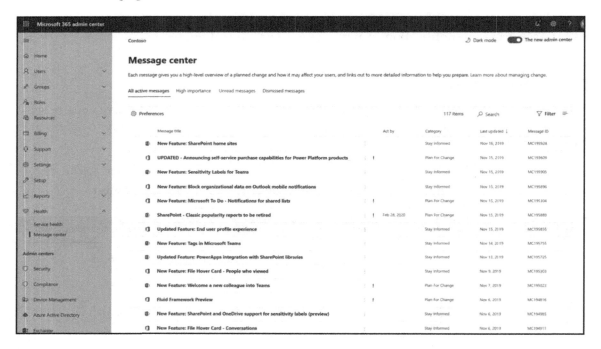

Notifications for upcoming changes and features are posted here. Some periodically require administrative intervention, so be sure to monitor the Message center regularly.

Service ticket

Should support issues arise, you can open a service ticket with Microsoft. Resources will be assigned to assist you. Follow these steps to initiate a service ticket:

1. Log in to the Microsoft 365 admin center (`https://admin.microsoft.com`) with an account that has one of the roles required to create a support ticket.

2. Click **Support** in the navigation bar, and then click **New Service Request** to launch the **Support Assistant:**

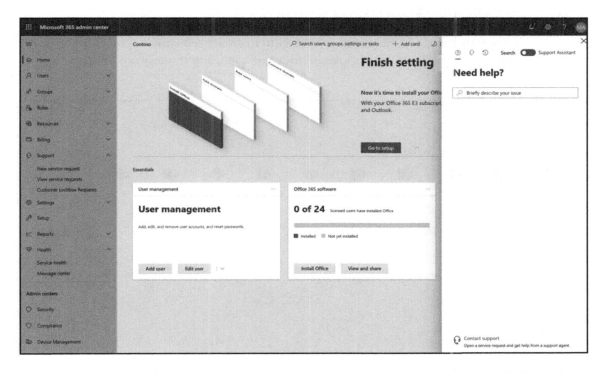

3. If the support assistant is unable to answer your question, select the link at the button to **Contact support.**

Administrators can also see past service requests as well.

Now that you've seen some of the basic features of the admin center, let's take a look at the user experience.

Navigating the Microsoft 365 portal

Users will navigate to the Microsoft 365 portal when accessing services and applications through a web browser. The address for the Microsoft 365 portal is `https://portal.office.com`, though some organizations may decide to create referrals or redirections from other sites they manage. When a user logs in, they see a landing page similar to the following:

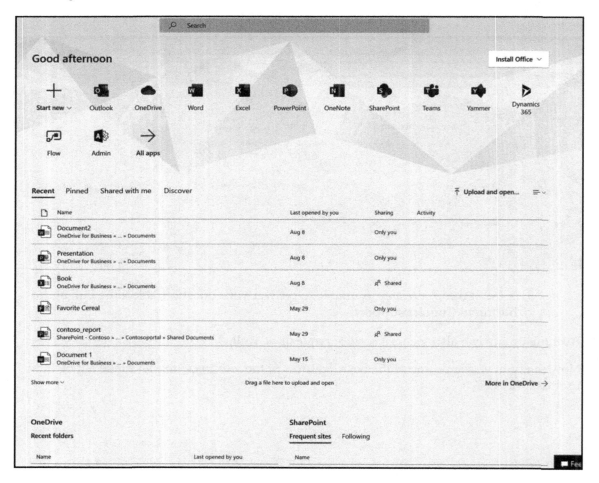

The home page has several features, including the following:

- There's a search bar at the top of the page that allows users to search for applications and files.
- There are tiles or icons for all of the applications that they are licensed to use.
- There's a list of files, organized into categories:
    - **Recent** shows files that a user has recently accessed across various services.
    - **Pinned** shows files that a user has pinned (similar to marking something as favorite in a browser).
    - **Shared with me** lists the files that other users have granted them permissions to access as well as items that they have pinned (similar to saving as a browser favorite).
    - **Discovery** shows files that may be relevant to you, based on Office Graph signals.
- There's a list of recently accessed OneDrive files.
- There are frequently visited or followed SharePoint sites.

Now we have covered both the administrator and user interfaces to the Microsoft 365 platform, as well as some of the features of both.

Summary

In this chapter, we discussed the new WaaS model for delivering Windows, including the feature updates, quality updates, servicing channels, and deployment rings. Understanding the deployment methodology is important from both the MS-900 exam perspective as well as real-world management one.

Additionally, we covered some of the features of the Microsoft 365 admin centers, including the various security roles and basic administrator tasks. Finally, we took a tour of the Microsoft 365 end user interface so you can understand how users will see and interact with the service.

In the next chapter, we will discuss some of the differences between Office 2016 and Office 365 ProPlus, as well as how to begin deploying Office.

Questions

Use the following questions to test your knowledge of this chapter. You can find the answers in *Assessment Answers*:

1. When deciding when users will get a Windows release, what concept would apply?
   1. Service branch
   2. Service channel
   3. Deployment ring
   4. Windows Insiders

2. What are the three primary servicing channels?
   1. Windows Insiders
   2. Semi-Annual Channel
   3. Long-Term Servicing Channel
   4. Monthly Channel

3. Which role has access to nearly every feature and role in the Microsoft 365 service by default?
   1. Enterprise admin
   2. Domain admin
   3. Global admin
   4. Azure admin

4. Which description identifies a feature update?
   1. Anything new such as improvements in a specific built-in application, visual refresh, or user experience
   2. Monthly release that contains both security and non-security maintenance fixes
   3. Security releases only
   4. Non-security releases only

5. Which description identifies a quality update?
   1. Anything new such as improvements in a specific built-in application, visual refresh, or user experience
   2. Monthly release that contains both security and non-security maintenance fixes
   3. Security releases only
   4. Non-security releases only

6. Application Administrators can administer aspects of Application Proxy.
    1. True
    2. False

7. Cloud Application Administrators can administer aspects of Application Proxy.
    1. True
    2. False

8. Which of the following tasks is *not* part of the License Administrator role?
    1. Removes licenses from users
    2. Assigns licenses to users
    3. Edits usage location on user objects
    4. Purchase licenses

9. Which of the following tasks is *not* part of the Message center reader role?
    1. Access to regular messages in the Message center
    2. Access to data privacy messages in the Message center
    3. Read-only access to users and groups
    4. Read-only access to subscriptions

10. Which of the following tasks is *not* part of the Customer Lockbox Access Administrator?
    1. Approves Customer Lockbox requests
    2. Denies Customer Lockbox requests
    3. Enables or disables the Customer Lockbox feature
    4. Create and manage service requests

6
Understanding Office 365 ProPlus

Office 365 ProPlus is the new, subscription-based edition of the familiar Office application. The applications you're familiar with (Word, Excel, Outlook, Access, PowerPoint, and OneNote) are still part of the Office 365 ProPlus package.

In Chapter 5, *Understanding the Concepts of Modern Management*, we introduced the concept of **Windows-as-a-Service (WaaS)** and the Windows Deployment and Release model for Windows 10. In this chapter, we will shift the discussion to Office desktop applications. Similar to the WaaS model, Office 365 ProPlus has unique considerations. In this chapter, you'll learn about the deployment and licensing options for Office 365 ProPlus and how to choose the right options for your organization.

One of the core differences between retail or volume license editions and the Office subscription model is the concept of channels in Office 365 ProPlus. Like Windows 10, Office 365 ProPlus has update channels and release cadences to understand.

Office 365 ProPlus has both deployment and licensing differences from traditional software, both of which we will address:

- Deploying Office editions
- Licensing Office editions

Let's get started!

Deploying Office editions

As we discussed in Chapter 3, *Core Microsoft 365 Components*, Office 365 ProPlus contains the same applications (Outlook, PowerPoint, Word, and Excel) as the traditional Office software package. In that sense, **Office 365 ProPlus (OPP)** and Office 2016 are very similar. Office 365 ProPlus is also available in both 32-bit and 64-bit versions. Microsoft recommends the 64-bit editions for new deployments, but you'll need to verify which edition is right for your organization based on hardware and third-party plugin compatibility requirements.

While they have many similarities, there are some differences. We'll start with Office Professional.

Deploying Office Professional

Microsoft Office has been available as a traditional, Windows Installer-based media package for quite some time. However, Office Professional 2016 is the last Windows Installer-based version of the Office suite. All future versions (including Office 2019) will be based on a newer deployment architecture called Click-to-Run, which we'll discuss later.

All Office media packages up to this point have relied on fixed installers, meaning that all of the software components are present on the media at the time of installation. Any updates or service packs are normally applied either after the installation has been completed or slipstreamed (downloading the updates and manually integrating them into the deployment package). Microsoft would publish updates or service packs that would need to be downloaded and applied individually.

From a feature perspective, Office Professional is normally only updated when another version of the product suite is released. Office Professional is serviced through a traditional release cadence, meaning that new features only become available with a new version.

While the Click-to-Run deployments *do* support side by side installations, it only applies to different versions (for example, Office 365 ProPlus can be deployed side by side with Office 2010 Professional). You cannot simultaneously install the Windows Installer-based edition and Click-to-Run edition of the same Office build on a computer.

You can use traditional methods to deploy and update Office Professional, such as Group Policy or System Center Configuration Manager. Let's go over some examples of each.

Group Policy

If your organization doesn't have a software distribution platform, you can use Active Directory Group Policy to deploy the Windows Installer-based builds of Office Professional. Follow these steps to do so:

1. Create a network share on a server accessible to all computers that you will deploy Office Professional on. You'll need to enable the Share and NTFS permissions to allow Authenticated Users and Domain Computers.
2. Copy the contents of the Office media (extracted ISO image, extracted compressed EXE, or CD/DVD media) to the share.
3. If desired, run the Microsoft **Office Customization Tool (OCT)** by running `setup.exe /admin` in the folder where you copied the media in the previous step to choose which product options you want to install or configure.

   The OCT allows you to configure product keys, accept the **End User License Agreement (EULA)**, configure additional network sources, provide the organization name to be used in the registration process, as well as some additional security and setup options.

4. Select **Create a new Setup customization file** and click **OK:**

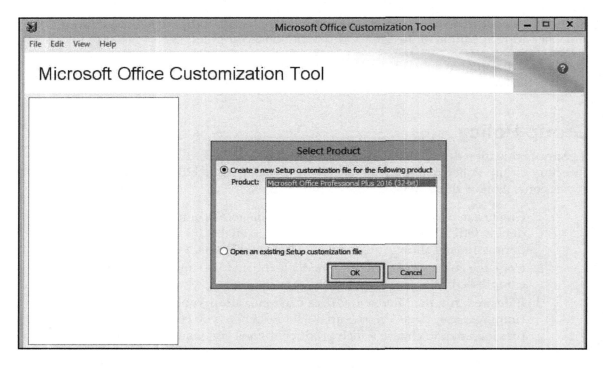

You'll want to configure the unattended installation settings inside the OCT. If you don't want to run the OCT, you'll need to edit the configuration file manually to support a Group Policy-based installation.

5. If you did not use the OCT to edit the configuration file, you'll need to edit it manually. The config.xml file is located in the source files folder where you copied the media. By default, it will be in \\server\share\Office16\ProPlus.WW\config.xml. Locate the line that contains the <!-- <Display Level --> element and update it with the following settings:

```
<Display Level="none" CompletionNotice="no" SuppressModal="yes"
AcceptEula="yes"/>
```

6. Create a `.bat` script in Notepad that contains the path to the installation media and configuration file and save the file. For example, the contents of the script might be as follows:

```
@ECHO OFF
SET LOCATION="C:\Program Files (x86)\Microsoft
Office\root\Office16"
IF NOT EXIST ""%LOCATION%\MANIFEST.XML""
\\server\share\Office16\setup.exe /config
\\server\share\Office16\ProPlus.WW\Config.xml
```

 A more complex example of the previous script sample is available at https://www.undocumented-features.com/2020/02/03/flashback-to-what-it-took-to-do-math-in-dos-batch-files/.

7. On a domain controller, launch the Group Policy Management Console (`gpmc.msc`).

8. Create a new Group Policy object in the Group Policy Objects container and edit it.

9. **Navigate to** `Computer Configuration\Policies\Windows Settings\Scripts (Startup/Shutdown)` **and double-click on Startup:**

10. Click **Show Files...** to open the GPO folder under SYSVOL.
11. Copy the file you saved in *Step 5* to this folder and click **OK.**
12. In the **Group Policy Management Editor**, select **File** | **Close.**
13. Link the GPO to a container that has one or more computers that you want to install Office 2016 to.

After configuring a Group Policy and linking it to a container that has computers in it, restart one of the computers. Group Policy should trigger the Office installation.

System Center Configuration Manager

If your organization does have a software deployment tool such as **System Center Configuration Manager (SCCM)**, you can follow these steps to deploy the Windows Install-based editions of Office as well:

1. Create a network share that will be accessible to you for the entire configuration process on the System Center Configuration Manager.
2. Copy the contents of the Office media (extracted ISO image, extracted compressed EXE, or CD/DVD media) to the share.
3. Run the Microsoft OCT by running setup.exe/admin in the folder where you copied the media in the previous step to choose which product options you want to install or configure. The Office Customization Tool allows you to configure product keys, accept the EULA, configure additional network sources, provide the organization name to be used in the registration process, as well as some additional security and setup options. You'll want to configure the unattended installation settings inside the OCT.

4. Select **Create a new Setup customization file** and click **OK**:

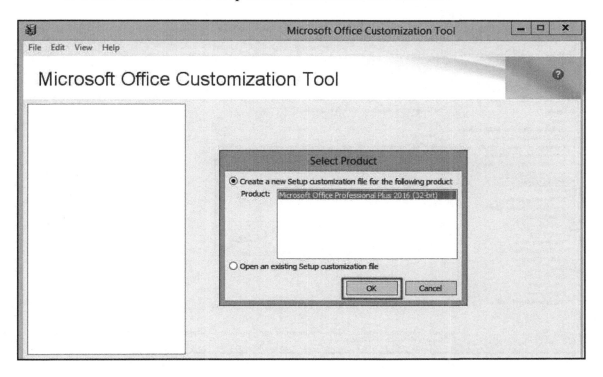

5. Select **Modify Setup properties**. Add a new property called SETUP_REBOOT with a value of Never and click **OK**:

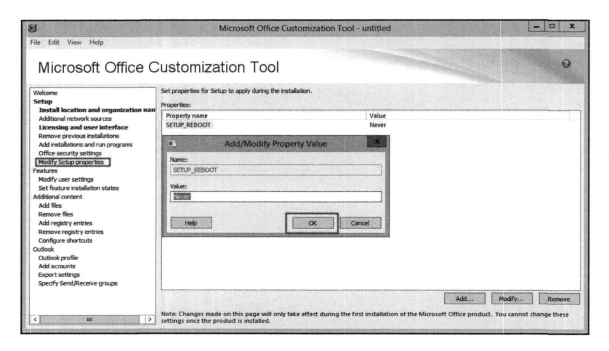

6. Perform any additional customizations and save the file under the \Office 2016\Updates folder.

7. Launch the System Center Configuration Manager console.

8. Expand **Application Management**, right-click **Applications**, and select **Create Application.**

9. Select **Automatically detect information about this application from installation files**, provide the path to the installation media (typically in the form of `\\server\share`), and click **Next**:

10. On the **View imported information** page, click **Next.**
11. On the **Specify information about this application** page, edit the information as necessary. Select **Install for system** under **Install behavior** and click **Next:**

12. Click **Close** after the wizard completes.
13. Right-click the **Office 2016** application and select **Properties.**
14. Select the **Deployment Types** tab, select the MSI file, and click **Edit.**
15. On the **Content** tab, set the content location to the folder root (removing `ProPlus.ww`) and click **Apply:**

16. On the **Programs** tab, update the installation program value to `setup.exe`. Then, click **OK.**
17. Right-click on the Office 2016 application, select **Distribute Content**, and select a distribution point that you wish to make the content available to.
18. Deploy the Office 2016 application to the desired collection.

After following these steps, the Office 2016 Professional suite should be installed on the desired computers.

Deploying Office 365 ProPlus

Whereas older versions of the Microsoft Office suite are deployed as a Windows Installer package, newer versions of Office Professional (starting with the 2019 version) and all versions of Office 365 ProPlus are packaged with **Click-to-Run** (**C2R**) technology.

Visio and Project are **not** included with Office 365 ProPlus. These products are available separately for purchase.

Click-to-Run installations are primarily designed to use the Microsoft Content Delivery Network to stream the installation media to endpoints. C2R deployments can also be configured to cache content on a local network share to minimize internet bandwidth for clients.

Microsoft uses a distributed CDN to deliver content and updates for Office 365 ProPlus. Individual clients typically need access to the CDN to install the Office 365 ProPlus software, obtain updates, and download shared files (such as icons and images) for the Office 365 service. Depending on your organization's requirements, you can configure local servers to host the Office 365 ProPlus content updates.

Part of deploying Office 365 ProPlus is determining which update cadence (referred to as a *channel*) you will be deploying to users, as you'll see in the next section.

Servicing and Update channels

Like Windows 10, Office 365 ProPlus uses **Update channels**. Update channels are used to determine the schedule of software updates to endpoints. There are four update channels:

- **Monthly Channel**: Users in the monthly channel will receive updates for the newest Office features on a monthly cadence. Updates may include performance improvements and security updates. Microsoft recommends configuring a small percentage of your users as a Monthly Channel as a way to test upcoming features for your organization. Builds in the Monthly Channel release are supported until the next Monthly Channel release is available. This channel is not recommended for business users who have a heavy reliance on macros, embedded application integrations, or third-party app integrations as part of their daily role.

- **Monthly Channel (Targeted):** If you have users that are looking for the newest features and are willing to provide feedback on behalf of the organization to Microsoft regarding new features, you can select this channel. It's not intended for broad distribution. Monthly Channel (Targeted) builds are released approximately 1-2 weeks before the regular Monthly Channel build.

- **Semi-Annual Channel:** The Semi-Annual Channel is the default channel for Office ProPlus updates. Users in this channel will receive updates twice a year – one in January and another in July. These updates will include new feature updates that have previously been available to those in the Monthly Channel. While security updates are part of this update as well, critical security updates are deployed during the normal security update release cycle. Microsoft recommends configuring most of your users for this channel, including users that rely heavily on line-of-business applications, plugins, or custom and complex macros. Support for semi-annual releases lasts 18 months, starting from the initial release.

- **Semi-Annual Channel (Targeted):** For those that want to test out features in the Semi-Annual Channel, but don't want the features every month, they can subscribe to the Semi-Annual Channel (Targeted). These users also receive these updates twice a year, but four months prior to the Semi-Annual Channel release. Users that have been configured for the Semi-Annual Channel (Targeted) will receive updates in March and September. That way, they can test the features that will be in the next release of the Semi-Annual Channel. This release will also contain new features but also security and non-security updates. Critical security updates are deployed monthly. The Semi-Annual Channel (Targeted) channel is designed to be used for testing before the Semi-Annual Channel release.

Once you have selected an update and servicing cadence for Office ProPlus, you'll need to decide on how to deploy the software to endpoints.

Deployment methods

As we mentioned earlier, Office 365 ProPlus uses C2R packaging. There are four ways to deploy Office 365 ProPlus. Let's go over each method here (in order of complexity):

- **Self-install from the cloud:** This is the simplest option – allowing end users to self-configure Office 365 ProPlus on their workstations. They can click a download link directly in the Office 365 portal to initiate the installation process.
- **Deploy from the cloud with the Office Deployment Tool**: Administrators can use Microsoft's **Office Deployment Tool** (**ODT**) to deploy Office from the Office Content Delivery Network (**Office CDN**). In this scenario, an administrator can connect the client devices to Office CDN using the OD for distributing media. The ODT will help IT administrators determine OPP configurations such as language, update channel, and products (exclude Word, or include Visio, for example). This can be a good option for mobile devices that are not connected to a corporate network very often or for remote workers.
- **Deploy from a local source with the Office Deployment Tool:** With the local source option, administrators can use their own infrastructure to create their own local source repository in order to store the latest Office updates and services. In this local source infrastructure, administrators maintain current updates for each of the channels. The ODT is then used to control which configurations are delivered to endpoints.
- **Deploy from a local source with Configuration Manager:** Finally, if organizations have a current version of System Center Configuration Manager, they can use it to deploy and update Office 365 ProPlus. Since the Configuration Manager already has a dedicated service for Office 365 ProPlus (Office 365 Client Management), the Office Deployment Tool is not required.

Now that you understand some of the deployment options, let's look at some configuration examples.

Self-installing from the cloud

The cloud is the default mechanism for deployment and updates. To configure a cloud deployment, users only need to click the **Install Office** button on the portal. Users must have administrative rights on their devices. For self-installs, follow these steps:

1. Navigate to the Office 365 portal and sign in (`https://portal.office.com`).
2. Select the **Install Office** dropdown and select **Office 365 apps:**

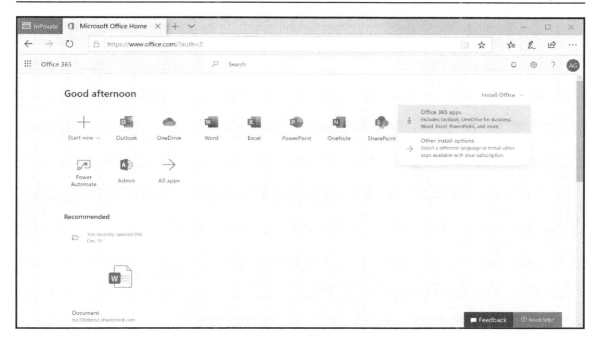

3. Follow the prompts to install the software.

By default, the setup will install the 64-bit version of Office 365 ProPlus (if you have a 64-bit system). You can also select the **Other install options** link and select other download options, such as the 32-bit version of the Office 365 ProPlus suite. You may need to do this if you already have existing 32-bit Office applications installed or need to use add-ins or plugins that only support 32-bit deployments.

Deploying from the cloud with the Office Deployment Tool

In this scenario, you'll be creating a configuration file that will be executed on user desktops. This configuration file will instruct the installer to configure specific applications, as well as use the Office CDN for obtaining media. To create the configuration, you'll use the Office Deployment Tool, which you can obtain from the Microsoft Download Center: `https://go.microsoft.com/fwlink/p/?LinkID=626065`. Follow these steps to get started:

1. Create a network share, such as `\\server\share\Office365ProPlus`, that all users will have to be able to access.

2. Download the Office Deployment Tool and double-click to extract the files to the previously created network share. Agree to the license terms and click **Continue**:

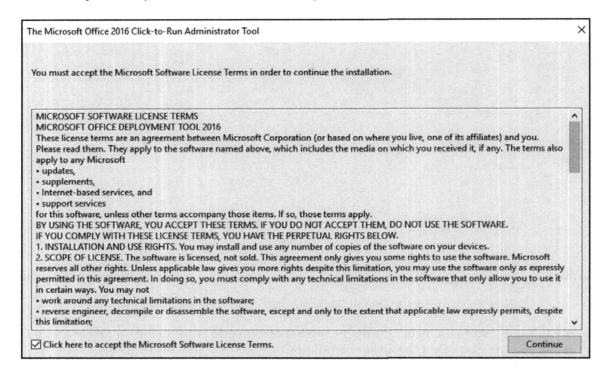

3. Open a browser and launch the Office Customization Tool (`https://config.office.com`). Sign in if necessary.

4. Using the Office Customization Tool, you can either create a custom configuration or download existing base configurations that you can then reimport and customize. In this example, expand **Customization**, select **Device Configuration**, and select **+ Create:**

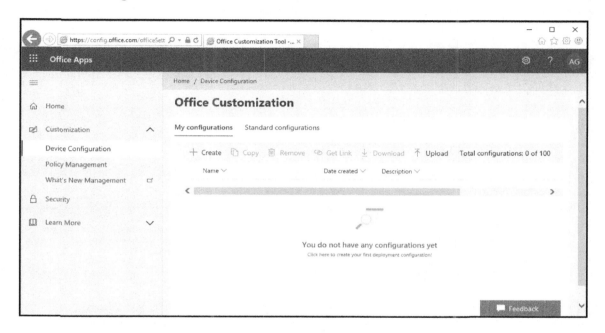

5. Select the Office Suite, additional application, and update and upgrade options you want:

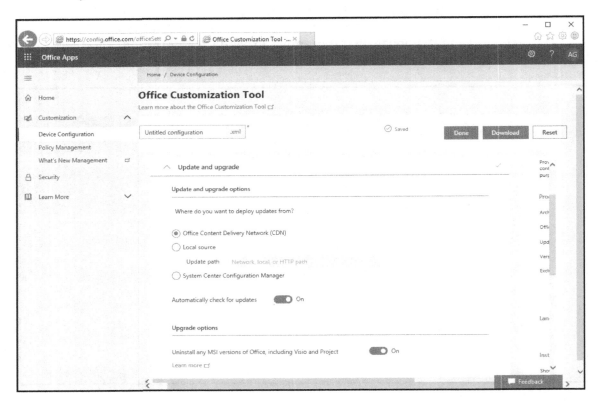

The recommended settings are as follows:

- **Products**: Select Office 365 ProPlus (this tool can also be used for C2R-based volume license editions, as well as Office 365 for Business). You can also include Visio and Project if you plan to deploy those applications. Users must be licensed for any applications that are deployed.
- **Update channel**: Choose **Semi-Annual Channel** to configure the installation package for a broad group or **Semi-Annual Channel (Targeted)** for deploying to a pilot group.
- **Language**: Include all the language packs you plan to deploy. Microsoft recommends selecting *Match operating system* to automatically install the same languages that are in use by the operating system and any user on the client device.

- **Installation**: Select **Office Content Delivery Network** *(CDN)*.
- **Updates**: Select CDN and set *Automatically check for updates* to *On*.
- **Upgrades**: Choose to automatically remove all previous MSI versions of Office. You can also choose to install the same language as any removed MSI versions of Office, but you need to make sure to include those languages in your installation selection.
- **Additional properties**: To silently install Office for your users, set the **Display level** to **Off** and **Automatically accept the EULA** to **On**.
- **Application preferences**: Define any additional Office settings.

6. Click **Done** when you're finished.
7. Click **Download** to download the XML file to the network location where you'll save the media, such as \\server\share\Office365ProPlus.
8. On a workstation where you wish to deploy Office 365 ProPlus, launch an elevated Command Prompt and type the following, replacing the network path and filenames with yours:

    \\server\share\Office365ProPlus\setup.exe /configure
    \\server\share\Office365ProPlus\FullDeployment.xml.

After the installation has completed, verify that it works correctly. If everything has worked as intended, you can then instruct users to run that command or deliver the command line using a method such as Group Policy Computer Startup Scripts. For more information on using this method, go to https://docs.microsoft.com/en-us/DeployOffice/deploy-office-365-proplus-from-the-cloud.

Deploying from a local source with the Office Deployment Tool

In this scenario, you'll be creating a configuration file that will be executed on user desktops. This configuration file will instruct the installer to configure specific applications as well as to use the local media source where we've saved the installation media. To create the configuration, you'll use the Office Deployment Tool, which you can obtain from the Microsoft Download Center at https://go.microsoft.com/fwlink/p/?LinkID=626065. Let's get started:

1. Create a network share, such as \\server\share\Office365ProPlus, that all users will have access to.
2. Create a network folder for each channel that will be deployed with this method. In this example, we're going to deploy the Semi-Annual Channel, so we'll create a folder called \\server\share\Office365ProPlus\SemiAnnualChannel.

3. Download the Office Deployment Tool and double-click to extract the files to the previously created network share. Agree to the license terms and click **Continue:**

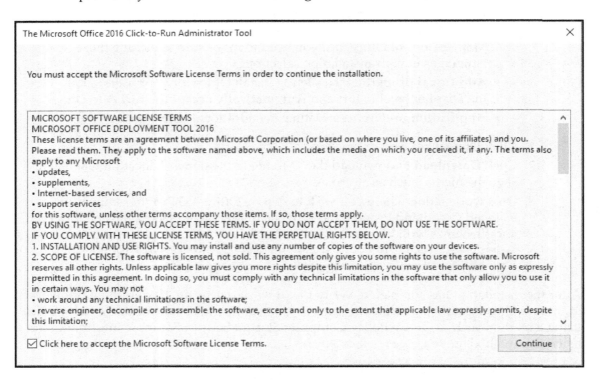

4. Open a browser and launch the Office Customization Tool (`https://config.office.com`). Sign in if necessary.

5. Using the Office Customization Tool, you can either create a custom configuration or download existing base configurations that you can then reimport and customize. In this example, expand **Customization**, select **Device Configuration**, and select **+ Create:**

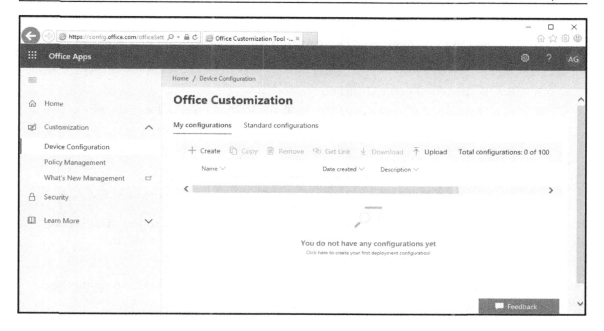

6. Select the Office Suite, additional application, and channel options that you want. The recommended settings are as follows:

- **Products**: Select Office 365 ProPlus (this tool can also be used for C2R-based volume license editions, as well as Office 365 for Business).You can also include Visio and Project if you plan to deploy those applications. Users must be licensed for any applications that are deployed.

- **Update channel**: Choose *Semi-Annual Channel* to configure the installation package for a broad group or *Semi-Annual Channel (Targeted)* for deploying to a pilot group.

- **Language**: Include all the language packs you plan to deploy. Microsoft recommends selecting *Match operating system* to automatically install the same languages that are in use by the operating system and any user on the client device.

- **Installation**: Choose the local source, and then enter the path we created in *Step 1* (`\\server\share\Office365ProPlus\SemiAnnualChannel`).

- **Updates**: Select CDN and set *Automatically check for updates* to *On*.

- **Upgrades**: Choose to automatically remove all previous MSI versions of Office. You can also choose to install the same language as any removed MSI versions of Office, but you need to make sure that you include those languages in your installation selection.

- **Additional properties**: To silently install Office for your users, set the **Display level** to **Off** and **Automatically accept the EULA** to **On.**
- **Application preferences**: Define any additional Office settings.

7. Click **Done** when you're finished.
8. Click **Download** to download the XML file to the network location where you'll save the media, such as `\\server\share\Office365ProPlus`.
9. Launch Command Prompt and type the following, replacing the network path and filenames with yours:
   ```
   \\server\share\Office365ProPlus\setup.exe /download
   \\server\share\Office365ProPlus\FullDeployment-LocalSource.xml
   ```

The `/download` switch that's specified will cause the ODT to download the installation media to the location you previously specified in the OCT (in this example, this is `\\server\share\Office365ProPlus\SemiAnnualChannel`).

Once the files have been downloaded, you can deploy it to a test workstation using the following command:

```
\\server\share\Office365ProPlus\setup.exe /configure
\\server\share\Office365ProPlus\FullDeployment-LocalSource.xml
```

After the installation has completed, verify that it works correctly. If everything has worked as intended, you can instruct your users to run that command or deliver the command line using a method such as Group Policy Computer Startup Scripts.

 For more information on using this method, go to `https://docs.microsoft.com/en-us/DeployOffice/deploy-office-365-proplus-from-a-local-source`.

Deploying from a local source with Configuration Manager

With this method, you'll be configuring new application deployments for an existing System Center Configuration Manager installation.

This section assumes that you have a working knowledge of configuring System Center Configuration Manager settings, collections, and applications. The MS-900 exam doesn't require that you have deep knowledge of SCCM, though it does require some knowledge of concepts and terminology.

From a best practices perspective, Microsoft makes these recommendations:

- Use the Current Branch of Configuration Manager for deploying Office 365 ProPlus.
- Enable peer cache on your client devices, which will provide benefits during both initial deployment and updating.
- Deploy Office using the Office Client Management Dashboard and Office 365 Installer wizard.
- Ensure your endpoints have internet access so they can complete Office 365 ProPlus activation.
- Ensure the Configuration Manager server can reach `https://config.office.com` on port `443`.
- If Enhanced Security Configuration for Internet Explorer is enabled on the Configuration Manager server, add `https://.office.com` and `https://.officeconfig.msocdn.com` to Trusted Sites.

Before configuring the application, you should identify or configure a collection with at least one device so that you can test the configuration.

To configure Office 365 for deployment, follow these steps:

1. Create a share on the Configuration Manager where you will store the Office 365 ProPlus setup files, such as `\\server\share\Office365ProPlus`.
2. In the Configuration Manager console, expand **Software Library | Overview** and select **Office 365 Client Management.**
3. Select **Office 365 Installer** and wait for the Office 365 Client Installation Wizard to start.
4. On the **Application Settings** page, provide a name and description for the app (such as **Office 365 ProPlus**) and enter the target download location for the files that you created in *Step 1*.
5. Click **Next.**

6. On the **Office Settings** page, select **Go to the Office Customization Tool**. As we mentioned previously, ensure the Configuration Manager server can reach `https://config.office.com`.

7. Configure the settings for this Office 365 installation. Microsoft recommends the following options:

   - **Software**: Select Office 365 ProPlus. You can also include Visio and Project if you plan to deploy those applications. Users must be licensed for any applications that are deployed.
   - **Update channel**: Choose **Semi-Annual Channel** to configure the installation package for a broad group or **Semi-Annual (Targeted)** for deploying to a pilot group.
   - **Languages**: Include all the language packs you plan to deploy.
   - **Upgrades**: Choose to automatically remove all previous MSI versions of Office.
   - **Additional properties**: To silently install Office for your users, set the **Display level** to **Off** and **Automatically accept the EULA** to **On**.
   - **Application settings**: Define any additional Office settings. Ensure you select default Office formats.

8. After you have selected the required options, click **Submit.**

9. On the **Deployment** page, select **Yes** to deploy the application, and then click **Next.**

10. On the **General** page, select the test collection you previously identified or created.

11. Complete the wizard.

Using these steps, System Center Configuration Manager will configure the clients so that they automatically update from the Office CDN. You can go through an additional process to enable the Configuration Manager so that it manages the update cycle for Office 365 ProPlus applications as well.

For more information on managing updates with Configuration Manager, go to `https://docs.microsoft.com/en-us/DeployOffice/manage-office-365-proplus-updates-with-configuration-manager`.

By now, you should have a good idea about the deployment differences between Office Pro Plus and Office 2016. There are many more methods that you can use to deploy and manage Office 365 ProPlus, which is especially advantageous for organizations with workforces that have varied network configurations or have remote workers that don't often connect to corporate resources.

Now, we'll look at some of the differences in licensing between Office 2016 and Office 365 ProPlus.

Licensing Office Editions

Just as there are different types of product technology available when it comes to Office software, there are also different licensing and acquisition methods. In this section, we'll look at the following differences:

- Licensing Office Professional 2016
- Licensing Office 365 ProPlus

Licensing Office Professional 2016

Traditionally, Office products have been licensed with what is known as a **perpetual license**. This means you purchase it once and you're never obligated to make another payment again for the product unless you want to upgrade to a new version or need support on it. If Office 2016 meets your needs, you can purchase it once through a channel (such as a retail or volume license) and then continue to use Office 2016 until you no longer have a means to run the software, whether that's next year or 10 years from now.

There are some benefits to this licensing model, as follows:

- It's a fixed cost and can be capitalized easily, from an accounting point of view.
- Software can be licensed per-device or per-user, depending on which scenario is most beneficial to the organization.

Some of the drawbacks of this model, however, include the following:

- It's possible to let the software grow stale and unsupportable.
- The software is a legacy architecture and requires complex migration planning to upgrade.

- It's very easy to under-license and over-deploy.
- Organizations may be responsible for paying for costs and penalties for *all* the licenses that are deployed (even if the media is stolen or taken home by an employee).

As such, Microsoft is shifting away from perpetual licensing models to subscription-based models like that of Office 365 ProPlus.

Licensing Office 365 ProPlus

From a licensing perspective, Office 365 ProPlus is part of the Microsoft 365 subscription. Because it's a subscription, there are certain important requirements and features. They are as follows:

- Licensing is user-identity based, meaning a user must have an Azure AD account and have an Office 365 ProPlus license associated with it.
- Office 365 ProPlus can be installed on up to five different computers (Windows PC or Mac), five tablet devices, *and* five mobile phones with one single-user license, for a total of 15 installations. Users activate their subscription by signing in with their tenant credentials.
- Office 365 ProPlus *does* support a shared computer activation configuration. Scenarios where this might be useful include if users share workstation devices (such as shift workers) or are configured to use non-persistent virtual desktop environments.
- Office 365 ProPlus is activated over the internet, so the licensing service that's deployed on the computer must be able to reach the internet to check in every 30 days and verify that the user still has a valid subscription. If the status cannot be verified, or if the user remains offline for more than 30 days, OPP goes into reduced functionality mode.

This is important and will show up on the exam. If a device is offline for more than 30 days, OPP will be in reduced functionality mode. In reduced functionality mode, users can **only view** or **print** their documents. Other features such as edit or create will be unavailable.

When looking at this, a few benefits emerge:

- Since licensing is user-based, it's very easy to understand how many licenses need to be acquired. Users get a total of 15 that they can tie to their user account.
- When a user leaves the organization, their identity is typically deactivated and their license returned to the organization's pool. There's no need to worry about licensed "installations in the field" as they will stop working in 30 days.
- The update servicing mechanism is built-in by default, so installations will always be up to date and in a supported state.

The only potential drawback is for organizations that like to maintain their software as an "asset," since the subscription is an operating expense instead of a capital expense.

As you can see, there are some important choices to make when deploying technologies, updating and servicing methodologies, as well as choosing a product and licensing model that achieves your organization's business needs.

Summary

In this chapter, we learned about the differences between Office ProPlus and the legacy Office 2016 platform.

We covered the four different installation options for Office ProPlus, including self-service and IT-driven deployments. You also learned about the update servicing methodology, along with the channels and differences between traditional Windows Installer-based installations and the new Click-to-Run technology.

By completing this chapter, you should be able to explain the benefits and advantages an Office 365 ProPlus subscription has over the traditional perpetual license of Office 2016 Professional.

In the next chapter, we'll discuss the collaboration and mobility options that are available with Microsoft 365, including how the Microsoft 365 options enable remote and mobile working scenarios for modern organizations.

Questions

Answer the following questions to test your knowledge of this chapter. You can find the answers in *Assessment Answers*:

1. You are the administrator of your organization. You need to deploy an Office 365 ProPlus configuration that allows users to get updates twice a year. Which two options should you choose?
    1. Monthly channel
    2. Monthly channel (targeted)
    3. Semi-annual channel
    4. Semi-annual channel (targeted)

2. You have several users who are part of the Office Business Insiders program. They need to be configured to receive the latest Office 365 ProPlus updates. Which option should you choose?
    1. Monthly channel
    2. Monthly channel (targeted)
    3. Semi-annual channel
    4. Semi-annual channel (targeted)

3. You are assisting a user in troubleshooting their Office 365 ProPlus installation. The user reports that while they are able to print or view documents, they cannot create a new document or edit an existing one. What are the two most likely causes of this issue?
    1. The user does not have a subscription for Office 365 ProPlus.
    2. The user's document is read-only.
    3. The user's profile is corrupt.
    4. The Office 365 ProPlus activation service has been unable to connect to the internet for 30 days.

4. Which two options best describe Office 365 ProPlus licensing?
    1. It is a subscription.
    2. It is a perpetual license.
    3. It is per-user based.
    4. It is device-based.

5. Which two options best describe Office 2016 Professional licensing?
    1. It is a subscription.
    2. It is a perpetual license.
    3. It is per-user based.
    4. It is per-user or per-device based.

6. Office 365 ProPlus uses the Windows Installer platform.
    1. True
    2. False

7. Identify the technology platform used for Office 365 ProPlus.
    1. Windows Installer
    2. MSI
    3. Click-to-Run
    4. Run-Anywhere

8. Identify the tool that's used to configure the options for the Office installation.
    1. Office Deployment Tool
    2. Office Configuration Tool
    3. Office Customization Tool
    4. Office Installation Tool

9. The Office configuration XML file can be configured through which of the following?
    1. `https://configure.office.com`
    2. `https://config.office.com`
    3. `https://config.office365.com`
    4. `https://configure.office365.com`

10. Which two options does Office 365 ProPlus require?
    1. Azure Identity
    2. Office 365 ProPlus subscription license
    3. Office perpetual license
    4. KMS server

7
Understanding Collaboration and Mobility

In Chapter 3, *Core Microsoft 365 Components,* and Chapter 4, *Comparing Core Services in Microsoft 365,* we discussed the core technologies that make up Microsoft 365: Exchange Online, SharePoint Online, Teams, Windows 10, and the Enterprise Mobility + Security suite. Chapter 6, *Understanding Office 365 ProPlus,* covered the basics of deploying the Office 365 ProPlus software platform.

In this chapter, we will bring all of those technologies together to highlight effective collaboration with Microsoft 365. We will be focusing on enterprise mobility, device management, and application management within an organization. This chapter will be split into two sections: the first will concentrate on effective collaboration with different parts of Microsoft 365 and the second will cover the benefits of enterprise mobility and device and application management.

These two sections will bring all of the Microsoft 365 technologies together so you can be equipped to address and think critically to meet an organization's collaboration, productivity, and security needs. Being able to evaluate and understand the scenarios presented here is critical for both the effective use of the Microsoft 365 platform as well as the MS-900 exam.

In this chapter, we will address the following:

- Discussing effective collaboration with Microsoft 365
- Understanding enterprise mobility and device and application management

Discussing effective collaboration with Microsoft 365

We discussed in `Chapter 3`, *Core Microsoft 365 Components*, the different platforms that can provide collaboration between coworkers:

- **Exchange Online** provides email communication and a calendar.
- **SharePoint Online** provides a single repository of sorts in which members can store, share, and edit files, data, and news.
- **Teams** provides a hub for people to chat and video conference, while incorporating SharePoint Online, **OneDrive for Business**, and other apps within a single interface.

These core technologies provide a basis for collaboration and productivity. We've mentioned these foundational services of Office 365 several times.

These apps and services may either work on top of the core Microsoft 365 technologies such as SharePoint Online or Teams or complement collaboration by providing different functions. In this section, we will cover the other collaboration products that also come with Microsoft 365 as part of the suite. MS-900 will have scenarios where you need to identify the correct service to meet an organization's needs.

The following table provides a list of additional Office 365 services and one-line descriptions for each:

Service	Description
Delve	Manage your Office 365 profile, and discover and manage personal insight and relevant data based on who you work with and what you work on.
Excel	This is a powerful spreadsheet program to discover and connect to data and model, analyze, and visualize insights.
Forms	Build simple surveys, quizzes, and polls to easily share with others and see results in real time.
Kaizala	This a phone number-based secure mobile chat app for work.
MyAnalytics	These help to build better work and productivity habits using analytics and insights from Office 365.
OneDrive	Store, access, and share files in one place from multiple devices.
OneNote	This is a digital notebook to capture and organize notes across all devices.
Outlook	This provides email and a calendar in one rich and familiar Outlook experience.
Planner	Easily create and manage simple plans, organize and assign tasks, share files, and get progress update with other teammates.

Power Automate (formerly Microsoft Flow)	Seamlessly integrate apps and services to automate time-consuming and repetitive tasks.
Power BI	Create coherent, interactive, and engaging dashboards from various data sources and easily share insights.
PowerPoint	This is a powerful presentation platform to deliver clear and engaging displays during meetings and proposals.
Power Apps	Build and publish modules, rich forms, and web apps with various data sources with little to no code.
Stream	This is a secure workplace video platform to manage video content such as recorded training, announcements, or meetings and share them within the organization.
Sway	This is a digital storytelling platform to create and share interactive reports, presentations, and personal stories.
To Do	Create task lists to manage, prioritize, and complete.
Whiteboard	This is a freeform canvas to ideate and collaborate, designed for pen, touch, and keyboard.
Word	This is a document platform for word processing, editing, and sharing.
Yammer	This is an enterprise social network platform to connect with coworkers and classmates, share information, and organize projects.

Each of these services is designed to seamlessly integrate with the Office 365 platform. They can operate individually or be integrated into SharePoint Online, Teams, or both to help with collaboration and productivity.

 Make sure that you know each app and the collaboration and productivity features it provides to an organization for the exam.

However, there are additional apps and services native to Office 365 that come alongside the core services and offer more features—services such as **Stream**, **Planner**, **Forms**, and **Yammer**. You'll need to know about these different services so you can both address any other collaboration needs within your organization and pass the MS-900 exam.

We'll take a look at some of the apps in a little more detail next.

Planner

A planner can be used to create simple projects or plans and allows for participants to assign and manage tasks. The planner can be integrated into Teams, as shown in the following screenshot:

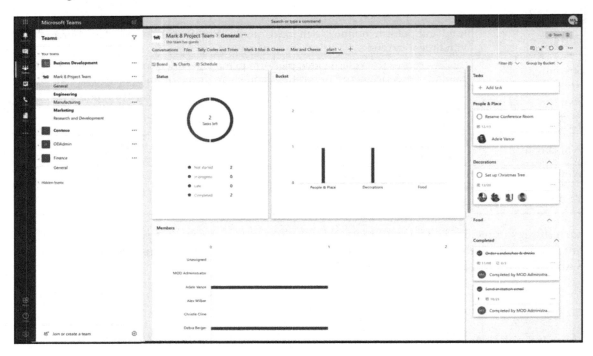

The planner can also be accessed directly through a browser, as the following screenshot shows:

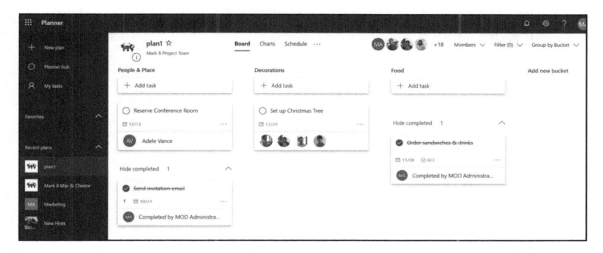

The planner can be incorporated into a Team to start a list of tasks, due dates, and assignments. The app provides different views to help to organize tasks and plans.

Forms

Forms is another way to engage both the organization and the community by creating and sending out simple surveys and forms for others to fill out.

Like Planner, Forms can be integrated within Teams:

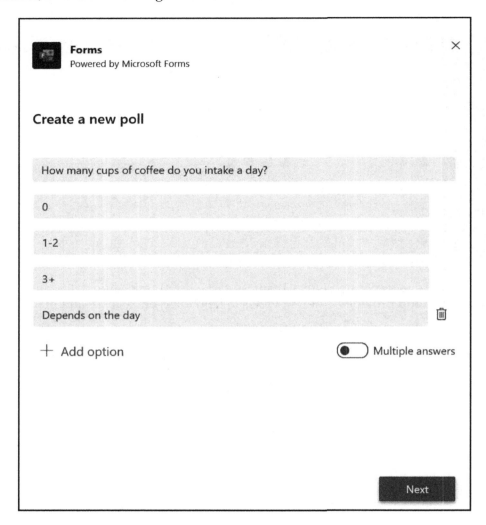

Forms can be used directly inside the Teams client. Forms also has a web interface, as shown here:

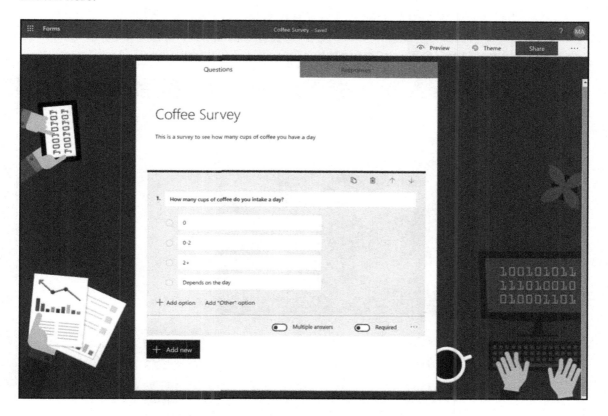

You can create a form and then send or share it with others. As responses start coming in, you can track the responses and export them to Excel for further analysis. You can also view them without having to leave the Teams interface.

Stream

Microsoft Stream is an enterprise video hosting platform. It can be used to host and share videos, including recorded team meetings or live events as well as training content.

Stream, like other Office 365 applications, has a powerful web interface:

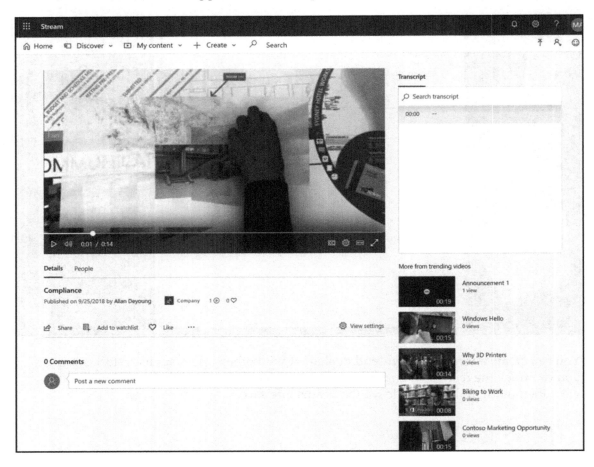

It can also be embedded inside other collaborative tools such as SharePoint Online, as shown here:

Stream videos and channels can also be added to Microsoft Teams channels.

Yammer

Yammer is a social networking platform, integrated into Office 365. Yammer has a feed-style interface and is organized by creating groups. Yammer can be used to post announcements, host live events, take polls, follow conversations, and participate in chats. It supports images, file attachments, GIFs, and @ mentions, like other popular social networking platforms.

Yammer can be used to replace the SharePoint Online newsfeed or configured as a part of the web interface on a modern SharePoint page, as shown here:

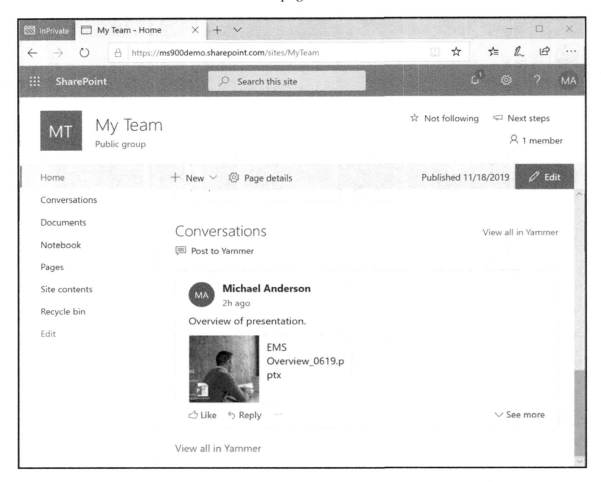

As you can see, these applications have a lot of integrations with other components in Office 365. The application integration allows you to move between applications and draw the user's attention to certain pieces of content, no matter which user interface experience they're using. For example, you can mention or tag a user in Teams, and they'll get an activity notification in Teams as well as one in Outlook. If you mention or tag a user in Yammer, they'll get notifications in Yammer and Outlook. You can use Teams to bring together Stream, video channels, or Yammer group content, making users aware of updates in a single user interface instead of relying on a user being logged in to the particular site or application you're commenting on.

In the next section, we will cover how enterprise mobility concepts of device and application management help to secure these services.

Understanding enterprise mobility and device and application management

Smartphones are essentially pocket-sized portable personal computers. Workers use their phones to check email, join meetings, make calls, view and share documents, and more. More than ever, workers are requiring flexible work hours and the ability to work remotely. Workers in the field can have more flexible and powerful options at their disposal.

Organizations need to find a way to balance performing such activities and enabling productivity without increasing risks such as accidental data leakage. Additionally, work responsibilities might require users to be able to access their work data or applications from a remote location using potentially insecure or non-managed devices. Administrators need to manage the assets of the organization and allow collaboration and productivity in the most secure way possible.

For some, the immediate response to some of thee these scenarios might be to block users from accessing data entirely. However, as the workforce changes, other organizations will adapt and find ways to empower their teams to get more done in non-traditional, flexible ways. The organizations that do this will have a competitive advantage over those that don't.

In the next three sections, we'll discuss enterprise mobility features, device management, and application management to help to address these needs.

Enterprise mobility

Enterprise mobility is a modern approach to business in which the workforce can do their jobs from anywhere using a variety of devices and applications. It typically refers to the use of mobile devices, such as smartphones and tablets, for business purposes. The concept of enterprise mobility also frequently encompasses **Bring-Your-Own-Device (BYOD)** scenarios, where the workforce uses personal devices for business purposes.

Enterprise mobility empowers end users to work in new and flexible ways. Mobile devices such as laptops, tablets, and smartphones have access to work data through the browser and/or apps. This section will go into detail about apps for iOS and Android devices.

Microsoft has released mobile versions of its popular collaboration and productivity tools on both Android and iOS platforms.

The following is a screenshot of the App Store for iPads and iPhones (`https://apps.apple.com/us/developer/microsoft-corporation/id298856275`):

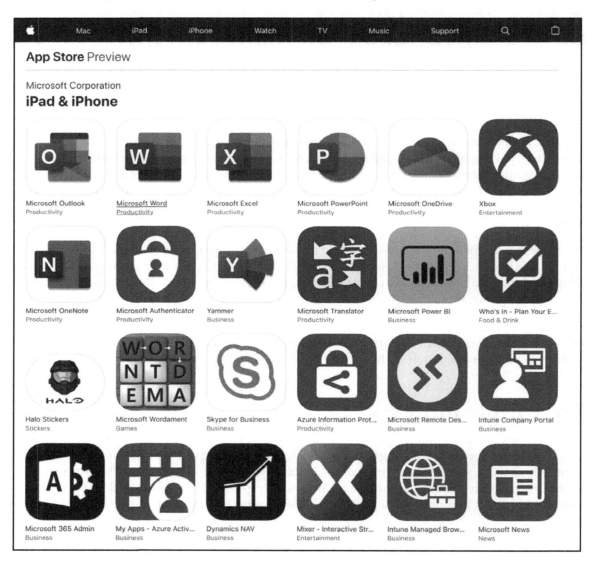

A similar experience is available for Android devices as well (`https://play.google.com/store/apps/developer?id=Microsoft+Corporation`):

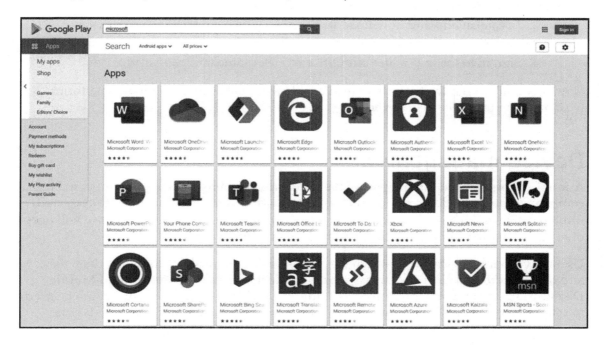

To use any of these apps, follow these steps:

1. Visit the Apple App Store or Google Play Store on your device.
2. Locate an app and download it.
3. Launch the app on your device.
4. Sign in to the app with your Office 365 username and password.

Now that you've seen the tools that are available for collaboration on mobile platforms, we'll move on to device management.

Device management

Administrators can use Intune (part of the Enterprise Mobility + Security suite) to manage a company or personal devices— any device that has access to corporate data. We covered Intune earlier in `Chapter 3`, *Core Microsoft 365 Components*, but in this section, we will deep dive into scenarios and capabilities for device management.

Users have many devices from which they can access, edit, or share company data, files, and other resources. To protect these, most organizations choose some form of **Mobile Device Management** (**MDM**). Intune is a full-featured MDM platform. Intune can be used to set or manage *device* configurations for macOS, Windows, iOS and Android devices.

For example, on any of the supported platforms (Windows, macOS, iOS, or Android), administrators can use Intune's MDM capability to configure device restrictions such as requiring a minimum password length or disabling the device camera. Intune also can be used to remotely reset, delete, or wipe all data on lost or stolen devices, prohibiting malicious parties from obtaining access to corporate assets.

Policies can be configured directly from the Azure management portal by going to `https:/ /portal.azure.com`. In the following example, we've configured a policy that sets the minimum password length to six alphanumeric characters and wipes the device if an incorrect passcode is entered five times:

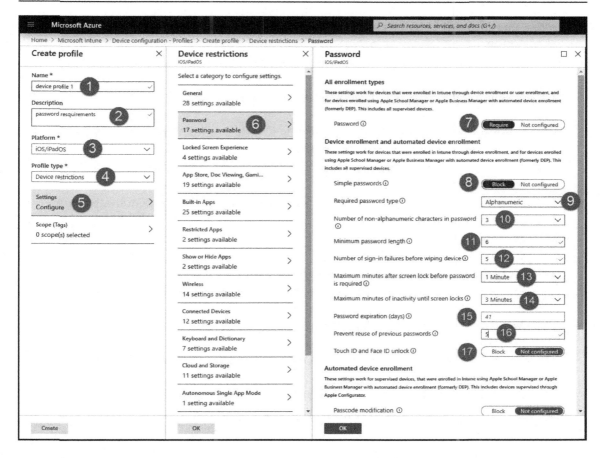

Let's examine the policy profile in a little more detail. Each of the numbered configuration items in the screenshot is referenced in the following list:

1. **Name**: Use this field to identify the policy.
2. **Description**: Use this optional field to provide a description of the policy.
3. **Platform**: Identify which platform these policies configure. In this case, the policy targets iOS devices. To configure additional platforms, you must create another profile.
4. **Profile type**: Select which type of configuration this profile manages. Profile types include device features, restrictions, email. For a complete list of profile types, see https://docs.microsoft.com/en-us/intune/configuration/device-profilesOne.

5. Once a profile type has been chosen, select **Settings** to expand the configurable options.

6. **Passwords**: This node contains all of the password options available for a given profile.

7. **Password**: This toggle controls whether or not a password will be required to unlock the device.

8. **Simple passwords**: This toggle controls whether or not simple passwords (passcodes such as 1234 or 0000) are blocked.

9. **Required password type**: An alphanumeric password is selected, though other options such as "**numeric only**" are available.

10. **Number of non-alphanumeric characters in password**: Three non-alphanumeric characters are required.

11. **Minimum password length**: The minimum length has been set to six characters, though it can go up to 14.

12. **Number of sign-in failures before wiping device**: The user has five tries before the device is wiped and all data erased. This is equivalent to performing a hard reset on the device.

13. **Maximum minutes after screen lock before password is required**: The password is required one minute after the screen is locked.

14. **Maximum minutes of inactivity until screen locks**: The screen locks after three minutes of inactivity.

15. **Password expiration**: This is unconfigured, so the password does not expire.

16. **Prevent reuse of previous passwords**: The previous five passwords are not allowed.

17. **Touch ID and Face ID unlock**: Touch ID and Face ID can be used to unlock the device if the user configures it on the device.

 For more information on other device configurations, please see https://docs.microsoft.com/en-us/intune/configuration/device-profiles.

By setting this simple password requirement profile, any user with an enrolled iOS/iPad device accessing corporate data would have to adhere to these rules. This way, access to company data is permitted once these passwords configurations are set. In this scenario, to unlock the device, end users can also rely on biometrics (Touch ID or Face ID).

To use device profiles, devices must be *enrolled* in Intune. Device enrollment involves allowing an organization to control settings on the device. Many users—especially those in bring-your-own-device scenarios—might be wary of this configuration or see it as an intrusion.

Fortunately, Intune can manage at an even more granular level, which we will cover in application management.

Application management

Intune also provides **Mobile App Management (MAM)** capabilities. Like MDM, MAM controls certain aspects of the user experience when connecting to organizational data. While MDM manages at the *device* level, MAM manages the *application* level.

As we've discussed throughout this book, Microsoft 365 relies heavily on the concept of identity-driven security. All Office 365 applications are accessed by signing into them, essentially securing them as containers. Intune can associate which data belongs to a profile signed in as a managed identity and which data is not (whether it's a managed identity from another tenant or a consumer identity).

This allows administrators to set requirements and configurations so that a user can safely use managed *apps* on an unmanaged (or managed) mobile device. MAM can not only be used to set security requirements, but it also has the capability for deploying, publishing, monitoring, and updating apps on a device as well.

To best illustrate MAM's capabilities, let's take an example of a user who frequently uses the Teams app to stay up to date with team activities and participate in chats and meetings from their personal, non-managed iOS device. This user utilizes their own iOS device to access both organizational data and their own personal data.

The following is a screenshot of an app policy that applies to Microsoft Teams:

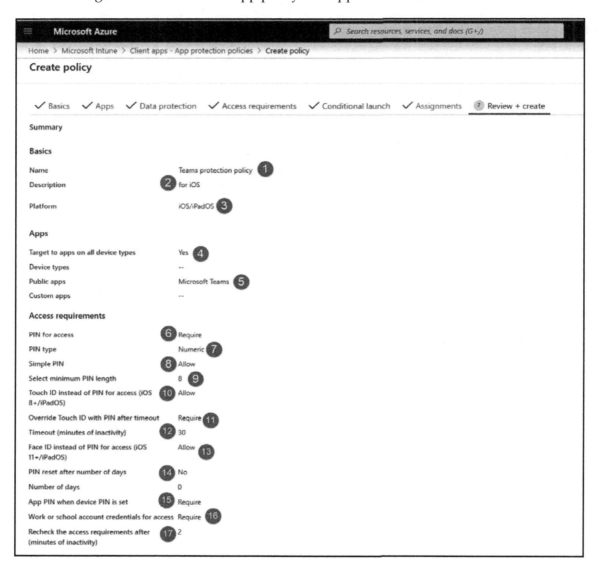

Let's walk through the configuration. The policies numbered in the preceding screenshot are explained as follows:

1. **Name**: Enter the name of the policy.
2. **Description**: Provide a description (optional).
3. **Platform**: Choose the platform for which this policy applies.
4. **Target to apps on all device types**: It is required that this policy applies to all device types.
5. **Public apps**: Choose the public app to target (Microsoft Teams, for this scenario).
6. **Pin for access**: Requires a PIN for access to the Teams app.
7. **Pin type**: Requires the PIN to be numeric. The other type is a *passcode*, which requires at least one alphabetic character.
8. **Simple PIN**: This allows users to use simple PINs, such as 1234 or 0000.
9. **Select minimum PIN length**: Requires the PIN to be at least eight characters.
10. **Touch ID instead of PIN for access (iOS 8+/ iPadOS)**: Allows Touch ID biometric input in place of the PIN for supported devices.
11. **Override Touch ID with PIN after timeout**: If configured, it requires a PIN after inactivity.
12. **Timeout (minutes of inactivity)**: Specify the period of inactivity that constitutes a timeout (30 minutes, in this case).
13. **Face ID instead of PIN for access (iOS 11+ / iPadOS)**: Allows Face ID biometric input in place of the PIN for supported devices.
14. **PIN reset after number of days**: Forces the PIN to be reset after the specified number of days or select **No** to disable this requirement.
15. **App PIN when device PIN is set**: Requires PIN input when the device PIN is set.
16. **Work or school account credentials for access**: Select *Require* to force the user to sign in with their work or school account instead of entering a PIN for app access. If you set this to **Require**, and PIN or biometric prompts are turned on, both corporate credentials and either the PIN or biometric prompts are displayed.
17. **Recheck the access requirements after (minutes of inactivity)**: Configures the number of minutes of inactivity before the app requires the user to again meet the access requirements. This setting is shared across all Intune-managed PIN-enabled applications from the same publisher. In the example, the setting is configured for *2 minutes*.

This policy requires the end user to input a simple eight-digit PIN (or use biometrics such as Face or Touch ID) every time a user wants to access Microsoft Teams on an iOS device.

 For more information on overall MAM capabilities, please see https://docs.microsoft.com/en-us/intune/apps/app-management. For more information on the iOS-specific settings shown earlier, refer to https://docs.microsoft.com/en-us/intune/apps/app-protection-policy-settings-ios.

Intune MAM can further publish, update, and monitor mobile apps. MAM can also support custom apps and third-party apps such as Salesforce that have incorporated the Intune SDK components. MAM can target and remove a company-related app only on a device instead of wiping the whole device, as well as control data movement between managed applications (one example of this might be prohibiting data from a managed identity in a Microsoft Word profile app from being copied to an insecure or unmanaged application, such as iMessage or SMS messages).

As you've seen, the combination of MDM and MAM can be used to ensure users are securely accessing organizational data.

Summary

In this chapter, we first identified other collaboration tools that come with the Microsoft 365 platform, such as Forms, Planner, Yammer, and Power BI. These services can drive additional productivity gains inside an organization.

We also explored what enterprise mobility means in terms of organizational productivity, as well as some scenarios where Microsoft Intune can help to secure mobile device experiences. Emphasizing the security features and capabilities will be important as organizations look toward moving more workloads to cloud services.

In the next chapter, we will discuss Microsoft 365 Analytics and how it can give users valuable insights about their daily habits.

Questions

Use the following questions to test your knowledge of this chapter. You can find the answers in *Assessment Answers*:

1. Enterprise mobility is _____.
    1. Only for Windows and Mac computers
    2. A business approach enabling users to accomplish their jobs from anywhere
    3. Insecure and should be avoided at all costs
    4. A legacy mindset not applicable to the Microsoft 365 platform

2. You need to enable your users to create and manage projects using the Office 365 suite. Which Office 365 application is best suited to accomplish this task?
    1. Microsoft Outlook
    2. SharePoint Online
    3. Planner
    4. Stream

3. You are the administrator of your organization. The marketing team has requested the ability to create a survey to send to external respondents. Which Office 365 application is best suited to accomplish this task?
    1. Planner
    2. To Do
    3. Forms
    4. Surveys

4. You host a live event. After the live event, users who were unable to attend want to view the recording. Which Office 365 application is best suited to accomplish this task?
    1. Stream
    2. Planner
    3. Forms
    4. Azure Active Directory

5. MAM requires Intune device enrollment.
    1. True
    2. False

6. MDM requires Intune device enrollment.
    1. True
    2. False

7. You need to create a profile for every _____ you wish to manage when configuring MDM.
    1. Platform
    2. Brand
    3. Laptop
    4. Application

8. Microsoft Enterprise Mobility + Security features rely on _____-driven security.
    1. Application
    2. Software
    3. Identity
    4. Platform

9. Users can connect their Microsoft mobile applications to their organization's process by doing what?
    1. Installing a certificate on their device
    2. Signing in to the productivity applications using their Office 365 identity
    3. Configuring their Apple ID or Google ID to match their Office 365 identity
    4. Configuring Azure Active Directory Identity Protection

10. You need to enable an internal social networking platform to allow users to communicate informally. Which Office 365 application is best suited to accomplish this?
    1. Stream
    2. Forms
    3. Planner
    4. Yammer

Microsoft 365 Analytics

8

Analytics is an important aspect of every corporate deployment. Among other benefits, it helps organizations understand how services have been deployed and how users are consuming those services. Analytics should be able to reveal complex insights, but they should also be accessible enough to allow organizations to answer important questions right away, such as who is using what, what features or services are the most popular, or which services are not being used at all. Ideally, an analytics solution should also be extensible or accessible using programmatic methods or interfaces such as APIs, so data can be easily imported into other applications.

Microsoft 365 Analytics provides this feature set. Besides service usage, these reports can be used to better understand current employee working habits. This will enable report viewers, from IT or **Adoption and Change Management (ACM)** teams, to be able to leverage continuously updated company usage data to build upon their adoption strategy. This can help organizations promote desired work habits or tools, which are in line with an organization's productivity strategy.

In this chapter, you will learn about the different reports available in Microsoft 365 that present this information. These tools and reports are as follows:

- Activity reports
- Microsoft 365 Usage Analytics
- MyAnalytics

Activity reports

Activity Reports in Microsoft 365 provide administrators and report viewers with the required data to understand how core components of Microsoft 365 are being used across the organization. In order to access Activity Reports, users should have at least one of the following built-in administrator roles:

- Global admins
- Exchange admins
- SharePoint admins
- Skype for Business admins
- Reports reader

 More information about the different administrator roles is available at https://docs.microsoft.com/en-us/office365/admin/add-users/about-admin-roles?view=o365-worldwide.

Activity Reports present data about specific activities being executed by users in services, as well as the device profile that is being used to access them. It provides the following reports:

- Email activity
- Mailbox usage
- Office activations
- Active users
- Email apps usage
- Office 365 groups
- OneDrive for Business user activity
- OneDrive for Business usage
- SharePoint site usage
- SharePoint activity
- Skype for Business Online activity

- Skype for Business Online conference organized activity
- Skype for Business Online conference participant activity
- Skype for Business Online peer-to-peer activity
- Yammer activity
- Yammer device usage
- Yammer groups activity report
- Microsoft Teams user activity
- Microsoft Teams device usage

The Activity Reports screen displays an overview of some of the popular service-based reports, as shown in the following screenshot:

 You can toggle between the current and the new admin center in the top right-hand corner by clicking on **Try the new admin center** to try the new admin center or click on **The new admin center** to return.

To access the Activity Reports, follow these steps:

1. Navigate to the Microsoft 365 admin center (`https://admin.microsoft.com`).
2. Select **Reports** | **Usage:**

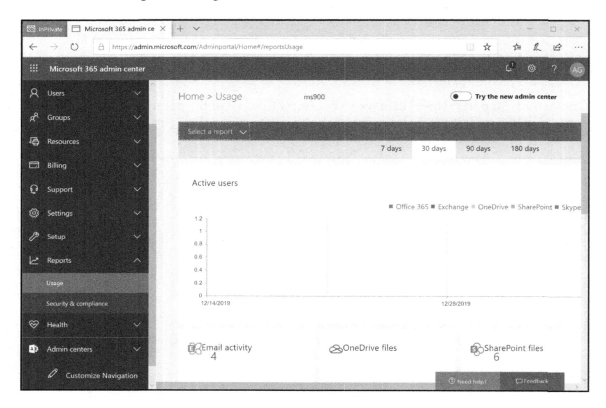

You can switch the report being viewed by using the **Select a report** drop-down menu at the top of the page. With the desired report selected, you can then use the steps in the next section to begin manipulating and exporting reports.

Exporting reports

Activity Reports are updated automatically, and, within the chart view of each one, report viewers can filter historical report data. Report ranges are available for 7 days, 30 days, 90 days, and 180 days, as shown in the following screenshot:

Below each report, report viewers can also have a detailed table view of the numerical data presented in the charts. To download and export a report's data, follow these steps:

1. Log in to the **Microsoft 365 admin center** (https://admin.microsoft.com).
2. Select **Reports | Usage.**

3. Click on **Select a report**, and then select a report for which you wish to download the underlying data:

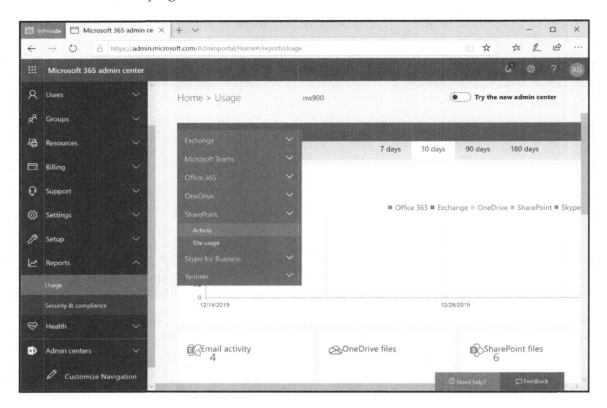

4. Select the **Export** link on the right-hand side of the page to download a CSV file containing the data presented on the graph:

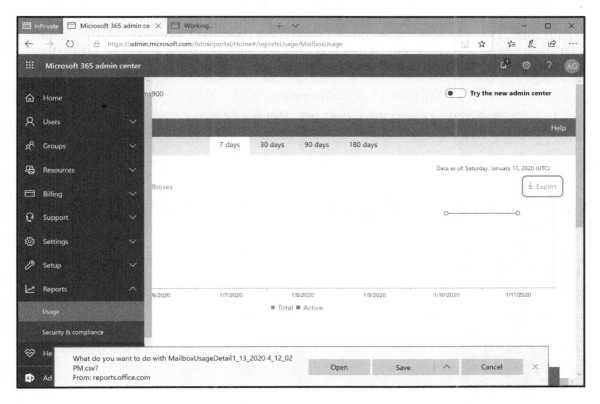

Once you have downloaded the data, you can further analyze it with Excel or Power BI.

Anonymizing data

Many organizations, due to regulatory obligations, don't want report readers to be able to display actual users or display names when reviewing statistical data about an organization. This data can sometimes be classified as **Personal Identifiable Information (PII)**, depending on your locality. Administrators can anonymize the report by using the following steps:

1. Log in to the **Microsoft 365 admin center** (`https://admin.microsoft.com`).
2. Expand **Settings**, and then select **Services & add-ins.**
3. Select **Reports**:

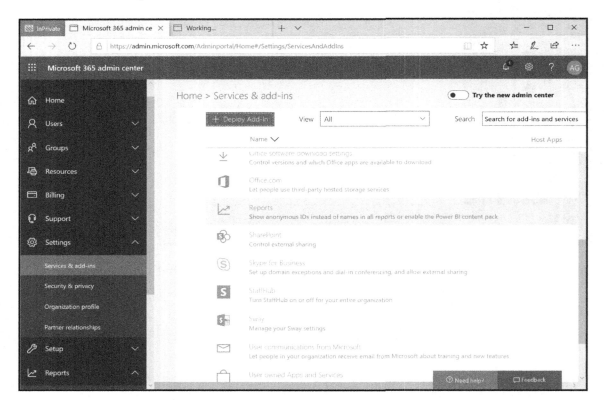

4. Move the slider for **Display anonymous identifiers instead of user, group, or site names in all reports** to **On**:

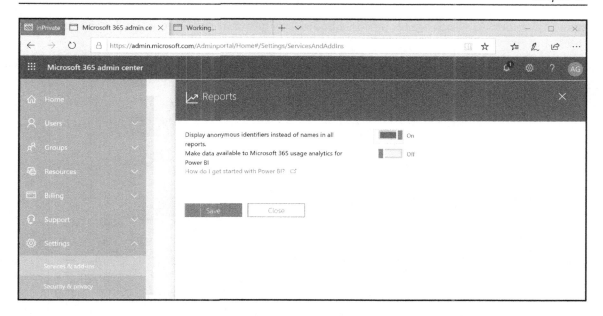

5. Click on **Save**.

Anonymization will be enabled for Activity Reports. When you download any reports where a username or display name is typically shown, it will be replaced with a randomized character string.

 More information about Activity Reports can be found at https://docs. microsoft.com/en-us/office365/admin/activity-reports/activity-reports?view=o365-worldwide.

Activity Reports are the easiest way to view a service's usage data across the organization as it is available automatically to all users with the appropriate roles. However, sometimes, organizations need to customize reports or even have a broader view of usage across the organization. For those use cases, Microsoft 365 Usage Analytics is the solution.

Microsoft 365 Usage Analytics

Some organizations may need a more customized or granular view of usage and analytics data. Microsoft 365 Usage Analytics enables users to view and customize reports using up to 12 months of data. Report data can be published in Power BI, making it available to be shared with other users across the organization.

The Microsoft 365 Usage Analytics dashboard, as shown in the screenshot, has a number of tiles showing usage snapshots:

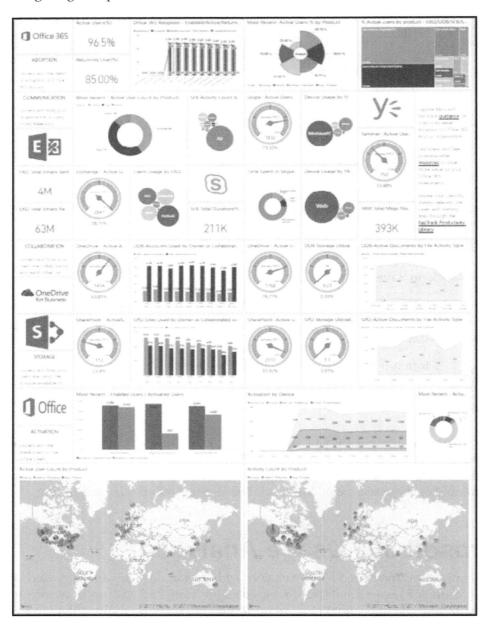

Microsoft 365 Usage Analytics is not enabled by default, but can be activated by administrators through to the following steps:

1. Navigate to the Microsoft 365 admin center (`https://admin.microsoft.com`).
2. Select **Reports | Usage**.
3. Scroll to the bottom of the page and select **Get started** in the **Microsoft 365 usage analytics** card:

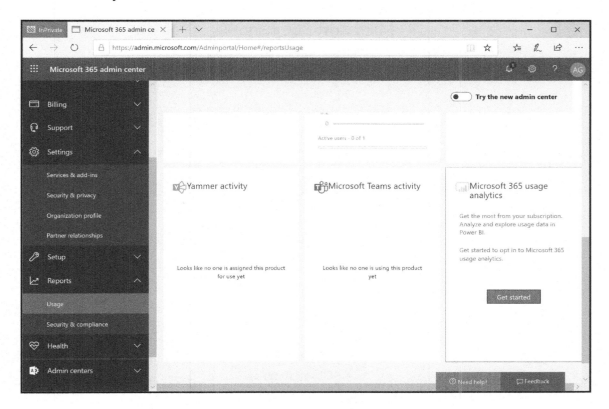

4. Slide the **Make data available to Microsoft 365 usage analytics for Power BI** toggle to **On** and click on **Save.**

5. Click on **Close.**

6. In the previous view, after the data has been made available to Microsoft 365 Usage Analytics, take note of the tenant ID and click on **Go to Power BI**, as shown in the following screenshot:

7. Select **Get Data** on the bottom-left portion of the page, search for Microsoft 365, and then click on **Get it now** on the **Microsoft 365 Usage Analytics** card:

8. Insert your tenant ID, copied from before, and sign in using the **OAuth2** authentication method:

9. If prompted to select a privacy source, select an option, such as **Combine data according to your Privacy Level settings for each source** or **Ignore the Privacy Levels and potentially improve performance**.

10. The app will be installed as follows:

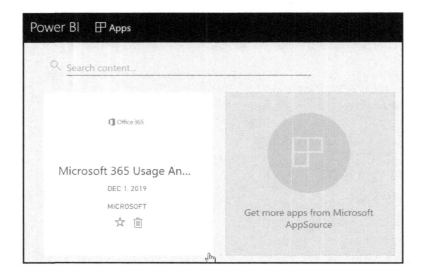

11. Click on the tile to launch the app and start viewing reports:

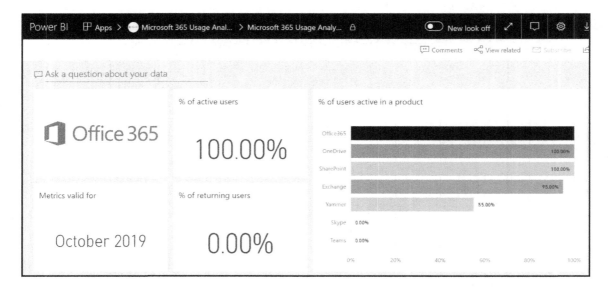

Microsoft 365 Usage Analytics can be also be customized, allowing organizations to integrate existing company information with the services usage data. In order to customize a Microsoft 365 Usage Analytics report, you can choose between the following options:

- Creating reports directly in the browser
- Creating reports from scratch with Power BI Desktop
- Editing the Microsoft 365 Usage Analytics Power BI template file

We'll go over these in more detail now.

Creating reports directly in the browser

In order to create a custom report in the Microsoft 365 Usage Analytics app, the following steps can be taken:

1. Navigate to Power BI (https://powerbi.microsoft.com).
2. From the default **Microsoft 365 Usage Analytics** dashboard page, click on the top of the ellipsis, and then select **View related:**

3. Under **My workspace** | **Datasets**, click on the create report icon (the vertical bar graph icon with a + symbol):

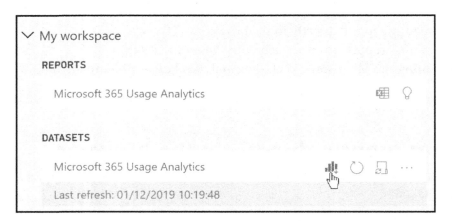

4. Start editing your report by applying filters and visualizations. When finished, select **File** | **Save:**

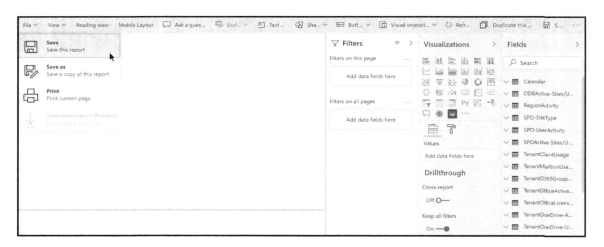

After the report has been saved, you can publish it and make it available to other users in your organization.

While it's important to know that Microsoft 365 Usage Analytics allows reporting with Power BI, you don't need in-depth knowledge of Power BI for the MS-900 exam.

Although custom reports and views can be configured through this approach, it is not possible to add custom data from different sources.

Creating reports from scratch with Power BI Desktop

In order to create a custom report from scratch with Power BI Desktop for the Microsoft 365 Usage Analytics data, the following steps can be taken:

1. Open the Power BI Desktop application.
2. Select **Get Data** and then select **OData feed:**

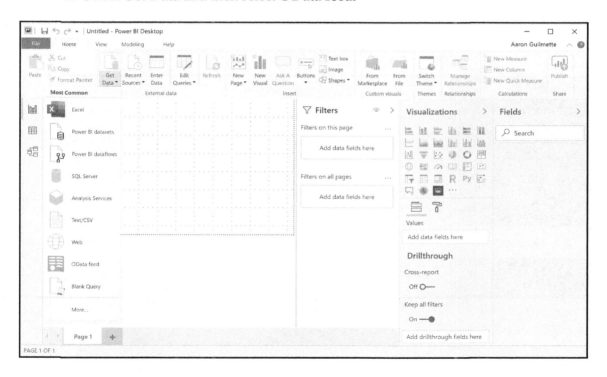

3. Insert the Office 365 reporting URL,
   `https://reports.office.com/pbi/v1.0/TenantID`, replacing `TenantID`
   with the value for your tenant, for example,
   `https://reports.office.com/pbi/v1.0/abcd1234-1234-abcd-ab12-123`
   `4abcd1234`. You can locate your tenant ID in the Azure Admin Portal, or in the
   Microsoft 365 admin center under **Reports** | **Usage** (on the Microsoft 365
   Analytics tile). Select the **Basic** radio button and then click on **OK**:

4. Select **Organizational account** and **Sign in** with an authorized user:

5. Selected your desired fields from the available data:

6. Create and customize your report:

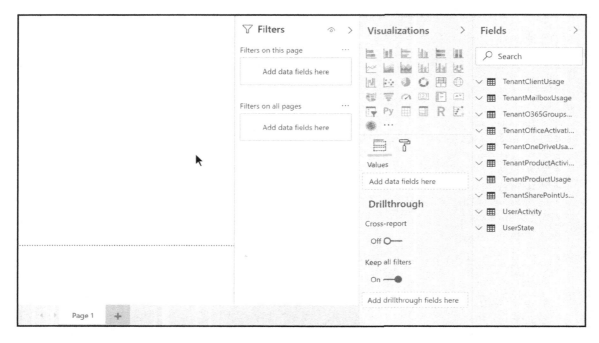

This approach allows you to add any desired custom data and customize the report as desired. Once you have finished customizing it to your liking, you can publish and share it.

Editing the Microsoft 365 Usage Analytics Power BI template file

You can also use Power BI to modify an existing definition or template to display more customized information. In order to use the existing Power BI template file to create a custom Microsoft 365 Usage Analytics report, the following steps can be taken:

1. Download and save the Power BI template file from Microsoft Download Center, which is available at `https://download.microsoft.com/download/7/8/2/782ba8a7-8d89-4958-a315-dab04c3b620c/Microsoft%20365%20Usage%20Analytics.pbit`.

2. Using Power BI Desktop, open the template file you saved in the previous step.

3. Insert your tenant ID, which can be obtained from the Activity Reports page in the Microsoft 365 admin center (`https://admin.microsoft.com` | **Reports** | **Usage** | **Microsoft 365 Analytics card**) and then click on **Load**.

4. After loading the data, customize the report as desired:

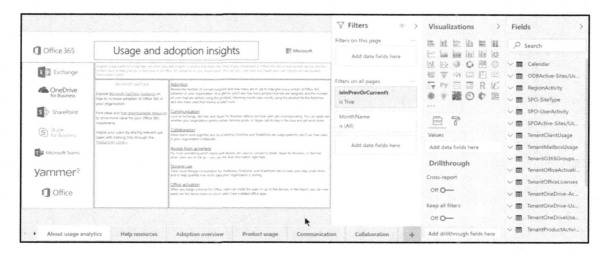

As in the previous option, it is up to the report owner to publish and make sure data stays current.

In addition to the usage reports targeted toward business owners or administrators already introduced in this chapter, there are also reports that help individual users understand and shape how they work, which we will cover next.

MyAnalytics

Almost every person approaches their work differently. Without dedicating time to taking measurements and understanding how you work, it may not be obvious how you're spending your time. MyAnalytics solves this by providing users with a personal view of their working habits, broken apart into measurable areas, such as the following:

- **Focus**: Time for individual work
- **Wellbeing**: Time disconnected from work
- **Network**: Relationship with people in your network
- **Collaboration**: Who you have collaborated with

The following screenshot illustrates an example of a MyAnalytics personal view:

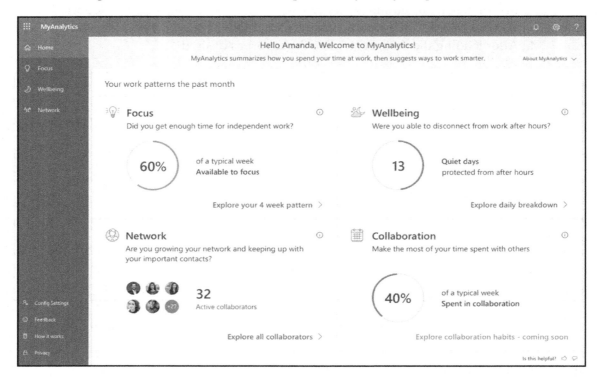

In addition to details about how users have spent their time and their connections, MyAnalytics provides suggestions for users to help them improve their collaboration, network, and focus time. The MyAnalytics dashboard can be accessed from the following URL: https://myanalytics.microsoft.com. There is also an Outlook add-in that you can use to share insights about working habits, as well as messages being sent or received, as shown in the following screenshot:

More information about MyAnalytics, including its add-ins, is available
at https://docs.microsoft.com/en-us/Workplace-Analytics/
myanalytics/use/mya-elements.

Understanding how and with whom we work is one of the first steps to start improving our working habits. MyAnalytics users can see their personal data and receive suggestions about how to improve in order to be more productive across different measures.

Summary

Microsoft 365 provides organizations with different data views and analyses that can be used to support their adoption strategy for services.

In this chapter, we learned about how report viewers can answer important questions regarding their service usage through Activity Reports and how Microsoft 365 Usage Analytics reports allow organizations to explore their own users' interactions. In addition to this, we also covered how MyAnalytics enables users to understand how they work, as a way to improve their working habits.

As you've seen, Microsoft 365 provides a number of analytics tools to help organizations realize the most from their investment.

In the next chapter, we will introduce security and compliance concepts with Microsoft 365 and what tools organizations have available to them to increase their security stance.

Questions

Use the following questions to test your knowledge of this chapter. You can find the answers in *Assessment Answers*:

1. You are a Microsoft 365 administrator for your organization. As part of a business initiative, you have been asked for both aggregate data and detailed dashboards of where your organization stands in relation to Microsoft 365 adoption. What two tools would be most helpful in providing this data?
    1. Microsoft 365 Activity Reports
    2. Azure audit logs
    3. Security & Compliance Center audit logs
    4. Microsoft 365 Usage Analytics
    5. Power BI
    6. Excel
    7. SharePoint Site Collection Reports

2. You want to enable users to review their own personal work habit analytics. Which service should you direct them to?
   1. Microsoft 365 Activity Reports
   2. MyAnalytics
   3. Microsoft 365 Usage Analytics
   4. Power BI

3. Identify four areas that MyAnaltics reports on:
   1. Focus
   2. Security
   3. Wellbeing
   4. Network
   5. Collaboration
   6. Teamwork

4. Microsoft 365 Usage Analytics can be imported into which two tools or services?
   1. Power BI
   2. Power BI Desktop
   3. Power BI Network
   4. Power BI Enterprise

5. In order to connect Microsoft 365 Usage Analytics to Power BI, what data must you provide?
   1. Activity report ID
   2. Tenant ID
   3. Power BI Template ID
   4. Global Administrator Object ID

6. Microsoft 365 Activity Reports are accessed through which interface?
   1. Security & Compliance Center
   2. Microsoft 365 Admin Center
   3. Report Center
   4. SharePoint Admin Center

7. In order to reduce exposure for personally identifiable information, administrators can enable what feature for Microsoft 365 Activity Reports?
   1. Randomization
   2. Anonymization
   3. Exfiltration
   4. Obfuscation

9
Understanding Security and Compliance Concepts

Data security and compliance with regulatory acts are important for nearly every organization. From privacy legislation (such as the European Union's General Data Protection Regulation or the United States' Health Insurance Privacy and Portability Act) to financial regulation (Sarbanes-Oxley) to industry compliance (Payment Card Industry Data Security Standard), organizations need to be mindful of how data is stored and transmitted.

With the rise of cybersecurity breaches and attacks, there is an urgent need to understand the proper configurations on available services and features. As we mentioned in Chapter 7, *Understanding Collaboration and Mobility*, cloud services have changed the way organizations plan and deploy technology and secure data.

A clear understanding of Microsoft 365's out of the box security and compliance-related features and services is the key to successfully deploying cloud services.

In this chapter, we will cover the key security pillars of protection and introduce the Secure Score, a tool that can help companies increase their security posture.

In this chapter, we will explore the following security and compliance concepts:

- Identity
- Documents
- Network
- Devices

We'll also look at a tool Microsoft provides that can be used to evaluate the tenant's security posture: Secure Score. Let's get started!

Identity

Cloud services pose new challenges. Traditionally, users do the following:

- Only access the organization's resources inside the organization's network perimeter
- Only access the organization's services, which are hosted on the organization's hardware

With cloud services, enterprise mobility, bring-your-own-device objectives, and the consumerization of IT, all that has changed. Users are accessing a variety of services from a multitude of vendors from both company-owned and personal devices. Identity is the new security perimeter for companies since it is the ultimate key to access.

From a cloud service perspective, identity defines who users are, what permissions they have, and what they can do with these permissions. With that, organizations need to plan how to protect users wherever they are.

As we have discussed throughout this book, Microsoft 365 already includes a directory service called **Azure Active Directory (AAD)**. Azure Active Directory stores the identity information for your Microsoft 365 tenant. AAD has several features that can be planned and deployed to further improve an organizational security stance, such as the following:

- Users and attributes
- Groups
- Permissions
- Audit logs
- Credential management

Let's look at each in more detail.

Users and attributes

AAD allows organizations to manage their users and attributes. The entire user life cycle, including their creation, license assignment, and deletion, can be managed directly from the cloud admin centers, or, if you prefer, you could manage users from PowerShell or Microsoft Graph. Moreover, if an organization already has a directory in place, such as **Active Directory (AD)**, it can also synchronize it with AAD in order to replicate users, attributes, groups, and even password hashes.

Microsoft Graph is a *unified programmability model* that ties in services such as Office 365, Dynamics 365, Azure, Azure AD, and more. For more information, please go to `https://docs.microsoft.com/en-us/graph/overview`.

A view of the list of users in a tenant, along with their current assigned licenses from the Microsoft 365 Admin Center, can be seen in the following screenshot:

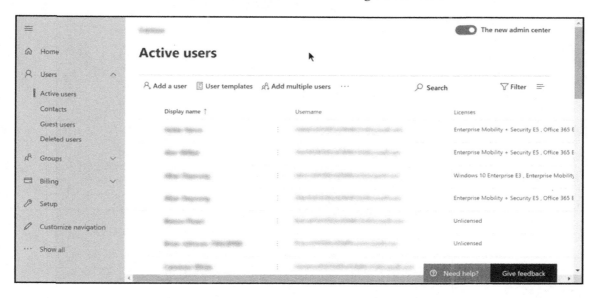

From this view, administrators can view users and their assigned licenses. If a user does not have a license assigned, the *Licenses* and **Apps** tab will show **Unlicensed**. Active users can either be *cloud-only users* or users in your Active Directory that have been synchronized to Microsoft 365.

Different cloud identity models, features, and scenarios will be covered in more detail in the next chapter.

In addition, AAD enables the management of users' attributes, such as **Display Name**, **User Principal Name** (which is how users are identified during the login process), **Job Title**, **Office Location, Usage Location, Sign-In Status** (Allowed or Blocked), and **manager**. These users and attributes are made available across the entire Microsoft 365 platform.

For every user in the organization, administrators can view their current attributes, as shown in the following screenshot:

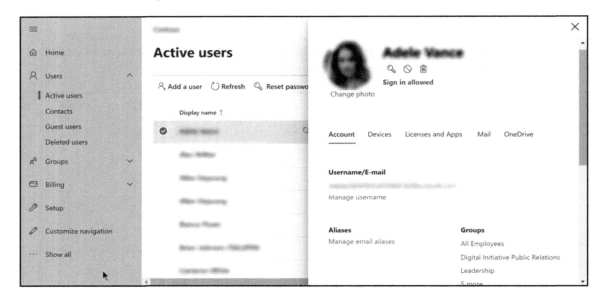

Next, we'll look at the concept of groups.

Groups

Microsoft 365 supports different types of groups that can be used across services for security permissions assignment, email distribution, team collaboration, and more. The different types of groups that are available in Microsoft 365, along with their recommended usage scenario, are as follows:

- **Distribution List Groups:** Used for sending emails to a group of users.
- **Security Groups:** Used for granting permissions to SharePoint resources, such as site administration.
- **Mail-enabled Security Groups:** Similar to security groups, but also allows emails to be sent to members, such as a distribution group.
- **Office 365 Groups:** A new security construct that has both security and collaboration features.

A complete list of all group types is available at the following documentation: `https://docs.microsoft.com/en-us/office365/admin/ create-groups/compare-groups?view=o365-worldwide`.

Through the admin center, as well as PowerShell or Microsoft Graph, administrators can view current groups, along with their group types, as shown in the following screenshot:

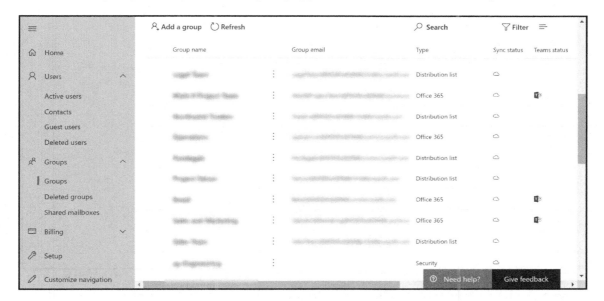

In addition, when creating a new group, the administrator can select the group type, as shown in the following screenshot:

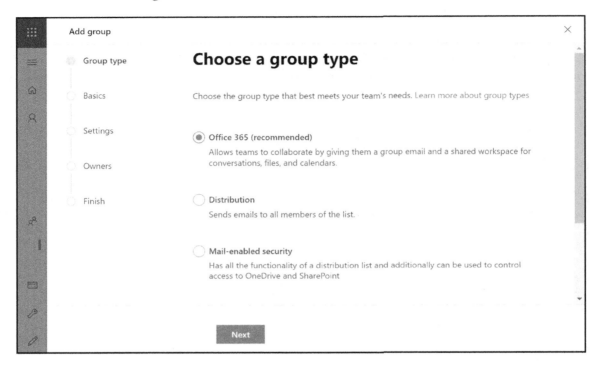

In the preceding screenshot, an Office 365 Group has been selected. As we've discussed throughout this book, Office 365 Groups are tightly integrated with many Microsoft 365 services, including Teams, Planner, SharePoint, and Yammer.

Depending on the organizational business and security requirements, Office 365 Groups can be configured to allow members to invite external users. When an Office 365 Group is created, Office 365 automatically assigns and provides access to several resources across the suite, such as the following:

- Shared mailbox for group emails
- SharePoint team site for document and content sharing
- Planner plan for tasks collaboration
- Teams team as the collaboration hub, if created in Microsoft Teams
- Yammer group for social networking, if created in Yammer
- Power BI workspace

Office 365 Groups has a wide variety of features available, such as the following:

- Group naming policies, to help ensure naming standards across groups
- Group expiration, to ensure old or unused groups are retired
- Dynamic membership, which is used to keep the group membership updated automatically
- External users
- Group writeback from Azure AD back to Active Directory, allowing the group to show up in an on-premises Global Address List

Each of these features should be carefully evaluated to make sure the best options are being selected for the organization's needs.

Permissions

Permissions allow organizations to provide certain individuals with elevated access so that they can perform specific operations in the service. A common strategy that's shared across different Microsoft 365 admin centers is the concept of **Role-Based Access Control (RBAC)**. RBAC will allow, under the minimum level of permissions needed, users, categorized by roles, to execute their tasks, and only their tasks.

Microsoft 365 has a granular permissions model that allows organizations to have multiple administrators whose administrative abilities can be scoped to certain groups of tasks. The roles that are available in Microsoft 365 are as follows:

- **Global admin**: The most permissive role with the rights to access and modify all configurations in all the Admin Centers. They can also reset the passwords of all users and add and manage domains.
- **Billing admin**: Makes purchases, manages subscriptions and service requests, and monitors the health service.
- **Help desk admin**: Can reset passwords for non-admin users, help users sign out, manage service requests, and monitor service health.
- **License admin**: Can assign and remove user licenses and usage location.
- **Reports reader**: Access reports dashboard, Power BI adoption content packs, sign-in reports, and the Microsoft Graph reporting API.
- **User admin**: Reset user passwords, manage user and groups, manage service requests, and monitor service health.

- **Exchange admin**: Full access to the EXO Admin Center, manages Office 365 groups and service requests, and monitors service health.
- **SharePoint admin**: Full access to the SPO Admin center, manages Office 365 groups and service requests, and monitors service health.
- **Teams admin**: Full access to the Teams Admin Center, manages Office 365 groups and service requests, and monitors service health.

A complete list with all possible permissions levels in AAD is available here: https://docs.microsoft.com/en-us/office365/admin/add-users/ about-admin-roles.

To assign a role to a user in the Microsoft 365 Admin Center, an administrator with proper permissions can edit a user's properties and assign an administrator role, as shown in the following screenshot:

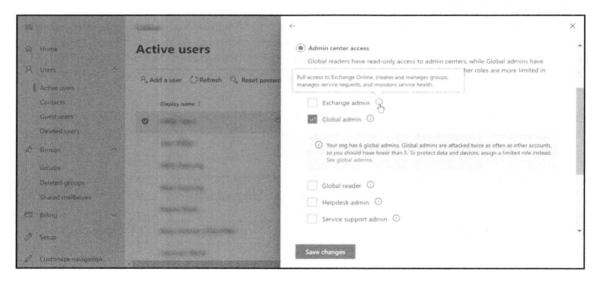

Additionally, more granular roles can be assigned in the Azure Active Directory Role and administrators blade, which is available in the Azure Portal (`https://aad.portal.azure. com`), as shown in the following screenshot:

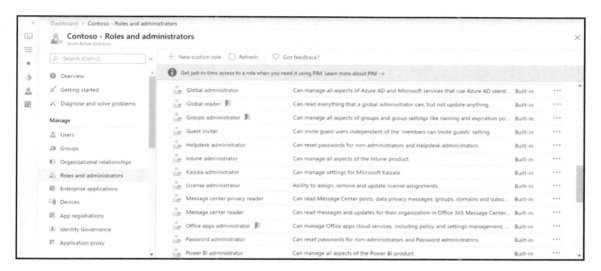

As part of a least-privilege model, organizations can also use **Privileged Identity Management (PIM)**. PIM allows designated users to be granted elevated permissions for a period of time. PIM can be configured with a series of workflows to ensure proper approval is granted before assigning the role permissions. With this feature, organizations are able to significantly limit the number of fully-privileged accounts in their environment, reducing their attack surface.

Azure Active Directory Privileged Identity Management is configured through the Azure Portal (`https://portal.azure.com`), as shown in the following screenshot:

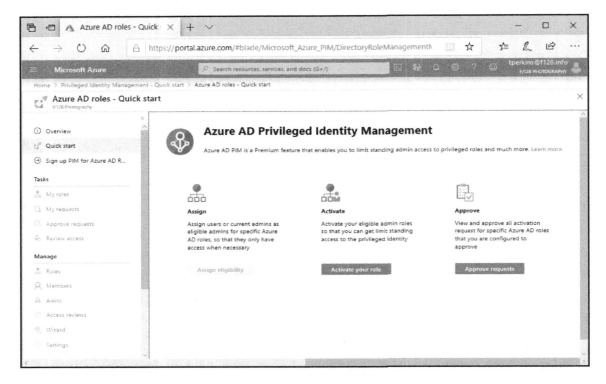

Organizations should follow best practices when considering their permission, role, and administration strategies. Some recommendations include the following:

- Have no more than four global admins or less than two.
- Whenever possible, assign the *least permissive* role to administrators.
- Require **Multi-Factor Authentication** (**MFA**) from all admins and end users.

We'll look at more recommendations later in this chapter.

Audit logs

Successful operations and governance strategy rely partially on being able to audit actions taken in the service. Microsoft 365 allows administrators to review activities that are performed either by users or administrators through the audit logs. Audit logs are available in the Security & Compliance Center, which is located at `https://protection.office.com`.

Some audited actions include the following:

- File and page operations
- Sharing and access request activities
- Exchange mailbox activity
- User administration activity
- Role administration activity
- eDiscovery tasks
- Microsoft Teams operations
- Exchange admin operations

 For a complete list of all the currently audited activities, please check out the following documentation: `https://docs.microsoft.com/en-us/office365/securitycompliance/search-the-audit-log-in-security-and-compliance`.

By default, audit logs are disabled. Administrators can enable them by opening the **Security and Compliance Center** and clicking **Turn on auditing**, as shown in the following screenshot:

When viewing audit logs, administrators can filter audit logs according to the following options:

- **Activities**
- **Start date**
- **End date**
- **Users**
- **File, folder or site**

Currently, Microsoft 365 audit logs are retained in the service for 90 days for users with a Microsoft 365 E3 license, or for 1 year for users with a Microsoft 365 E5 license. If an organization wants to retain data for a longer period of time, they will need to plan and deploy a solution to capture that data, such as Azure Sentinel, Log Analytics, or an on-premises **Security Information and Event Management (SIEM)** product. This can be accomplished through PowerShell or with the Office 365 Management Activity API.

To export a list of audit log entries, an administrator can open the audited data and click on **Export results**, as shown in the following screenshot:

A report will be made available to an administrator in CSV format.

Alerts

Another common scenario is to alert an operations team whenever specific activity occurs. An example would include any one of the following:

- Notifying a user who shared a document externally
- Blocking unauthorized administrators
- Blocking a potentially compromised account that is performing a suspicious activity

To do that, administrators can leverage *Activity Alerts*, which allows them to create rules based on conditions comprised of the following:

- Activities to be performed by one or more users
- Users who are under investigation

Whenever a user does anything that trips an alert, an email will be sent to the recipient configured in the alert, notifying them about the flagged activity. From here, the administrator can open the audit log search in Security & Compliance Center to review and investigate user activities.

The following screenshot shows an example of a notification email:

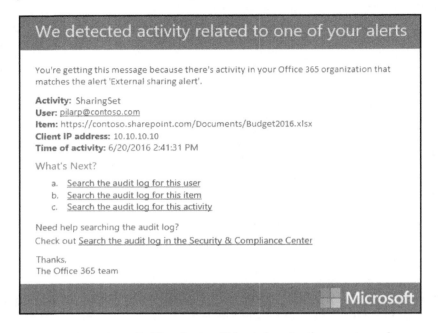

Administrators can automate activities that will be taken in the service whenever a set of actions occur. To accomplish this, they can leverage **Cloud App Security (CAS)**. CAS allows administrators to create policies to perform actions such as the following:

- Suspending a user
- Requiring a user to sign in again
- Notifying a user

 Cloud App Security policies, including activity, file, and anomaly detection, are out of the scope of this book. However, you can learn more about Cloud App Security here: https://docs.microsoft.com/en-us/cloud-app-security/what-is-cloud-app-security.

So, for example, a user triggers a specific activity alert that warrants that user to be suspended. Instead of an administrator performing the suspension manually, Cloud App Security can execute a workflow to automatically take action.

Administrators can also review alerts that were triggered and take action when appropriate, as shown in the following screenshot:

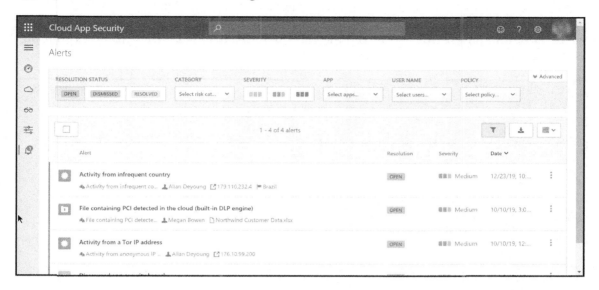

There are multiple ways to filter the results, such as by resolution status, category, and severity. Administrators can also export the results.

Credential management

Credentials confirm a user's identity during the sign-in process. Besides a password, Azure Active Directory supports different types of authentication challenges. Azure Active Directory already includes a password policy that can be adjusted to fit a company's requirements and can synchronize password requirements from an on-premises Active Directory as well. An organization may also be interested in a self-service password reset for its end users.

Password policy

A password policy can define the password characters' minimum length, when and if the password expires, and password strength. The password expiration policy determines the **Days before passwords expire** and the **Days before a user is notified about expiration**, as shown in the following screenshot:

The number of days before a password expires can range from 14 to 730 days, and the number of days before a user is notified can range from 1 to 30 days.

When an organization decides to sync user passwords from an on-premises Active Directory to Azure Active Directory, *existing local password policies* will govern the minimum requirements, such as the following:

- Length
- History
- Expiration time
- Complexity

Setting a simple password policy can help reduce user confusion and help desk support tickets within an organization.

Self-service password reset

Another common request from organizations regarding credential management is to allow users to reset their own passwords without needing to open a support ticket. Azure Active Directory provides a feature called self-service password reset that can allow users to confirm their identities and reset their passwords.

The Azure AD self-service password reset confirmation is validated based on a combination of the following methods:

- Mobile phone
- Office phone
- Security questions
- Email

In addition, if configured, passwords that have been reset in Azure AD can be written back to a local Active Directory, as shown in the following screenshot:

More information on Azure password management and policies is available at `https://docs.microsoft.com/en-us/office365/admin/misc/password-policy-recommendations`.

Password write-back is recommended to ensure users maintain the same password on-premises that they do in Azure AD.

Next, we will explore security and compliance concepts for documents within an organization.

Documents

Document authoring, storage, and sharing are the key components of every organization's collaboration strategy. Here, administrators need to implement policies such as the following:

- Where users will be able to store files
- How and where users will be able to access files
- How the files can be shared inside and, if enabled, outside the organization
- How long documents will be retained for
- How auditors can understand who accessed or deleted a document or find documents that contain specific information
- How documents can be classified and protected

This section will explore the following concepts:

- Document storage
- Sharing
- Auditing
- Retention
- eDiscovery
- Classification and protection

In the following sections, we will look at each of these in a more detailed manner.

Document Storage

Although documents can be accessed from almost all the services of the suite, Microsoft 365 has three primary interfaces where users can store, share, and collaborate on files. Both locations are automatically covered under the organization security and compliance requirements:

- **OneDrive for Business**: Personal documents
- **SharePoint Online Sites**: Team, group, or department documents
- **Teams**: Team, group, or department documents

The underlying storage component for all of the interfaces is SharePoint Online. Documents stored in SharePoint Online (or any service that leverages SharePoint) are automatically indexed, support custom metadata, have versioning enabled, and can be synchronized between desktop and mobile devices.

The following table depicts the main differences between OneDrive, SharePoint Online, and Teams for Document Storage:

Feature	OneDrive for Business	SharePoint Online or Teams
Storage space	Per user and varies according to the plan, ranging from 2 GB to unlimited storage. An administrator can increase the limit up to 5 TB of storage, but beyond that would require a service ticket up to 25 TB. Beyond 25 TB would require more storage.	Per tenant. Every user license will add to the tenant pooled storage, and administrators will be able to decide if sites will have a manually set amount of storage or if the site storage will be consumed automatically out of the tenant pooled storage
Ownership	Per user. Each user is accountable for managing what to do with the files in their personal storage	Per group or user. It is good practice to assign SharePoint site permissions to a security or Office 365 group, rather than individual users, but it is up to each user with the appropriate permissions to decide how to manage the storage space.
Teams integration	Yes. Users can access their personal storage inside the **Files** left rail icon in Microsoft Teams. In addition, inside individual or group chat conversations, files that have been shared are automatically uploaded to the OneDrive site of the user sharing the file.	Yes. Each Team automatically has a SharePoint site, which is where Team's channel files are stored and can be accessed or edited by users.

Sync client	Yes. Users can synchronize and access a local copy of their personal ODfB with the sync client.	Yes. Users can decide which SharePoint Online libraries they will choose to synchronize locally, and they can have more than one library synced at the same time. Users can also decide which folders of these libraries will be synced.
Mobile client	Yes (OneDrive for Business mobile app).	Yes (OneDrive for Business, SharePoint, and Teams mobile apps).
File storage limit (at the time of writing)	15 GB.	15 GB.
Sharing	Managed by the user, who is the owner of personal storage. Global sharing controls can be configured by administrators to prevent external sharing.	Managed by the SharePoint site, which includes its members, owners, and visitors. If a site is connected to a Microsoft Teams team, user permissions to access files are managed inside the Teams itself. In addition, users with appropriate permissions can also choose to share individual files or folders, without sharing the entire site. Global sharing controls can be configured by administrators to prevent external sharing.
Audit logs	Yes. Auditors can review sharing and file activities on OneDrive.	Yes. Auditors can review sharing and file activities on SPO sites.

We'll explore sharing in the next section.

Sharing

Among the benefits of storing documents in OneDrive, SharePoint, or Teams is the ability to share files without needing to send a copy to each recipient. Efficient file sharing is also important because it allows organizations to manage access to content. Documents sent as email attachments may be outside the management or oversight of security, compliance, or business administrators. When shared inside the framework of OneDrive for Business, SharePoint, or Teams, the file is kept in place and can be configured so that users cannot send files to another party.

Sharing can be done by almost all clients. Supported clients include the following:

- Mobile app
- Web client
- Desktop sync client
- Outlook client
- Teams client

Outlook sharing is particularly interesting because it allows users to attach files to email messages as "cloud attachments," thus automatically sharing those files out of their OneDrive personal storage. End users can even configure the permissions the recipients can have for these files, as shown in the following screenshot:

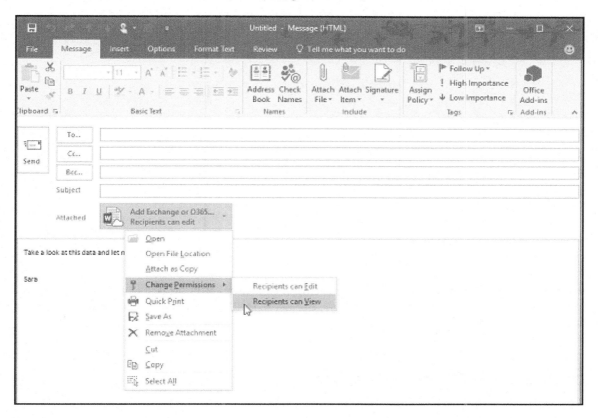

In addition, owners or users with the appropriate permissions can review and even revoke permissions that have been assigned to others at any time, as shown in the following screenshot:

If you click **Stop sharing**, the link to the document becomes invalid to external users. External users, as we discussed previously, are users that are outside the boundary of the tenant.

Sharing Admin Controls

Administrators can govern how sharing will be configured for the organization, under the following categories:

- **Anyone:** Users can create links to files that can be shared with people without requiring any type of authentication.
- **New and existing external users:** Users can invite existing or external users that aren't enrolled in their organization directory.
- **Existing external users:** Users can only invite external users who have already accepted an invitation.
- **Only people in your organization:** Users can invite internal users only. This means files can't be shared with external users.

OneDrive, SharePoint site administrators, and Team owners can invite internal and external users (if the overall tenant settings are configured to allow it).

However, if needed, organizations can leverage a Guest Inviter role, granting non-administrators the ability to invite guests.

 Organizations can also restrict which domains users can share with. By defining a whitelist or blacklist of domains for sites, administrators can allow or prohibit sharing with specific domains.

While many settings can be configured globally, exceptions can still be made for groups of individuals. Sharing controls can be modified to give different levels of permissiveness between **SharePoint** (which also governs Teams) and **OneDrive**, though the OneDrive setting may never be more permissive than the overall SharePoint setting, as shown in the following screenshot:

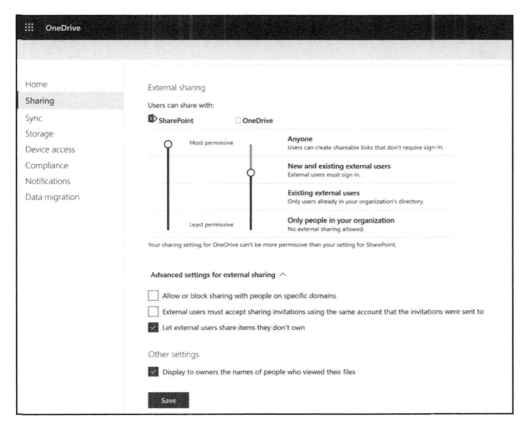

Several best practices can be considered to protect the organization while allowing guests to collaborate with them. Among them are the following:

- Defining group and team classifications (such as Internal Only, Confidential, and so on) and limiting which groups are eligible for guest access
- Defining authentication requirements for guests, such as multi-factor authentication
- Forcing guests to accept terms of use
- Frequently reviewing guest access to enforce that only allowed users are guests (such as with Access Reviews)
- Defining client access requirements for guests
- Frequently reviewing activities in the audit log search

Security, compliance, and governance conversations should include strategy on guest access.

 More information on configuring guest access for Microsoft Teams can be found here: https://docs.microsoft.com/en-us/microsoftteams/ guest-access.

Auditing

Auditing determines what actions were performed by what identity, and at what time those actions were performed. As we described earlier, Microsoft 365 allows administrators to audit actions that are made in the service regarding file sharing and collaboration, syncing, and deletion and access. The main auditing activities for files are as follows:

- Accessed file
- Copied file
- Deleted file
- Deleted file from the recycle bin
- Deleted file from the second-stage recycle bin
- Downloaded file
- Moved file
- Uploaded file

In addition, sharing is also part of the audited log activities, and the main sharing audited activities are as follows:

- Created access request
- Created a company shareable link
- Created a sharing invitation
- Shared file, folder, or site
- Used a company shareable link
- Withdrew sharing invitation

A view of the sharing activities inside the Security and Compliance Center can be seen in the following screenshot:

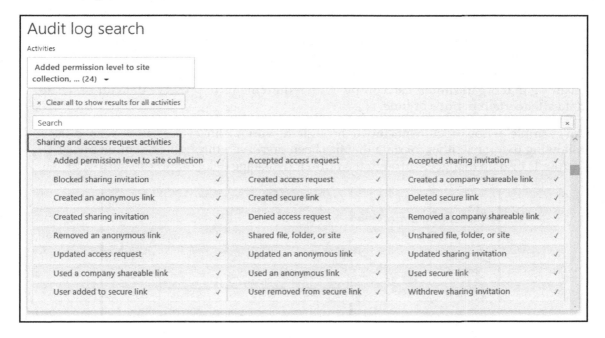

As we mentioned earlier, administrators should leverage audit logs, along with activity alerts and Cloud App Security policies, to understand what actions are being taken by users and administrators regarding files and sharing inside their organization.

Retention

The document life cycle describes what happens to documents as they are acted upon throughout a system. This includes activities such as renaming, deleting, moving to other sites or folders, and being labeled and retired. **Retention** is the process that preserves copies of that document data as it progresses throughout its life cycle. Retention is an important part of helping organizations comply with regulatory obligations and business requirements.

Microsoft 365 includes a default life cycle policy that preserves versions and can keep deleted documents for up to 93 days. Versioning (enabled by default) keeps copies of incrementally changed documents; deleted documents are retained a recycle bin. If no further actions are taken, documents can be restored or permanently deleted, within 93 days, across the two-stage recycle bin that's available in OneDrive and SharePoint.

If retention policies have been configured, deleted documents are moved to a secured location called the **Preservation Hold Library**. At the end of the retention period, they are permanently deleted. Retention policies can also control the deletion of documents, ensuring that organizations can comply with requirements to preserve data for or delete data after certain periods of time.

An example of how documents move through the various life cycles can be seen in the following diagram, either for data that has been preserved through a retention policy (arrow 1) or data that goes through the normal two-stage deletion process (arrow 2):

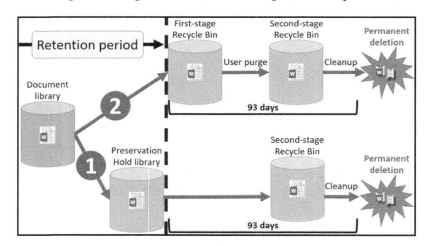

Retention policies can also be configured with a feature called *preservation lock*, which prevents data being protected by a retention policy from having its retention controls altered to a shorter or less restrictive period of time. This control is typically used for organizations that need to comply with SEC Rule 17a-4, which stipulates the regulatory standards. Enabling a preservation lock on a retention policy restricts the following actions:

- The retention period of the policy can't be decreased, though it may be increased or extended.
- Users can't be removed from the policy, though they may be added.
- The retention policy cannot be deleted.

Retention policies can be applied to storage in Office 365 in order to delete or retain information, based on a set of conditions. These policies allow administrators to select where policies will be applied and specify how content will be managed for each location:

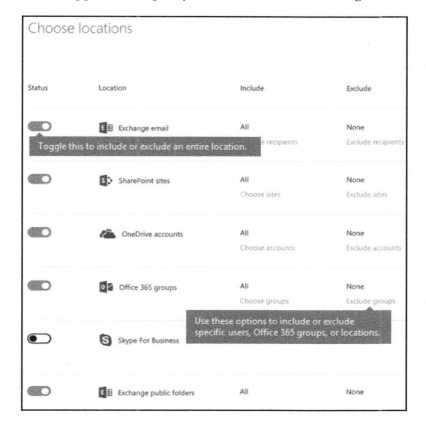

The following screenshot shows the delete or retain action in the **Security and Compliance Center** retention policy:

If this policy is applied to Document A, Document A will be deleted 7 days after it's been created, whether it's been retained or not:

For this policy, a document will be retained for 7 years after it's been deleted. So, within those 7 years, a user can delete the document but it will actually still be discoverable. After 7 years, it will be deleted.

eDiscovery

By default, every document stored in OneDrive and SharePoint is indexed. Content stored in Teams (messages and files), as well as email content, is also indexed, making it available for search.

eDiscovery searches can be configured to locate data based on certain conditions, such as the following:

- Attachment names
- Importance
- Has Attachments or not
- Date when the message was sent or received
- Size
- Subject
- Authors
- File types
- Created on
- Created by
- Modified on
- Modified by
- Detected Language
- Path
- Size
- Title

Administrators can configure which users will be able to search for content inside their organizations by defining a set of permissions. There are two main permission roles related to eDiscovery, as follows:

- **eDiscovery managers**: Search for content inside their organization and preview or export search results. However, eDiscovery managers can only access and manage the cases they have created.
- **eDiscovery administrators**: In addition to being able to perform the same search tasks as eDiscovery Managers, eDiscovery Administrators can also access and manage any search case that's created in their organization.

The eDiscovery process consists of a set of activities that can be performed, such as the following:

- Creating a case and assigning users to work on the case
- Optionally placing content to be searched on hold so that any changes that are made won't interfere with the search results
- Defining locations to be searched
- Creating one or more queries to find the desired information

- Reviewing result statistics
- Exporting search results for further analysis

 Microsoft 365 eDiscovery supports the **Keyword Query Language** (**KQL**) for creating searches. You can learn more about structuring KQL queries here: `https://docs.microsoft.com/en-us/microsoft-365/compliance/keyword-queries-and-search-conditions`.

All the activities that are performed during an eDiscovery investigation are audited and can be reviewed and exported. eDiscovery activities, like other auditable activities in Microsoft 365, can also be configured to trigger alerts. A view of part of the eDiscovery audited activities can be seen in the following screenshot:

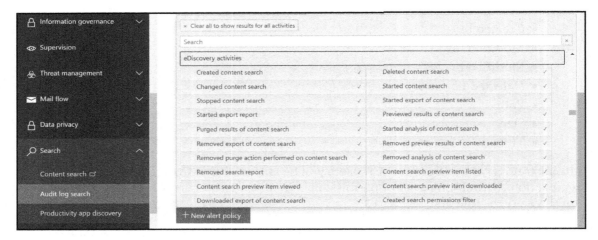

In addition to the core eDiscovery features for search, hold, and export, organizations can also leverage Advanced eDiscovery. Advanced eDiscovery is a technology-assisted review platform, designed to use a combination of machine learning and human training to teach the engine what is responsive to a particular query. It's generally recommended for large datasets that need a minimum of at least 10,000 items to perform many of the advanced functions. Advanced eDiscovery enhances native case and content searches with the following capabilities:

- Advanced data preparation, which removes duplicates, similar documents, and categorizes information according to themes
- Trains data based on relevance to the case so that reviewers can analyze the relevant data and decide on the right amount of data to be reviewed
- Exports relevant case data for further review

Advanced eDiscovery is outside the scope of the MS-900 exam, but more information on the capabilities of the platform are available at https://docs.microsoft.com/en-us/ microsoft-365/compliance/office-365-advanced-ediscovery.

Classification and protection

Microsoft 365 allows users and administrators to classify and protect documents stored in OneDrive, SharePoint, or locally, as well as email messages, using the **Azure Information Protection (AIP)** service.

Administrators create classification labels and configure the actions available to users of the label. For example, a label can be configured to allow or deny the ability to take screenshots, copy content, or print it. Labels can be used to prevent people from modifying the recipients of a message or forwarding it to others.

Once the labels have been configured and published, users can apply them to protect documents, files, and email.

Administrators can also audit and control how classification and encryption technologies are used across the organization. Content can be classified using a number of methods, including the following:

- Outlook
- Office applications such as Word or Excel
- Exchange Online transport rules, which modify specific message properties throughout its transport
- Security & Compliance Center Data Loss Prevention rules
- Windows Explorer using the Azure Information Protection unified labeling client

After classification has been applied, the email message or document will display its tag and users, if authorized to open the file, will be able to review what actions they are allowed to take on that information, as shown in the following screenshot:

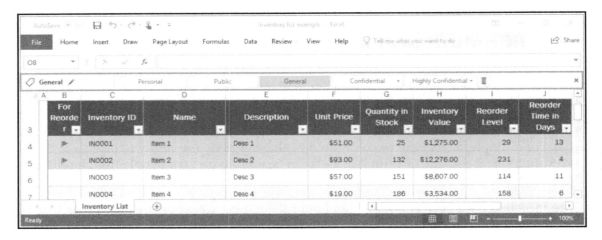

AIP is part of both Microsoft 365 E3 and Microsoft 365 E5. In Microsoft 365 E3, users must perform data classification manually. With Microsoft 365 E5, administrators can configure classification so that it happens automatically, such as when an application detects sensitive content such as credit card or social security numbers.

Next, we'll turn to security and compliance concepts for networking.

Network

Microsoft 365 services are generally accessed over the public internet. In this section, we'll discuss how users will access the Microsoft 365 service and how data will flow to, and be stored in, the service.

Administrators need to understand the following concepts when considering Microsoft 365 in terms of networking:

- Connectivity
- Encryption
- Performance

In the upcoming sections, we'll look at these in a detailed manner.

Connectivity

As a cloud service, Microsoft 365 components are not available on the internal network. Network administrators must allow internal users to access the internet endpoints for the Microsoft 365 service, which may mean configuring existing appliances such as firewalls and proxy devices.

Endpoints, which can be IP addresses or URLs, are classified into three categories:

- **Optimize:** Required for connectivity to Office 365 services and represent over 75% of the consumed bandwidth
- **Allow:** Required for connectivity, but not as sensitive to latency as optimize endpoints
- **Default:** Endpoints that can be treated as normal internet traffic

Organizations should plan for network best practices when planning their Office 365 deployment. Among the recommended practices are the following:

- Differentiating Office 365 traffic from normal internet traffic.
- Egress network connections locally so that users will be routed as quickly as possible to the Microsoft network.
- Bypassing proxies to reduce the amount of time needed for data to arrive at Office 365 services.

Microsoft 365 administrators and network administrators should work together to plan a network connectivity strategy. To help plan effectively, Microsoft provides a web service for obtaining the IP addresses and URLs that are used in the service.

 More information about the Office 365 endpoint web service is available in the following documentation: `https://docs.microsoft.com/en-us/office365/enterprise/office-365-ip-web-service`.

Microsoft typically recommends bypassing proxy devices for network traffic destined for Microsoft 365.

Encryption

Encryption is a mechanism that's used to protect information from unauthorized access. Microsoft 365 implements several encryption technologies across the platform. Encryption is enforced for data in two core states:

- **At rest:** Data that is stored in the service. This includes files and documents uploaded to OneDrive, SharePoint, and Teams, as well as email content. Data at rest is protected through the use of BitLocker, **Distributed Key Manager (DKM)**, and Customer Key for Office 365. Depending on the service, data may also be stored in blob storage, with each chunk being encrypted using the Key Store.
- **In transit:** Refers to data that is being transferred between clients and services, as well as between different endpoints within the service and data centers. Data in transit is protected via **Transport Layer Security (TLS)** and IPSec. TLS is typically used to secure traffic application-layer traffic between clients and services, while IPSec is used to secure the underlying physical or logical networking connections.

In addition to the built-in encryption technologies, customers can also apply unique content encryption to files and email messages using the Azure Information Protection client. Not only does Azure Information Protection provide data classification services, as we described earlier, but it can also be used to encrypt content at the file or document level.

The following diagram depicts how Azure Information Protection encryption works:

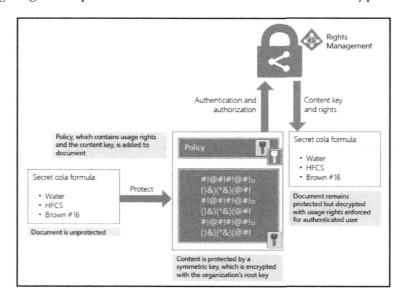

Customers in highly-regulated industries may be required to control the encryption keys that are used in the service. To accomplish this, organizations may use the Customer Key service, which allows them to manage the key life cycle and can be used to encrypt data in the following services:

- Exchange Online, including Skype for Business Online and Microsoft Teams data stored in user mailboxes
- Files stored in OneDrive and SharePoint Online

Setting up the Customer Key service requires additional Azure services, such as Key Vault, as well as further considerations that are out of the scope of this book. You can learn more about Customer Key here: `https://docs.microsoft.com/en-us/microsoft-365/compliance/controlling-your-data-using-customer-key`.

Performance

Since Microsoft 365 is a cloud service, organizations should follow best practices during the network planning phase. Customers should ensure adequate network capacity and redundancy is available so that users have consistent, reliable connectivity to the service. Network performance planning should consider the following, among other things:

- How to make sure that the correct ports, IP addresses, and URLs are allowed for Office 365 services
- How to reduce the latency between users and the Office 365 network
- How to prepare the customer network so that it supports additional internet traffic
- How to plan Office 365 features so that they use a local cache whenever possible

As we described previously, Microsoft provides a list of URLs and IP addresses that are used by its services. Organizations should use this data to configure their networking and edge devices. Depending on the security requirements and configurations, the network should be prepared to update devices, should Microsoft add or remove endpoints and services.

To reduce the amount of latency, organizations should consider Office 365 network best practices, such as bypassing proxies and local network egress (as opposed to backhauled connections to a central office) so that information arrives at the Office 365 network through the shortest path.

To help measure the latency, organizations can use tools such as PSPing or TraceTCP against Office 365 services such as the following:

- `outlook.office365.com`
- `<tenant>.sharepoint.com`
- `portal.microsoftonline.com`

There are also calculators and tools available to help measure latency, such as the Network Onboarding Tool and the Skype Network Assessment Tool, which help organizations understand where improvements need to be made, as shown in the following screenshot:

You can learn more about the Network Onboarding Tool at `https://techcommunity.microsoft.com/t5/Office-365-Networking/Updated-Office-365-Network-Onboarding-Tool-POC-with-new-network/m-p/711130`.

Also, to prepare the network for additional Office 365 traffic, customers that have currently been deployed with on-premises systems should plan to accommodate the network traffic that's necessary to communicate with Microsoft 365 services. Another planning tool, known as the Network Planner for Microsoft Teams (available in the Teams Admin Center at `https://admin.teams.microsoft.com`), can be used to estimate how much traffic the Teams workload will contribute to their overall internet bandwidth. The Network Planner for Microsoft Teams can be seen in the following screenshot:

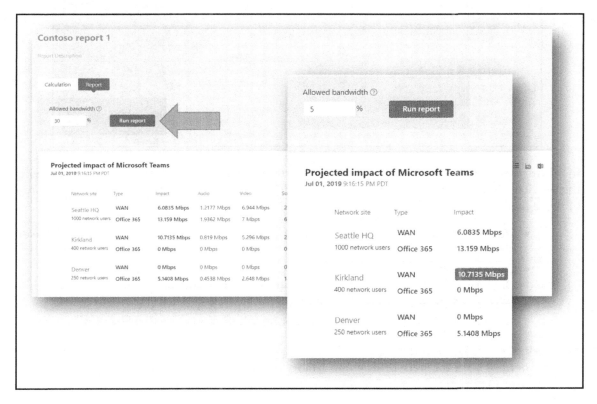

Organizations that are deploying services such as Microsoft Teams for phone systems, audio conferencing, and video or Microsoft Stream for video may also want to consider deploying **Quality of Service (QoS)**, which allows them to prioritize some types of network traffic over others to provide better real-time communication experiences.

The following diagram shows an example of how an organization might use QoS to shape their traffic:

In addition to network traffic, companies should understand what features are available in the service clients, which can help reduce the amount of internet traffic that's needed. Some of these features are as follows:

- **Outlook cache**, which stores a local copy of the user's email data that can be used offline
- **OneDrive sync client**, which can keep a local copy of both a user's personal OneDrive storage and their selected SharePoint Online libraries
- **Office 365 ProPlus binaries and servicing updates,** as we discussed in Chapter 6, *Understanding Office 365 ProPlus*, for installation update distribution

Network planning is an ongoing task, which requires, among others, the engagement and commitment of both the networking and Microsoft 365 administrative teams to ensure optimal user experience.

Finally, we will cover security and compliance concepts for devices.

Devices

Devices play an important role during the entire user experience with Microsoft 365 because services can be accessed from several clients, such as the web, desktop, and mobile devices. Administrators should plan for what devices users will be allowed to access Microsoft 365 services from if devices will be managed or not, and what protection controls are available in those devices, such as Windows 10 security features.

This section will explore the following concepts for devices:

- Device Access
- Device Management
- Device Protection

We'll look at each of these in the following sections.

Device Access

Managing device access for Microsoft 365 is key to ensuring that only known devices can access the service or store company data. There are two main strategies that can be used to control device access for Microsoft 365:

- **Network restriction:** Microsoft 365 services can only be accessed from authorized network locations, such as inside the organization perimeter, where managed devices reside. This scenario is enforced in the service during the authentication and authorization phase, where users identify themselves and their locations, before being granted access to services.
- **Conditional access:** Services can only be accessed when conditions, such as group membership, device compliance, network region, or multi-factor authentication, are satisfied.

A network restriction implementation can be implemented with one or more of the following four features:

- **Conditional Access:** As we mentioned previously, conditional access can be used to interrogate devices accessing the service for their IP address information and then grant or deny access based on that (among other conditions). Microsoft recommends configuring conditional access as the best way to manage device and application access.

- **Active Directory Federation Services (AD FS) claims rules**: In an identity federation scenario, claims are information about users that are exchanged between different identity providers, such as between a local Active Directory and Azure Active Directory. In this case, claims rules allow administrators to configure conditions that must be satisfied to enable the authorization. Organizations frequently use AD FS claims rules to limit access to services based on IP addresses.

 Active Directory Federation Services (AD FS) Claims Rules for Office 365 services do not work effectively for geofencing purposes. In most Office 365 application scenarios, users attempt to access the Office 365 service from their device and are redirected to the on-premises environment. The result is that the "client IP address" being presented to AD FS is from Office 365, not the originating client device.

- **Exchange Online Client Access Rules**: Administrators can configure conditions to authorize access to Exchange Online services. Among the services that administrators can configure Exchange Online Client Access rules for are **Exchange Admin Center (EAC)**, PowerShell, Exchange ActiveSync, and **Exchange Web Services (EWS)**.

- **OneDrive for Business and SharePoint Online Device Access**: Administrators can configure which networks users are authorized to access OneDrive and SharePoint content. This setting also applies to external users and administrator access, so it is recommended to be well planned before they're rolled out to users. It affects all services that use SharePoint (such as OneDrive, SharePoint Online, and Microsoft Teams). Misconfiguring the allowed networks will prevent users from being able to access the service and will require a phone call to be made to Microsoft support that they will resolve.

The following screenshot shows the device access configuration options in the OneDrive admin center:

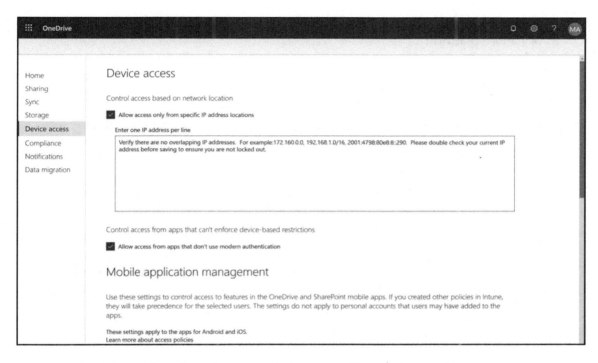

The most flexible (and preferred) approach for controlling authorized locations is to create Conditional Access policies, which, like the previous options, define conditions and actions.

The following diagram shows the main components of a Conditional Access Policy:

The core conditions for building a Conditional Access Policy are as follows:

- Users and groups
- Sign-in risk
- Device platform
- Location
- Client apps
- Device state

After being validated, administrators can configure actions such as the following:

- Blocking access
- Granting access, but requiring multi-factor authentication
- Granting access, but requiring a device to be compliant with Intune requirements
- Enforcing limited session usage, such as preventing users from opening SharePoint documents locally

 As part of testing a Conditional Access policy, administrators can simulate a set of conditions, such as user and location, to understand what policy would take place and what would happen as a result of this policy being implemented.

We'll talk about Device Management in the next section.

Device Management

Microsoft 365 allows administrators to manage devices that are used to connect to services. Administrators can enforce features and stipulations, such as requiring a password to unlock a device, making sure that the device is not rooted or jailbroken, and being able to selectively wipe company data from the device. There are two services that can be used to manage devices. They are as follows:

- **Intune**: Intune offers the ability to manage device certificates, Wi-Fi, VPN, and email profiles, deploy apps to users and manage app protection, as well as device compliance, preventing jailbroken/rooted devices from accessing corporate resources, defining password policies, and disabling cameras.
- **Mobile Device Management (MDM) for Office 365**: Mobile Device Management for Office 365 provides a subset of Intune features, such as preventing the connection of jailbroken or rooted devices, disabling cameras, and defining a password policy.

The following table lists the main differences between MDM for Office and Intune capabilities:

Feature	Intune	MDM for Office 365
Where devices are managed	In the Intune management portal.	In Security and Compliance Center.
Supported devices	iOS, Mac OS X, Android, and Windows devices.	iOS, Android and Windows devices.
Main capabilities	Requiring a password, defining a number of sign-in failures before the device is wiped, password expiration, jailbreak or rooted detection and corporate wipe, pushing certificates to devices for Wi-Fi networks or VPNs, viewing reports on compliant and not compliant devices, and pushing applications to devices.	Requiring a password, defining a number of sign-in failures before the device is wiped, password expiration, and jailbreak or rooted detection and corporate wipe.

In addition to Device Management scenarios, Intune provides **Mobile App Management (MAM)** capabilities, allowing controls to be applied to specific applications, such as the following:

- Requiring a pin to open the app
- Encrypting corporate app data
- Data wipe for a full or selective wipe
- Blocking copy and paste between corporate and personal applications

Organizations that already have an MDM solution to manage corporate devices can still use Intune to manage applications with MAM. For more information on Mobile Application Management, go to `https://docs.microsoft.com/en-us/intune/apps/app-protection-policy`.

Device Protection

Windows 10 devices include several security features that administrators should consider during their device planning phase, such as the following:

- **Windows Defender Antivirus**: Anti-malware that can protect Windows 10 and Windows Server computers.

- **Microsoft Defender Advanced Threat Protection**: Advanced protection against threats leveraging behavioral sensors, security analytics across different Microsoft services, and threat intelligence by Microsoft hunters and security teams.
- **Windows Defender Application Guard**: Isolates untrusted sites that are opened in an isolated Hyper-V-enabled container, separate from the host operating system.
- **Windows Hello for Business**: Replace passwords with strong two-factor authentication on PCs and mobile devices using a device-specific PIN or biometric credential that can't be captured and replayed on other devices.
- **Credential Guard**: The component responsible for isolating the secrets that are used throughout the machine to prevent unauthorized access.
- **Windows Defender Application Control**: Allows only authorized applications to run in users' machines.
- **BitLocker**: Whole-disk encryption, integrated with a device's Trusted Computing Module chip and the Windows 10 operating system.
- **Windows Information Protection**: Protects against data leakage separating personal and corporate data.

Microsoft Defender **Advanced Threat Protection (ATP)** can also protect Windows 7, Windows 8.1, Windows Server, and Mac OS X. More information about Microsoft Defender ATP can be found here: `https://docs.microsoft.com/en-us/windows/security/threat-protection/microsoft-defender-atp/microsoft-defender-advanced-threat-protection`.

 More information about Windows 10 security features can be found in the following documentation: `https://docs.microsoft.com/en-us/microsoft-365/enterprise/windows10-enable-security-features`.

Secure Score

Microsoft 365 has several security features that can be configured in different ways, depending on an organization's requirements. However, many organizations aren't aware of all of the settings, which order to address them in, or how they might impact the user experience.

Additionally, organizations are faced with the following questions:

- How can they understand the current security best practices?
- How does their current deployment compare to the best practices?

Secure Score is a service that's included with Microsoft 365 that contains a list of dozens of security-focused features (each with a point value), compares an organization's current settings against the Microsoft-recommended best practices, and assigns the tenant a score. It allows organizations to understand their current security posture and understand what actions need to be taken to improve their current score. Microsoft Secure Score can be seen in the following screenshot:

Actions settings are organized according to the following categories:

- Identity
- Data
- Device
- Apps

The following screenshot shows various improvement actions, sorted by category:

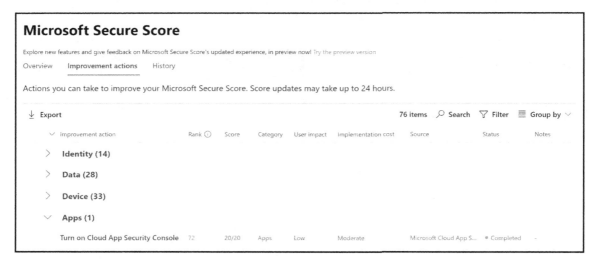

For each improvement action, administrators can review a description, what attacks or risks it mitigates, related compliance controls, and how its implementation will impact users. The score is recalculated (typically after 48 hours) and the updated score is shown on the dashboard. The Secure Score console provides links to the admin centers where actions need to be taken. The Secure Score console also includes an acknowledgment toggle that lets organizations indicate if they have implemented an action in a third-party system that isn't tracked by Secure Score, allowing them to maintain an accurate score for their environment.

As organizations make changes over time, they can see the history of the actions they've taken and the impact their modifications have had, as shown in the following screenshot:

Microsoft recommends reviewing Secure Score controls and reports frequently to make sure they are implementing current best practices, enabling and configuring new security controls as features become available, and continuously improving the security of their Microsoft 365 deployment.

Summary

Microsoft 365 was built with security features in mind. Administrators should take some time to understand the wide range of features and controls that are available to them for delegating and administering the security aspects of tenants.

In this chapter, you learned about the security concepts and controls for managing identity, documents, networking, and devices. In addition, we discussed managing access to resources through credentials, network perimeter controls, and Conditional Access. Finally, we discussed the benefit and visibility that Secure Score brings to an organization and how it can be used to continuously improve and monitor an organization's security.

In the next chapter, we will cover identity protection and management.

Questions

Answer the following questions to test your knowledge of this chapter. You can find the answers in *Assessment Answers*:

1. Identify two features or capabilities of the Secure Score.
    1. Recommend security configurations for Microsoft 365 services
    2. Track user security policies
    3. Provide configuration steps for security recommendations or links to configuration controls
    4. Administer user risk policies

2. Identify two features of Intune Mobile Application Management.
    1. Define application-based security policies
    2. Wipe managed device
    3. Wipe managed application profile
    4. Require device PIN

3. Where is Intune managed?
    1. Microsoft 365 admin center
    2. Azure portal
    3. Security & Compliance Center
    4. Intune Control Panel

4. Where is Microsoft Mobile Device Management managed?
    1. Microsoft 365 admin center
    2. Azure portal
    3. Security & Compliance Center
    4. Intune Control Panel

5. Identify the four types of groups available in Microsoft 365.
    1. Office 365 groups
    2. Security groups
    3. Mail-enabled security groups
    4. Domain local groups
    5. Distribution List Groups
    6. Global groups
    7. Universal groups
    8. Local groups

6. eDiscovery managers can see what?
    1. All cases
    2. Only cases that they created or are assigned to them

7. eDiscovery administrators can see what?
    1. All cases
    2. Only cases that they created or are assigned to them

8. Secure Score actions are grouped into which four categories?
    1. Identity
    2. Network
    3. Data
    4. Windows
    5. Azure
    6. Device
    7. Apps
    8. Multi-factor authentication

9. You are the SharePoint administrator for your organization. You need to allow OneDrive users to share documents with external users who have already been added to your organization's Azure Active Directory tenant. Which option should you choose?
    1. Anyone
    2. New and existing external users
    3. Existing external users
    4. Only people in your organization

10. Identify the two true statements about OneDrive sharing controls.
    1. They can be the same level of permissiveness as SharePoint sharing controls.
    2. They can be more permissive than SharePoint sharing controls.
    3. They can be less permissive than SharePoint sharing controls.
    4. They must be the same as the SharePoint sharing controls.

11. Which three terms apply to the SharePoint online document life cycle?
    1. Two-stage recycle bin
    2. Azure AD recycle bin
    3. Preservation Hold Library
    4. Versioning

12. When deploying Azure Active Directory Connect Password Hash synchronization, what happens to the Azure AD Password Policy?
    1. Nothing.
    2. The Azure AD password policy wins.
    3. The on-premises Active Directory password control settings are synchronized to Azure AD.
    4. Organizations must choose which password policy controls to deploy.

13. You are a security manager for your organization. You need to configure document classification. Which tool should you use?
    1. Classification explorer
    2. Azure Information Protection
    3. Azure Identity Protection
    4. Exchange Data Loss Prevention Policies

14. In which two ways does Microsoft 365 encrypt data?
    1. At rest
    2. At bay
    3. In transit
    4. In utero

15. Password change management recommends customers configure _____ so that password changes in Azure are updated in the on-premises Active Directory.
    1. Password change management
    2. Password write-back
    3. Exchange hybrid write-back
    4. Privileged identity management

16. Microsoft Defender Advanced Threat Protection can protect Mac OS-based computers.
    1. True
    2. False

17. You are the compliance administrator for your organization and need to perform a search for users who have accessed certain SharePoint sites. Which tool should you use?
    1. Microsoft 365 admin center
    2. Audit Log Search
    3. SharePoint Report Server
    4. SharePoint Admin Center

10 Understanding Identity Protection and Management

In the previous chapter, we saw the importance of protecting identity, since users can potentially access cloud services from anywhere with an internet connection.

Traditionally, identity has been managed internally with directory services such as Active Directory. When incorporating cloud services into your organization's infrastructure and service portfolio, you'll need to understand how to provide access to those cloud resources. Ideally, you'll want to use single sign-in features that enable users to authenticate with a single identity across multiple platforms and services.

In this chapter, we're going to talk about the kinds of identity models available and their applications, and some of the ways to protect identity. We will cover the following topics:

- Understanding identity models
- **Multi-factor authentication (MFA)**

Understanding identity models

When describing how users access a service, the identity and authentication processes are the key concepts to understand. In this section, we're going to discuss three core identity models (as well as some sub-features of each) and how they work in the context of Microsoft 365. The three models are as follows:

- Cloud identity
- Hybrid or synchronized identity
- Federated identity

Let's look at each in detail.

Cloud identity

Cloud identity is the simplest form of identity. It's the same form of identity you typically use when you sign up for other consumer cloud services or access retail shopping and personal banking sites.

With regards to Microsoft 365 and cloud identity, the identity is stored and completely managed inside of **Azure Active Directory (Azure AD)** and Microsoft 365. You can manage this identity through the **Microsoft 365 Admin Center** (`https://admin.microsoft.com`), through the Azure Portal (`https://aad.portal.azure.com`), or by scripting with PowerShell or Microsoft Graph.

When a user authenticates with the service, they are providing an identity that has been created in the service. This user identity is separate from any other identity they may have (such as the username and password they use to log on to their computer or other services).

Hybrid or synchronized identity

Hybrid or synchronized identity refers to the integration of an on-premises **Identity Provider (IDP)** with a cloud identity provider. Changes made in one environment (typically, the on-premises environment) are synchronized and made available in the cloud environment.

To utilize a hybrid or synchronized identity in your Microsoft 365 deployment, you should install and configure a directory synchronization service to copy your identities from an on-premises directory to Azure AD. Microsoft has a free software appliance, **Azure Active Directory Connect (AAD Connect)**, that performs this function.

There are also third-party vendors that provide similar solutions, though they are outside the scope of the MS-900 exam and may not support all of the identity protection features of the Microsoft 365 platform.

The concept of synchronized identity has two core sub-configuration concepts:

- Synchronized identity with cloud authentication
- Synchronized identity with pass-through authentication

Both of these configuration subcomponents include the optional ability to synchronize user password data.

Objects synchronized with Azure AD are linked to their on-premises account by way of a property called the `ImmutableID`. The `ImmutableID` value in Azure AD as a `base64` conversion of an object's on-premises Active Directory object GUID. You can obtain the `ImmutableID` value for any on-premises directory object with the following PowerShell command, where `sAMAccountName` is the pre-Windows 2000 account name for an identity whose `ImmutableID` you wish to compute:

```
$ImmutableID = [system.convert]::ToBase64String((Get-AdUser
sAMAccountName).objectGuid.ToByteArray())
```

The resulting value in the `$ImmutableID` is a `base64` string value, such as `goOHPqiAEkSwHaRd2bQZ9g==`.

Here are the core capabilities of each method of authentication:

- Synchronized identity with cloud authentication
- Synchronized identity with pass-through authentication

We'll explore both of these methods.

Synchronized identity with cloud authentication

With synchronized identity, you are essentially configuring your organization's directory objects to be replicated in Azure AD. This includes a number of properties (first and last names, email addresses, office information, manager reporting configuration, physical addresses, and phone numbers, among others). You have the option to configure this *with* or *without* password hashes.

 For an exhaustive list of the attributes synchronized to Azure AD, see `https://docs.microsoft.com/en-us/azure/active-directory/hybrid/reference-connect-sync-attributes-synchronized`.

Password hash synchronization enables an Azure AD user to use the same password as the corresponding on-premises account. If you choose to synchronize identity *with password hashes* (the default configuration), then a hash of the user's on-premises password is computed and synchronized to Azure AD. Authentication will be performed by Azure AD using the synchronized credential when a user attempts to access resources. In order to synchronize password hashes, the account specified in the Azure AD Connect setup must have two specific Active Directory rights granted (**Replicating Directory Changes** and **Replicating Directory Changes All**). These rights can be delegated manually (using a tool such as the Azure Active Directory Connect Advanced Permissions tool at http://aka.ms/aadpermissions) or by making the synchronization service account a member of either Domain Admins or Enterprise Admins. While the default synchronization time for Azure AD Connect is every 30 minutes, password changes on-premises are processed and synchronized to Azure AD immediately as a separate process.

 For a deeper understanding of how Azure AD Connect password hash synchronization works, see https://docs.microsoft.com/en-us/azure/ active-directory/hybrid/whatis-phs.

If you choose to synchronize identity *without* password hashes, then all of the same account details are synchronized *except* the password. Users have to maintain the password separately. This option is commonly configured if you are going to configure a federation service outside of AAD Connect, though you are not required to do so. Authentication will be performed by Azure AD using the synchronized user identity with a cloud password (if no federated authentication has been configured), or the request will be redirected to the federated IDP if the federation has been configured.

Password hash synchronization doesn't rely on any on-premises infrastructure to validate passwords or authentication attempts. If the on-premises environment is unavailable, then users will still be able to log in to Azure AD-protected resources, since the authentication attempt is processed against the service.

With or without password hash synchronization, users are able to change their passwords independently in Office 365. If you deploy password hash synchronization, Microsoft recommends you also deploy password writeback or self-service password reset so that when a user changes their password in Office 365, it's synchronized back to the on-premises Active Directory.

Synchronized identity with pass-through authentication

Pass-through authentication is an authentication method which, like standard synchronized identity, replicates account information to Azure AD; however, with the default pass-through authentication configuration, no password hashes are synchronized. Instead, password validation happens in the on-premises environment.

After this option is configured, Azure AD Connect Setup installs an authentication agent on the Azure AD Connect server that maintains a persistent outbound connection to Azure AD. Azure AD authentication agents register with the Azure AD service. Since pass-through authentication relies on an on-premise infrastructure to validate login requests, it is recommended that you install multiple pass-through authentication agents for redundancy. The Azure AD authentication agent's service communication is secured with public-key cryptography. Each agent has its own public and private key, which are used in the authentication process.

When a user attempts to sign into a resource protected by Azure AD authentication, the sign-in process encrypts the user's identity with the public keys of all registered Azure AD authentication agents and places this request in a queue. Through the persistent connection maintained by the Azure AD Connect authentication agent, an on-premises agent picks up the request in the queue, decrypts it with its private key, and then validates the credentials against the on-premises Active Directory. The response (success, failure, password expired, or locked out) is returned to the Azure AD service to complete the sign-in process.

Azure AD pass-through authentication only requires outbound connectivity on port 443 from the Azure AD Connect server (and any additional servers where redundant pass-through authentication agents have been configured).

 You can learn more about pass-through authentication at https://docs. microsoft.com/en-us/azure/active-directory/hybrid/how-to-connect-pta-how-it-works.

Now let's get started with federated identity in the next section.

Federated identity

Similar to the Azure Active Directory pass-through authentication, federated identity processes the identity validation in the on-premises environment. Federated identity requires directory objects to be synchronized to Azure Active Directory.

Azure AD Connect provides a mechanism to configure federated identity directly for both **Active Directory Federation Services (AD FS)** and PingFederate, a third-party federation IDP, from the setup wizard:

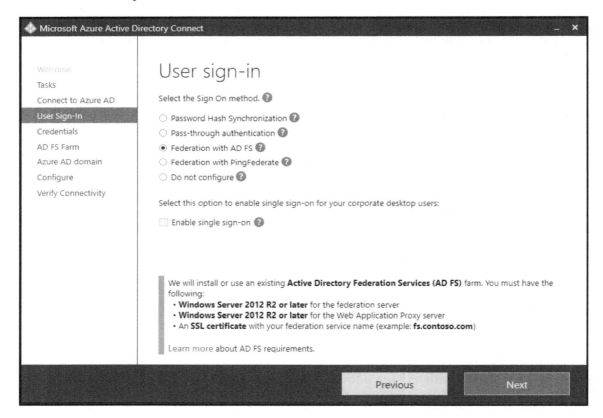

When federation is configured for an environment, authentication attempts are redirected from the Azure AD login portal to a web server hosting the federated identity provider service endpoint. When a user is redirected to the IDP endpoint, they enter their credentials if necessary and the on-premises federation service authenticates the user against the on-premises directory.

When determining which identity model fits your organizational needs, you can refer to a table such as the following:

Requirement	Potential identity and authentication models	Notes
Simplest identity	Cloud identity	Requires no on-premises infrastructure, but also provides no integration with on-premises applications or domain features.
On-premises credential verification	Pass-through authentication, federated identity	Both pass-through authentication and federated identity provide the ability to verify user credentials on-premises. Cloud identity and password hash synchronization perform identity verification in the cloud.
Easy integration with conditional access	Cloud identity, pass-through authentication, password hash sync	Of the identity models presented, federated identity and third-party identity providers may prove the most difficult to integrate with conditional access.
Integration with third-party identity provider	Only third-party identity providers	Third-party identity providers frequently require their solution end to end, so AAD Connect or other Microsoft-provided identity management services typically won't be deployed.
Leaked credential detection	Password hash sync; pass-through authentication or federated identity with password hash sync enabled and Azure AD Premium P2 license	Azure AD Premium P2 licensing is required in conjunction with an identity and authentication model that includes password hash sync.

Once you have chosen an identity and authentication model, you should think about securing the identity. One of the tools available to all users of the Microsoft 365 platform is MFA, which we'll discuss next.

Multi-factor authentication (MFA)

For most authentication or login attempts, users provide some form of credential (usually a username and a password). The methods of authenticating a user's identity typically fall into one of the following three categories:

- **Something the user knows**: A password is the most common example of this method.
- **Something the user has**: This can some sort of login device, such as a smart card, or it can be a text or phone call to a phone number previously registered with the system that the user is attempting to access.
- **Something the user is:** With this method, the user must supply some sort of biometric input, such as a fingerprint, iris scan, or voice passcode.

There are a lot of scenarios, however, where a simple username and password or even a single method may not be enough to secure valuable resources. In such cases, organizations may wish to further challenge a user during the login process to verify their identity. Multi-factor authentication provides this ability by adding a second method of authentication.

Azure Active Directory has a native multi-factor authentication service that can be used to further protect users and administrators and only needs to be enabled. Today, the following options can be used to further authenticate users with Azure multi-factor authentication:

- SMS or text message
- Phone call
- One-time passcode on a hardware or software token
- Confirmation prompt on registered authentication app

Azure multi-factor authentication has several features, such as self-service secure registration or the ability for users to bypass multi-factor authentication if they are connecting from secure, known networks. More in-depth information about the configuration capabilities of Azure multi-factor authentication, including steps to configure third-party tokens for verification, can be found at `https://docs.microsoft.com/en-us/azure/active-directory/authentication/concept-mfa-howitworks`.

Microsoft Azure Active Directory provides several different identity and authentication models, as well as security controls to provide a strong level of protection for your organization. Implementing conditional access and Azure multi-factor authentication can help organizations verify that users who are presenting credentials and attempting to obtain access to resources are authorized to do so and are using compliant devices.

Summary

As you've seen, there is a multitude of configuration options available to help organizations of all sizes meet their identity, authentication, and security needs.

In this chapter, we discussed the differences between cloud, synchronized, and federated identity, as well as the security controls available with Enterprise Mobility + Security, such as conditional access and access reviews. We learned which identity model can be used to help meet specific requirements—for example, if your organization needs on-premises identity authentication to comply with your security needs, you'll now know that you should choose between pass-through authentication and federated identity.

In the next chapter, we're going to look at technologies that enable endpoint security control and management.

Questions

Use the following questions to test your knowledge of this chapter. You can find the answers in *Assessment Answers*.

1. You are the compliance officer for your organization. You need to implement a policy to schedule the periodic verification of Azure Active Directory group memberships. Which tool should you use?
    1. Conditional Access
    2. Access Reviews
    3. Privileged Identity Management
    4. Privileged Authorization Management

2. You need to configure an authentication method where users are authenticated on-premises. Which option should you choose?
    1. Cloud identity
    2. Password hash synchronization
    3. Active Directory Federation Services
    4. Enterprise Mobility + Security

3. You need to configure an authentication method where password validation for authentication happens on-premises. Which two methods meet this requirement?
    1. Password hash synchronization
    2. Pass-through authentication
    3. Active Directory Federation Services
    4. Cloud identity

4. You need to configure an authentication method that does not depend on the availability of the on-premises infrastructure. Which two methods should you choose?
    1. Password hash synchronization
    2. Pass-through authentication
    3. Active Directory Federation Services
    4. Cloud identity

5. Identify three verification methods for Azure multi-factor authentication:
    1. SMS or text message
    2. Desktop popup
    3. Phone call
    4. One-time passcode

6. Which of the following are the three main things that are required to authenticate a user?
    1. Something a user knows
    2. Something a user has
    3. Something a user is
    4. Something a user does

11
Endpoint and Security Management

At the core of Microsoft 365 is the concept of identity-based security management. One of the benefits of using Microsoft 365 is that it includes a directory service, **Azure Active Directory (AAD)**, which can be used to define an organization's cloud-service security baseline.

Identity and security administrators alike should understand the main security features that can be integrated between their new and existing solutions. In the case of Microsoft 365, this will likely mean integrating an existing AD on-premise deployment with Azure AD.

In this chapter, we'll highlight some of the basic security features present in both AD (part of an organization's on-premise identity infrastructure), and AAD. Specifically, we'll look at the following:

- Understanding directory-based security features
- Addressing common threats with AAD

By the end of this chapter, you should have an understanding of how some AD security features such as Group Policy and password management, can be used in conjunction with AAD to mitigate threat risks.

Understanding directory-based security features

Both AD and AAD have a number of identity and security features built-in to help prevent or mitigate threats. In this section, we'll look at some core security features of AD, as well as features available with both AAD Premium Plan 1 and AAD Premium Plan 2, that can be used to help protect organizations.

Active Directory

Active Directory (**AD**) is an on-premise identity store service. It's used to authenticate and authorize computers and internal applications. The core functional container for a security boundary in AD is called a *domain*. A domain contains all of an organization's related security principals, groups, and other objects. Domains are grouped into *trees*, which are logical collections of related objects from either a security or organizational perspective. At the top level, *forests* are made up of one or more trees. Domains in a tree share a contiguous namespace. Each tree in a forest has its own namespace, as shown in the following screenshot:

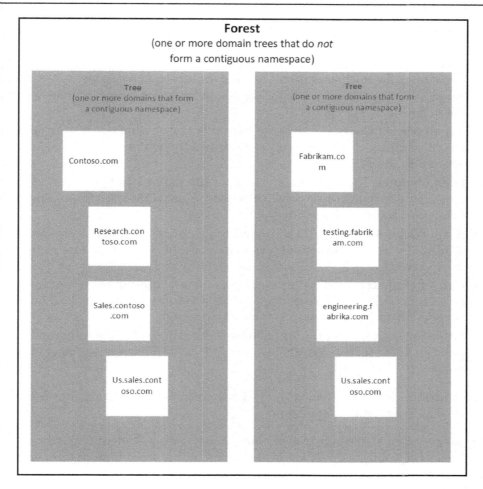

AD has the following features that can be used to define a security strategy:

- **Group Policy**: While not solely a security feature, Group Policy is used to administratively manage the configuration of policies and features throughout an AD environment. From a security perspective, Group Policy can be used to manage what software can run (through Software Restriction Policies), password policies, application or operating system features are available for users.

- **Logon hours**: The logon hours feature is used to define at what days and times a given user can authenticate against AD. This can be used to limit access to certain hours of the day (such as hourly employees who should only be logging in during normal business hours). Administrators can use Group Policy to enforce behaviors such as automatically logging users out of their machines when their logon hours expire.
- **Logon workstations**: While logon hours control at what *time* a user can log into an environment, the logon workstations feature determines which *devices* an account is allowed to use.
- **Logon banner**: The logon banner is a pop-up dialog box that appears when a user attempts to log on to a device. Many organizations use this dialog box to display an acceptable use policy.
- **Resource permissions**: AD allows administrators to apply permissions to file shares, printers, or individual files to manage the access that a user might have over a resource.
- **Roles-based access**: AD comes with a number of built-in roles, such as Account Operators and Print Operators, that can be used to delegate well-defined permission scopes over objects in an environment.
- **Password management**: Administrators can enforce a set of minimum requirements (such as length, history, and special characters) that should be applied to passwords.

Using a combination of written policy and technology enforcement, organizations can use AD to secure their on-premise organizations.

From a cloud perspective, though, organizations must use AAD identity to manage access control. For purposes of the MS-900 exam, we'll look at the two premium licensing levels available in **AAD**: **Premium Plan 1 (P1)** and **Premium Plan 2 (P2)**.

AAD Premium Plan 1

AAD Premium Plan 1 (commonly referred to as **AAD P1**) is the first AAD premium tier. It includes several features that can be used as part of an organization's security posture, as detailed here:

- **Conditional Access**: With Conditional Access, administrators can define what conditions must be satisfied to allow or block a user from accessing a specific application. Conditional Access policies can be configured based on the following factors: the user, group membership, IP or geolocation information, device compliance, and the application being used.

- **Custom banned password list**: Administrators can configure a list of banned passwords that shouldn't be allowed in their organization. With configuration, this process can be extended to on-premise AD deployments. The banned password list feature also performs common character substitutions (a and @, o and zero, and so on) when evaluating user passwords. For example, if you put **FABRIKAM** on the banned password list, AAD will also ban **F@BRIK@M**.

- **Self-service password reset (SSPR)**: Users may forget passwords periodically. The SSPR feature allows them to reset their passwords from anywhere with an internet browser. Password reset is subject to conditions or requirements (such as successfully answering security questions) configured by administrators. After successful validation, user passwords can also be written back to an on-premise identity AD environment.

- **Azure Multi-Factor Authentication (MFA)**: MFA prompts users for a second form of identification to confirm their identity when attempting to access a resource. Azure MFA provides administrators with advanced MFA features, such as the ability to configure trusted IP address ranges, custom greetings for phone call authentications, PIN mode, and fraud alerts. Azure MFA can even integrate with on-premise applications and allow organizations to use their own compatible tokens for authentication, as opposed to the Azure Authenticator phone app.

- **Microsoft Cloud App Discovery**: Frequently, an organization's security team needs to understand what applications are being used across the organization. Sometimes, this leads to the discovery of "shadow IT," or applications that are being used without the consent of the business. With Microsoft Cloud App Discovery, administrators can import firewalls and proxy logs can discover application traffic. These logs are analyzed and the discovered applications and the amount of traffic they are generating are made available.

- **Azure Application Proxy**: Many organizations host internal line-of-business applications. These applications sometimes need to be available to users outside of the corporate environment. **Virtual Private Networks (VPNs)** are commonly used to fulfill this need. Azure Application Proxy is another method that can be used to achieve this goal without the complicated configuration of VPN tunnels. One added benefit is that applications configured to use Azure Application Proxy can also take advantage of Azure MFA.

All AAD tiers have a feature that enables a number of security configurations and can be used to ensure default levels of protection in organizations. These policies originally called "baseline policies," are being deprecated and replaced with a newer feature: "security defaults." Security defaults will also be available to all tiers. These are binary switches for enabling defaults (such as disabling legacy authentication protocols); tenant-wide. Organizations that wish to use more granular controls must upgrade to Azure AD Premium P1 or P2 in order to use Conditional Access policies.

As you can see, AAD Premium Plan 1 provides a significant security benefit to organizations. Even more, benefits are available in the next tier, which we'll look at next.

AAD Premium Plan 2

AAD Premium 2 (or **AAD P2**) is the highest tier of the AAD service. In addition to the features already included in AAD P1, AAD P2 also provides organizations with the following tools:

- **Identity Protection**: Azure AD Identity Protection is an intelligence service that is able to understand current signals (data gathered from security and data interactions) and calculate the risk and vulnerabilities of user sessions across the organization. Identity protection can detect risky behaviors, such as when MFA registration is not configured, or the use of unsanctioned cloud apps unmanaged by Privileged Identity Management. Moreover, risk can be detected based on one of the following activities:
    - Users with leaked credentials
    - Sign-ins from anonymous IP addresses
    - Azure AD threat intelligence pattern detections
    - Sign-ins from IP addresses with suspicious activity
    - Sign-ins from unfamiliar locations

Identity Protection can be used along with Azure AD Conditional Access to enforce MFA or block access whenever an access attempt is identified as a potential risk is detected (referred to as *risk-based Conditional Access policies*). Identity Protection also allows administrators to export risk detection data so it can be analyzed with third-party tools.

- **Privileged Identity Management (PIM)**: PIM allows administrators to configure workflows for times when elevated permissions are required to perform a job duty. Once configured, PIM workflows can grant specified permissions for a limited duration of time and then revoke them once the time period has expired, thereby helping organizations implement a least-privilege administrative model.
- **Access reviews**: Access reviews allow organizations to recommend and automate permission or group management, such as removing users from groups after periods of activity.

With these tools in place, administrators should find it easier to reduce the attack surface of their organizations. While having access to these tools is important, it's equally important to know how the security features of AAD can help protect organizations. In the next section, we'll outline a few common threats and how AAD can help mitigate them.

Addressing common threats with AAD

Attackers are constantly developing new threats. Microsoft 365 provides organizations with a number of tools, guidance (such as Secure Score at `https://securescore.office.com`), and built-in features that can be used to improve security.

In this next section, we will explore some examples of common threats and see which Microsoft 365 capabilities can be used to protect against them:

- Compromised accounts
- Compromised devices
- Phishing attempts

First, let's look at compromised user accounts.

Compromised accounts

Credential compromise is one of the most common threats an organization can face. This can happen through any number of mechanisms, such as brute-force password cracking attempts, malware, or social engineering. This can lead to several security issues in the organization, such as the loss of intellectual property or the exposure of customer data.

Microsoft 365 has several features that can be used to protect against compromised accounts, such as the following:

- Enforcing MFA for users
- Detecting risky sign-ins and automating responses, such as prompting for MFA or denying access to resources
- Implementing risk-based Conditional Access
- Enforcing Privileged Access Management to restrict the number of users granted "always-on" administrative access
- Creating activity alerts or Cloud App Security activity policies to detect anomalous activity and act on them
- Creating a Conditional Access policy to enforce which applications users are allowed to access from certain locations on certain devices (such as managed ones), and under which circumstances this is allowed to happen
- Leaked credential reporting

Managing compromised accounts (or preventing them) is key to sustaining a secure computing environment.

Compromised machines

Besides protecting against compromised accounts, administrators should plan to implement measures to prevent or address compromised machines. The following Microsoft 365 features can be used:

- Configuring Windows Defender ATP policies to further detect anomalies and protect against malicious activity
- Deploying Azure ATA policies to detect malicious login attempts in AD Domain Services
- Configuring Windows Defender Credential Guard policies to isolate and protect machine secrets

- Configuring Windows controlled folder access to prevent malware from corrupting data
- Deploying Intune Mobile Device and Mobile Application Management policies to protect data on devices
- Deploying BitLocker for device-level encryption

A comprehensive device management policy is necessary to prevent damage from compromised machines.

Phishing

Phishing is one of the most common attacks experienced by organizations. With phishing, an attacker is attempting to obtain information from a victim, typically by pretending to be a trusted source (such as a business partner, a well-known brand or organization, a friend, or another employee). Attackers may attempt to compromise users by getting them to click on links pointing to malicious websites or by emailing confidential information. No matter the attack vector, phishing can result in both data and financial loss.

Microsoft 365 provides organizations with a number of tools to help combat email phishing attempts:

- **Exchange Online Protection (EOP)**: EOP is included with all Microsoft 365 subscriptions, and can be used to detect and block spam and virus-infected attachments. EOP uses multiple antivirus engines and is continuously updated with new antivirus signatures. EOP also has protections against anomalous message patterns and includes anti-phishing controls to block suspected attempts. Anti-phishing mechanisms can be configured to detect targeted impersonation attempts.
- **Office 365 Advanced Threat Protection (ATP)**: In addition to signature-based malware detection, Office 365 ATP includes heuristic technology to the sandbox, detonate, and examine the behavior of message attachments. ATP also maintains a reputation database and checks each link embedded in an email message to see if the destination website contains known malware or phishing characteristics.

- **Attack simulator:** While stopping threats before they reach users is critical, it's also very important to teach users how to respond should a threat evade detection. Microsoft 365 has an attack simulator that can be used to run phishing campaigns against your users, catalog the results, and help you target training at users who need it:

 Attack Simulator, shown in the preceding screenshot, is part of Office 365 ATP Plan 2. You can learn more about the features of ATP Plan 2 at `https://products.office.com/en-US/exchange/advance-threat-prot ection`

Microsoft 365 has a wide variety of tools to enable organizations to protect themselves against attacks as well as train users to respond correctly.

Summary

Both AAD Premium and AD provides organization administrators with several security features that can be used to safeguard critical data and systems. As we saw, there are controls available to verify and authenticate access, enforce MFA based on a number of usage and risk scenarios, and detect anomalous behavior patterns.

You also learned about how additional tools in the Microsoft 365 suite, such as Attack Simulator, can be used to help train users to respond appropriately to threats. You should now understand some core features of Azure AD Premium (such as Conditional Access) and how they can be used to enhance an organization's security.

In the next chapter, we'll begin examining the Service Trust Portal and Compliance Manager, which can be used to help organizations achieve and manage compliance with industry standards.

Questions

Use the following questions to test your knowledge of this chapter. You can find the answers in *Assessment Answers:*

1. Conditional Access is a feature of _____.
    1. AAD Premium P1
    2. AD
    3. Cloud App Security
    4. Privileged Identity Management

2. Risk-based Conditional Access is a feature of _____.
    1. AAD Premium P1
    2. AAD Premium P2
    3. AD
    4. Privileged Identity Management

3. Self-service password reset can update on-premise and cloud passwords.
    1. True
    2. False

4. Office 365 Attack Simulator is part of _____.
   1. Office 365 Advanced Threat Protection Plan 1
   2. Office 365 Advanced Threat Protection Plan 2
   3. AAD Premium Plan 1
   4. AAD Premium Plan 2

5. The feature that allows just-in-time rights management and access rights elevation is which of the following?
   1. Privileged Identity Management
   2. Access Reviews
   3. Baseline Security Policies
   4. Security Defaults
   5. Conditional Access

6. You are the security administrator for your organization. You want to automate a process to check on group memberships and remove stale accounts from groups. What tool or feature should you use?
   1. Privileged Identity Management
   2. Access Reviews
   3. Baseline Security Policies
   4. Security Defaults
   5. Conditional Access

7. You are a network administrator for your organization. You need to provide secure remote access to internal applications and want to use existing AAD Conditional Access policies. What tool or feature should you use?
   1. Azure Application Proxy
   2. Azure Reverse Proxy
   3. Azure Proxy Authentication Service
   4. Azure Remote Applications

8. Microsoft Cloud App Discovery can be used to do which of the following?
   1. Find new applications compatible with Office 365.
   2. Report on application compatibility.
   3. Provide cloud applications to Windows 10 devices.
   4. Identify "shadow IT"

9. After a security audit, you discover that several users have poor passwords that include your organization's name. What tool or feature can you use to prevent users from choosing passwords that contain specific words?

    1. Self-service password reset

    2. Custom banned password list

    3. Security defaults

    4. Baseline security policies

10. The Service Desk manager reports that her team spends a significant amount of time helping users who forgot their passwords. What tool or feature can you implement to help increase your organization's productivity?

    1. Multi-factor authentication

    2. Custom banned password list

    3. Self-service password reset

    4. Identity protection

12
Service Trust Portal and Compliance Manager

Most organizations have an assessment process, both from technical and compliance perspectives, that they must go through before authorizing the acquisition or use of a cloud solution. Some questions may arise during this process, such as the following:

- Is Microsoft 365 safe?
- Where is my data stored?
- Who has access to my data?
- What happens to my data if I decide to leave the service?

IT administrators, compliance administrators, legal representatives, and security officers typically have some or all of the responsibility for providing these answers to the business. It is imperative that everyone has a clear understanding of the principles by which Microsoft operates its data centers.

In this chapter, you will learn about two components available in Microsoft 365 that can help you answer these questions:

- Service Trust Portal
- Compliance Manager

As you'll see in this chapter, the Service Trust Portal and Compliance Manager will help both the business and operational sides of an organization address common concerns and questions when deciding on a Microsoft 365 strategy.

Let's begin!

Service Trust Portal

Many organizations need to have some level of evidentiary data that confirms cloud service providers are adhering to agreed-upon standards for security and data handling. The Microsoft Service Trust Portal is where all of these critical documents are stored.

The core components of the Service Trust Portal include the following:

- Compliance Manager
- Trust documents

Let's look at each of these briefly. First, we'll examine the trust documents.

Trust documents

There are several documents available in the Service Trust Portal that can enable organizations to better understand how the Microsoft 365 platform is designed and operated. With these documents and whitepapers, organizations can be confident about how their data is being collected, stored, and used in the service. The following sections will provide an example of how these documents can be used to address some of the organization's most common questions.

The areas we'll look at are as follows:

- Tenant isolation in Office 365
- Data residency
- Encryption in the Microsoft Cloud
- Audit reports
- Data resiliency in Office 365

Let's get started.

Tenant isolation in Office 365

Tenant isolation answers the question, *How is my data separated from other organizations?*

Microsoft 365 enables customers to share physical resources such as computing power and storage in a model called *multi-tenancy*. In order to isolate one organization's data from another, several forms of protection are implemented, such as the following:

- Logical isolation through Azure Active Directory
- Encryption for data at rest
- Encryption for data in transit

The tenant is a logical security boundary, and all information and data related to that organization are held within that container. You can learn more about how Microsoft's tenant isolation procedures are used to separate organizations' data at `https://docs.microsoft.com/en-us/office365/Enterprise/office-365-tenant-isolation-overview`.

Data residency

Data residency answers the question, *Where is my data stored?*

When an organization signs up for Microsoft 365, they indicate where their primary place of business is. This decision maps their tenant to a region, which in turn is used to define which data centers will be used to store their data. Organizations using sovereign clouds (such as 21ViaNet or Government Community Cloud) have very explicitly designated storage regions. For security purposes, Microsoft does not disclose the exact address of its data centers. Customers can leverage public documents, however, to learn where in the Microsoft cloud their data is stored, depending on which type of service they are using.

You can learn more about where data is located by visiting `https://products.office.com/en-us/where-is-your-data-located`.

Encryption in the Microsoft Cloud

Microsoft uses several encryption technologies to secure data. Encryption technologies and platforms used include the following:

- BitLocker
- Azure Storage Service Encryption
- **Distributed Key Manager (DKM)**
- **Internet Protocol Security (IPsec)**
- **Transport Layer Security (TLS)**

Depending on the data's activity status (at rest or in transit) and in which service it resides, encryption may be 128-bit or 256-bit AES. Many Microsoft 365 services also allow customers to manage their own encryption keys, further restricting access to their data.

 You can learn more about the encryption protocols and standards used at https://docs.microsoft.com/en-us/microsoft-365/compliance/ office-365-encryption-risks-and-protections.

Audit reports

Many organizations adhere to a variety of compliance standards or protocols. Some organizations choose to do this for their own benefit, while others are required to by their customers, constituents, or other statutory obligations.

Whatever the reason driving compliance, Microsoft 365 provides tools to help organizations achieve and maintain compliance. One of the benefits of using Microsoft as a cloud service provider is being able to leverage the investments they make in security and compliance efforts.

When compiling documentation for their own audits, organizations can include attestations and audited controls documents as part of their compliance package. The Audit Reports can be grouped and filtered by technology, industry, and report types, as shown in the following screenshot:

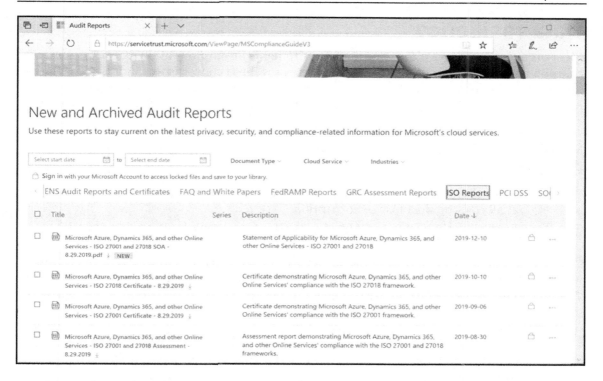

Audit reports are freely available but do require a sign-in to a Microsoft 365 tenant.

You can view all of the audit reports at `https://servicetrust.` `microsoft.com/ViewPage/MSComplianceGuideV3`.

These audit reports and trust documents can be used as part of an organization's overall auditing and compliance package. Microsoft provides another service, Compliance Manager, for organizations to track their progress toward completing various compliance goals.

Data resiliency

Most organizations have either question requirements around retention, backup, compliance, and recoverability. Microsoft addresses these concerns through a framework of data replication, physical backups, and highly-available or fault-tolerant designs. Resiliency refers to the concept of being able to continue to provide services, regardless of what types of failures occur.

Microsoft's goal in Microsoft 365 is designed with the following data five resiliency principals:

- **Critical and non-critical data**: Critical data (such as content) must be preserved at all costs against loss or corruption.
- **Fault domains**: Data must be separated into as many fault zones as possible to provide failure isolation.
- **Data must be monitored to detect whether it fails the Atomicity, Consistency, Isolation, and Durability test**: Atomicity, Consistency, Isolation, and **Durability** (ACID) are a set of properties that ensures the validity of a data transaction.
- **Customer data must be protected from corruption**. In order to ensure that data is in a continuously good state, it must be scanned or monitored, repairable, and recoverable. This includes physical and logical monitoring at both the hardware and software layers.
- **Allow customers to be able to recover their own data**. Tools are provided to allow customer autonomy when recovering accidentally deleted data.

Microsoft 365 addresses the potential for data corruption (whether due to hardware, human, application, or operational errors) by replicating data and performing continuous checks on transactions to ensure they are valid. In addition, during the development stages of applications and services, Microsoft conducts thorough code reviews to ensure that all code contributes to the overall efficacy of the system. Application data is monitored and replicated so that transactions can be rolled back to previous good states if necessary.

In addition to corruption, malware, and ransomware present challenges to both on-premises and cloud environments. Microsoft 365 uses mechanisms to prevent malware from being introduced through clients or servers, including both heuristic and signature-based detections. Microsoft 365 environments are scanned at regular intervals as well as during times when files are downloaded, opened, or executed. SharePoint Online and OneDrive for Business each include document versioning, which can be used to recover files that may have been encrypted, and Cloud App Security can be used from a customer's perspective to detect anomalous behaviors executed in their environments.

Microsoft 365 also makes use of extensive monitoring with native, third-party, and open-source products, using data analytics to predict problems and synthetic transactions to verify that services are responding correctly.

With this understanding of how Microsoft manages its resources, we can move into how organizations can manage audit and regulatory compliance activities with the Compliance Manager.

Understanding Compliance Manager

As organizations adopt new services, they need to make sure that doing so enables them to maintain or improve their compliance posture. Compliance Manager enables organizations to review and understand, under a shared responsibility model, what controls are being maintained by the provider (that is, Microsoft), and what controls or actions must be completed by the customer.

A sample of the Compliance Manager dashboard is shown in the following screenshot:

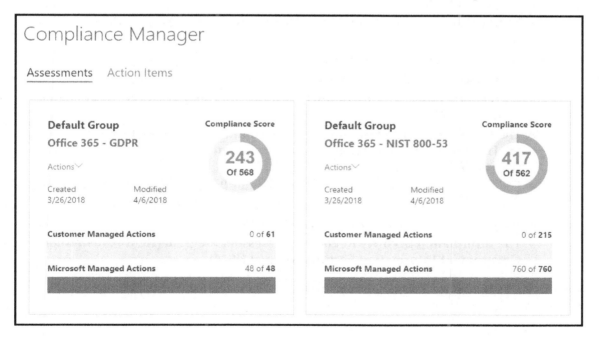

Compliance Manager displays the controls for a given certification and identifies which controls are managed by Microsoft and which controls the customer needs to review to confirm they are being applied in their own organization. For each control, there is a description of what needs to be accomplished that customers can use to help during the assessment process.

Additionally, Compliance Manager allows organizations to upload their own documents in support of their attestation of compliance. As a result of completing their required actions and attestations, organizations will be able to raise their **Compliance Score**. The **Compliance Score** is a risk-based score that measures progress in completing actions that help reduce risks.

Compliance Manager has a number of templates, pre-populated with the controls that are managed by both Microsoft and the customer. The default templates, as of this writing, are as follows:

- **International Standards Organization (ISO)** 27001:2013
- ISO 27108:2014
- ISO 27701:2019
- **National Institute of Standards and Technology (NIST)** 800-53 Revision 4
- NIST 800-171
- NIST **Cybersecurity Framework (CSF)**
- **Cloud Security Alliance (CAS) Cloud Controls Matrix (CCM)** 3.0.1
- The **Federal Financial Institutions Examination Council (FFIEC)** Information Security Booklet
- The **Health Insurance Portability and Accountability Act (HIPAA)** and the **Health Information Technology for Economic and Clinical Health Act (HITECH Act**, sometimes abbreviated **HITEC)**
- **Federal Risk and Authorization Management Program (FedRAMP)** Moderate
- The European Union **General Data Protection Regulation (GDPR)**
- The **California Consumer Privacy Act (CCPA)**
- The **Information Security Registered Assessors Program (IRAP)/Australian Government Information Security Manual (ISM)**

You can add any of these templates to Compliance Manager, as well as build or import your own templates using Microsoft Excel.

Compliance Manager templates are formatted in a Microsoft Excel workbook—not a standard CSV file. The Excel workbook must have several tabs, including tabs for Assessment, ControlFamily, Actions, and Owner. You can learn more about the structure of compliance templates at `https://docs.microsoft.com/en-us/microsoft-365/compliance/working-with-compliance-manager#templates`.

Compliance Manager allows organizations to assign and track compliance-related activities, such as managing the evidence or artifacts that can later be provided to auditors. While Compliance Manager does not guarantee that an organization is compliant with a given standard or regulation, it certainly helps in the compliance journey.

To learn more about Compliance Manager, see `https://docs.microsoft.com/en-us/microsoft-365/compliance/compliance-manager-overview`.

Summary

In this chapter, we discussed both the Service Trust Portal and Compliance Manager. Together, the Service Trust Portal and Compliance Manager can help organizations achieve and maintain compliance with industry-based standards and regulatory controls. We also covered some of the most common questions organizations have when assessing a cloud service, such as how data is secured, where data is stored, and what data resiliency protections are in place.

In the next chapter, we'll begin reviewing licensing options, including which cloud services may be available on licensing styles or agreements.

Questions

Use the following questions to test your knowledge of this chapter. You can find the answers in *Assessment Answers*.

1. Which Microsoft 365 tool can organizations use to track their progress against industry compliance standards?
   1. GDPR Accelerator
   2. Compliance Accelerator
   3. Compliance Manager
   4. Compliance Dashboard

2. Identify three of the encryption technologies or platforms used to secure data in Microsoft 365 from the following:
    1. Bitlocker
    2. Bootstrapper
    3. Encryption Manager
    4. Internet Protocol Security (IPSec)
    5. Transport Layer Security (TLS)

3. Data residency answers which of the following questions?
    1. What encryption is used to protect my data?
    2. Where is my data stored?
    3. Who has access to my data?
    4. What security standards are applied to my data?

4. Tenant isolation refers to which of the following concepts?
    1. Separation of organizational data in a single-tenant environment
    2. Separation of organizational data in a multi-tenant environment
    3. Securing records storage in a third-party system
    4. GDPR compliance

5. Which two terms apply to how data in Microsoft 365 is encrypted?
    1. At rest
    2. In transit
    3. In potente
    4. En masse

6. Compliance Manager allows you to import custom templates.
    1. True
    2. False

7. GDPR stands for which of the following?
    1. General Data Privacy Regulation
    2. General Data Protection Regulation
    3. General Data Primary Regulation
    4. General Data Proposed Regulation

8. Compliance Manager contains built-in templates for which three standards?
    1. NIST 800-53
    2. NIST CSF
    3. PCI-DSS
    4. GDPR

Licensing Options in Microsoft 365 **13**

As organizations advance through their assessment of Microsoft 365, they will usually discuss it in terms of understanding business value, technical features and requirements, and security and compliance features. Once the business conversations are complete, they will look at acquiring licenses to support their decision. Finally, they'll work through determining the best implementation and deployment options.

In this chapter, we will cover the following topics:

- Microsoft 365 subscription and management options
- Understanding key Microsoft 365 selling points
- Licensing and payment models
- Determining and implementing best practices

By the end of this chapter, you should have an understanding of how Microsoft 365 licensing is structured and what decisions you'll need to make when procuring or advising organizations on the available options.

Microsoft 365 subscription and management options

Deciding which Microsoft 365 subscription to acquire is not a trivial task. Organizations need to plan and should consider various business factors, which will ultimately drive the purchase decision. The following list details some of the common aspects and decision points:

- **Per-user, rather than per device**: For most cloud-based services, organizations should plan on acquiring licensing based on the user rather than device counts. While some industries or roles rely on shared devices or equipment, it will be important to determine which models apply to you. Most organizations will require a mix of individual or user-based licensing, as well as shared or common device licensing. Plan on identifying the numbers of individual users as well as the numbers of shared devices when estimating costs.

- **Service family**: Depending on your organization's size, type, or region, you may be eligible to acquire different licenses. Some of the service families include Business (maximum of 300 users), Enterprise, Education (only available for educational institutions), Government (only available to public sector organizations), as well as sovereign cloud environments such as Office 365, which are operated by 21Vianet in China or Office 365 Germany.

- **Standalone versus bundle**: If your organization plans to use only one particular piece of Microsoft 365 software, you may have an option of acquiring plans for standalone services (such as Exchange Online or SharePoint Online). As you choose services to acquire, however, bundled SKUs frequently provide better value. Most organizations choose to acquire bundles, which includes several services and provide a cost advantage.

- **Bundle service availability**: Not all services are available in an SKU bundle; bundles may have different levels of service associated with them. It's important to evaluate the exact features that are driving the business decision so you can purchase them accordingly.

- **Short-term versus long-term**: Even though licenses can be changed, whenever possible, organizations should attempt to predict what their users will need and plan accordingly to avoid surprise reconciliation bills at the end of their billing term.

After deciding on the user and service requirements, organizations can acquire licenses. The license assignment to end users is managed through the **Microsoft 365 admin center** or Azure AD portal, as shown in the following screenshot:

Under each user's account properties, administrators with proper permissions can also see which licenses have been assigned to particular users, as well as remove or edit these license assignments, as shown in the following screenshot:

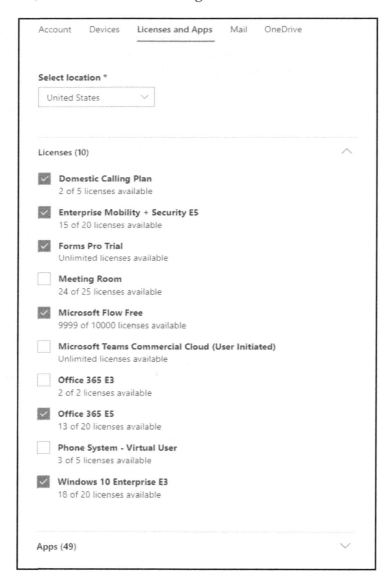

Moreover, license assignments can be automated or made in bulk through PowerShell or Azure group-based licensing (`https://docs.microsoft.com/en-us/azure/active-directory/fundamentals/active-directory-licensing-whatis-azure-portal`).

Many applications and services also include the ability to enable or disable features, so it is up to the business and technology teams to discuss what options or features can be managed.

Next, let's look at some of the things that go into the decision-making process, such as working with business stakeholders and requirements gathering. Part of building a Microsoft 365 strategy requires understanding the business requirements and how they map to the key features or selling points in the platform.

Understanding key Microsoft 365 selling points

When making purchasing decisions, some organizations may need different stakeholders' approval before being authorized to acquire a service. This may include needing to document current requirements and why a particular service solves them.

In this section, we'll review some of the key Microsoft 365 selling points.

Productivity

One of the primary design goals of Microsoft 365 is to enable personal and group productivity. This is possible largely due to the integration of the different products and services that comprise the suites, which can be accessed on a variety of devices in a secure and compliant manner.

Under a **Software-as-a-Service (SaaS)** model, users have access to a wide variety of applications that are always up to date, managed by Microsoft, which facilitates email, file sharing, chat, meetings, presentation, social networking, storage, business process automation, and low-code development.

Collaboration

People collaborate and work with teams more now than they ever have. Studies performed by organizations such as McKinsey (`https://www.mckinsey.com/industries/technology-media-and-telecommunications/our-insights/the-social-economy`) show that social networking and collaboration lead to increased productivity and output.

In the business landscape, this collaboration happens with both internal and external users, from both a corporate and consumer perspective. Microsoft 365, as a SaaS model, provides services that enable this collaboration in all of these types of scenarios.

For example, organizations can store and share files with users both inside and outside the organization using Teams, OneDrive for Business, and SharePoint Online, or by delivering attachments to external individuals using consumer email systems. Other scenarios involve creating and coauthoring files across different Office clients and users or creating a common workspace for groups to collaborate with Microsoft Teams. These collaborative workspaces can reduce context switching while providing access to the relevant tools and experiences for chat, files, meetings, and calls in a single tool.

Security

Microsoft 365 was designed to enable productivity and collaboration while staying secure. Security, one of the pillars of the service, can be seen across the suite, from the tenant isolation and data encryption to risk-based conditional access. Microsoft 365 allows organizations to deploy multi-factor authentication services and even extend those to their on-premises applications, in addition to creating and applying data classification tags to documents and messages.

Microsoft 365 also allows organizations to apply data management policies to mobile devices, ensuring that data can't move from managed or privileged applications to unmanaged applications or wipe data in managed devices or applications if users fail to authenticate. These capabilities allow organizations to protect on-premises, cloud, and hybrid environments against attacks such as compromised accounts by detecting unknown activities through several behavioral and heuristic strategies.

In addition, security administrators can access tools such as Secure Score (`https://securescore.office.com`) so that they can understand their security posture and evaluate actions they can perform in order to improve.

Compliance

Microsoft 365 supports organizations throughout their compliance journey. Microsoft is committed to building and maintaining a trusted computing environment and, as such, submits to numerous third-party audits to ensure compliance with industry security standards. Azure and Microsoft 365 services have obtained a number of industry certifications, such as **Payment Card Industry (PCI)**, **International Standards Organization (ISO) 27001**, **National Institute of Standards and Technology (NIST) 800-53**, **Health Insurance Portability and Accountability Act (HIPAA)**, the **General Data Protection Regulation (GDPR)**, and the **Federal Risk and Authorization Management Program (FedRAMP)**.

Microsoft provides something known as Compliance Manager (`https://servicetrust.microsoft.com/ComplianceManager`), a compliance reporting and management tool, to help organizations track their compliance against various industry standards. Compliance Manager allows administrators to download Microsoft's attestations and compliance certification documents so that they can be included in the organization's documentation. Compliance Manager also catalogs audited controls and allows compliance administrators to track their own organization's compliance actions. The **Compliance Manager** dashboard looks as follows:

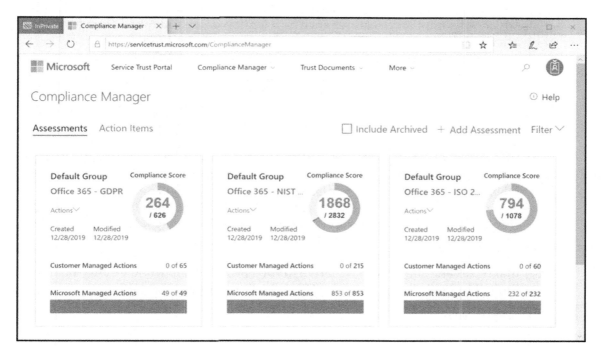

From a service perspective, Microsoft 365 provides mechanisms such as the Security & Compliance Center (`https://protection.office.com`) for administrators to enforce data governance and life cycle policies, encryption, data loss prevention, and eDiscovery case management activities.

While many of the service's features, capabilities, and selling points are available across all service offerings, there are some differences based on which product family an organization purchases. We'll explore some of those differences next.

Licensing and payment models

As you'll see in `Chapter 14`, *Planning, Predicting, and Comparing Pricing*, there are many different license acquisition and payment models available. Microsoft 365 has these different licensing and payment options so that they are suitable for their wide range of customer requirements. The main licensing service families and SKU bundles, as we discussed earlier in this chapter, are as follows:

- **Microsoft 365 Business**: This bundle is intended for small to medium-sized businesses with up to 300 employees. Microsoft 365 Business offers a compelling mix of features and basic service plans. Microsoft 365 business does not include advanced compliance features such as retention or the unlimited storage of Microsoft 365 Enterprise plans. It also does not include Windows 10.
- **Microsoft 365 Commercial (E-series or F-series)**: These SKU packages are intended for enterprise organizations with variations across the employee usage profile (sometimes referred to as *personas*). Most larger commercial organizations pick a mix of SKUs from this family of services, including SKUs for personas, termed as *information works* or *knowledge workers*, as well as personas such as *Firstline workers* (sometimes referred to as *line workers, front-line workers, front-of-house employees*, or *shift workers*). These SKUs are available worldwide, though some may be reformulated slightly due to encryption and export restrictions or when there are restrictions in place due to sovereign cloud agreements. Microsoft 365 includes Windows, as well as advanced features. Microsoft 365 E-series plans come with two licensing levels (E3 and E5), with E5 having additional advanced compliance, productivity, and security features available. Some of the key differences between E and F series are that E-series plans include 100 GB mailboxes and unlimited OneDrive for Business storage, while F-series plans are limited to 2 GB mailboxes and 1 TB of OneDrive for Business storage.

- **Microsoft 365 A-series**: This set of SKUs is typically used for educational institutions. Educational SKUs exist in the commercial environment and share the same infrastructure, but are available at deeply discounted rates to qualifying organizations. Microsoft 365 A-series SKUs are comparable to their E-series counterparts.

- **Microsoft 365 G-series**: The G SKUs are reserved for US government public sector entities, such as federal, state, and local municipality governments or dedicated contractors. These SKUs are not available in commercial or other sovereign clouds. These SKUs are tied to a separate sovereign infrastructure that is wholly inside the United States and is FedRAMP certified. These FedRAMP-certified environments are commonly referred to as **Government Community Cloud (GCC)** Moderate, GCC-High, and GCC-DOD. Organizations that require compliance with IRS Publication 1075 and **Criminal Justice Information Services (CJIS)** typically choose the GCC environments, as do organizations that require United States-based data residency. Like Microsoft 365 E-series, the G-series is also available in two licensing levels (G3 and G5), with a higher level having more advanced productivity, security, and compliance features. G-series SKUs typically don't feature all of the services of commercial SKUs, as products must go through additional certification and validation before being offered.

- **Individual licenses**: In addition to the ability to acquire bundled SKU licenses, organizations in any cloud (commercial, public sector, or sovereign) can also acquire individual licenses, either as add-ons to bundles or as standalone products.

It's important to note that you cannot mix SKU service families between the commercial and government ones. If you are purchasing for a government or public sector organization, you should evaluate whether you require compliance with **IRS Publication 1075 (Pub1075)** or the CJIS. If you don't require compliance with those services, it may be more beneficial to choose a commercial cloud offering, despite being a public sector organization. Government and public sector organizations are not required to be in a GCC offering, though many choose to be, depending on their reporting, compliance, data residency, or other security requirements.

In addition, some of the different payment models of Microsoft 365 are as follows:

- **Credit card or bank account**: Schedule a recurring credit card charge or bank account draft to pay for services.

- **Invoice**: An organization can receive an invoice with payment terms for Microsoft 365 services.
- **Prepaid product key**: Products and services can be purchased with a pre-paid license key at some retail locations.

 The frequency of these payments can be set to a monthly or yearly basis. You can learn more here: `https://docs.microsoft.com/en-us/ office365/admin/subscriptions-and-billing/change-payment-method? view=o365-worldwide`.

As you can see, while there are a number of decisions to make when choosing the right Microsoft 365 SKU licensing options, your market vertical (small business, enterprise commercial, academic, or public sector) largely defines which family of SKUs you can purchase. We'll look at the exact pricing models more closely in `Chapter 14`, *Planning, Predicting, and Comparing Pricing*.

In the next section, we'll review some of the best practices for designing a licensing strategy.

Determining and implementing best practices

With several options to choose from, especially from a licensing perspective, companies often have questions about which licenses to acquire. The following is a list of best practices that can help an organization decide how to proceed:

- **Define service and feature requirements**: As we mentioned previously, organizations should evaluate their business requirements and map what services and features that are in the various products map to their business goals and objectives.
- **Define user profiles or personas**: Especially in larger organizations, Microsoft recommends categorizing employees in profiles or *personas* based on their location within the organization (such as C-suite users, Firstline workers, or knowledge workers), job roles, or some other business criteria. Once the users have been profiled and organized, identify the particular service and feature requirements that those roles or profiles have and map them to the appropriate features in Microsoft 365. This can be used to drive licensing and SKU assignments. As part of this exercise, organizations should plan for labor force changes (such as seasonal workers).

- **Plan for a baseline**: While different user profiles may allow organizations to choose different products, SKUs, or bundles, it's also important to establish a baseline of required features or services that apply to all users. For example, if you have one requirement that can be fulfilled with Exchange Online Plan 1, but then have an organizational requirement for retention policies, you'll need to either acquire an archiving add-on or an Exchange Online Plan 2 license to support the business goal.

- **Individual versus bundle**: It may be beneficial to perform an analysis of which features are requirements and can be purchased a la carte or as individual items, as organizations typically don't deploy all the features or products present in a bundle. Frequently, though, if there are two or more required services or features, it's more cost-effective to look at an SKU bundle.

- **Consider add-ons**: Sometimes, though, there are situations where *only* an add-on solves a problem (if a product isn't included in a bundle) or only an add-on service is needed. One example is licensing for Exchange Online shared mailboxes. Organizations are entitled to "shared and resource" mailboxes *free of charge*. However, the "shared or resource" mailbox license doesn't support mailbox archiving or retention policies. In this case, if there is a requirement for archiving or retention policies, organizations may want to look at an add-on SKU for Exchange Online Archiving for those mailboxes.

- **Consider the internal deployment roadmap**: If an organization doesn't have plans to deploy a service to all their users at once, they could consider acquiring the service in cycles, ramping up their acquisition as they prepare to onboard more users.

After the licensing requirements have been worked out, organizations need to decide on their license acquisition plans, as well as their service deployment and implementation plans.

Summary

In this chapter, we covered some of the key points an organization should consider when formulating their cloud services purchase plan. A proper Microsoft 365 licensing management plan requires a careful understanding of an organization's requirements and user profiles. In particular, organizations should seek to understand the benefits (directly or indirectly) that a service can provide from productivity, collaboration, and security and compliance perspectives. These benefits are typically articulated to make the case for purchase. This chapter showed you the importance of mapping business requirements to selling points or features in the Microsoft 365 platform to ensure the right services are acquired.

In the next chapter, we'll dive deeper into understanding the purchase and payment subscription models that are available.

Questions

Use the following questions to test your knowledge of this chapter. You can find the answers in *Assessment Answers*:

1. You are the IT director for a medium-sized commercial organization with 220 employees. You are looking for the most cost-effective solution to provide Microsoft 365 services to your users. Which should you choose?
    1. Microsoft 365 E3
    2. Microsoft 365 E5
    3. Microsoft 365 G3
    4. Microsoft 365 Business

2. When purchasing Enterprise, Government, or Education plans, all the plans must be the same. It is not possible to mix and match E3 and E5 (or G3 and G5) SKUs in the same tenant.
    1. True
    2. False

3. You are the IT director for a public sector organization and you require data residency in the United States. What service family should you choose?
    1. Microsoft 365 Commercial
    2. Microsoft 365 GCC
    3. Microsoft 365 Business
    4. Microsoft 365 Education

4. You are the IT director for a large commercial organization with 15,000 employees worldwide. Which Microsoft 365 product service family should you choose?
    1. Microsoft 365 Commercial
    2. Microsoft 365 GCC
    3. Microsoft 365 Business
    4. Microsoft 365 Education

5. Identify three best practices for determining your licensing strategy:
    1. Plan for a baseline
    2. Define user profiles or personas
    3. Define service and feature requirements
    4. Sign a non-disclosure agreement

6. Identify two of the key Microsoft 365 selling points:
    1. Productivity
    2. Expensive
    3. Vulnerable
    4. Compliance

7. Identify two of the key Microsoft 365 selling points:
    1. Security
    2. Collaboration
    3. Static
    4. Disconnected

8. Microsoft 365 is licensed _____.
    1. Per-organization
    2. Per-tenant
    3. Per-user
    4. Per-device

9. Organizations can choose Microsoft GCC if they meet which requirement?
    1. Public sector
    2. Compliance
    3. Educational institution
    4. Desire

10. Identify three benefits for public sector organizations choosing the GCC sovereign cloud:
    1. IRS Publication 1070 Compliance
    2. IRS Publication 1075 Compliance
    3. Criminal Justice Information Services Compliance
    4. United States Data Residency

14
Planning, Predicting, and Comparing Pricing

In addition to deciding what features and licenses need to be acquired for an organization's business needs, it's important to decide how best to procure the licenses. While a number of different purchase models exist, a proper agreement should take into consideration the costs over time of a cloud solution when compared to any current or on-premise solution.

In this chapter, we'll tackle the following:

- Licensing models
- Cost-benefit analysis
- Billing options

Licensing models

At the time of writing, there are two core license acquisition models: direct licensing and indirect licensing.

Direct licensing refers to when an organization makes a direct purchase, such as through Microsoft Admin Center.

Indirect licensing refers to when an organization makes a purchase through a partner or reseller agreement. There are currently six indirect licensing methods available to acquire Microsoft 365. They are as follows:

- **Cloud Solution Provider (CSP)**: Organizations establish a billing relationship with a provider, who purchases on their behalf and sells the licenses to the customer.
- **Microsoft Open (includes Open Value, Open Value Subscription, and Open License)**: The Open License program allows customers to buy licensing through a reseller, typically for smaller organizations (more than 5 seats and typically fewer than 500).
- **Enterprise Agreement (EA)**: A program that is designed for larger organizations (more than 500 users or devices) and can include cloud services and software licenses together.
- **Microsoft Products and Services Agreement (MPSA)**: A purchasing account structure designed for organizations that use product pools and groupings to determine the price of services. Organizations must have more than 250 users or devices.
- **Services Provider License Agreement (SPLA)**: License structure designed for independent software vendors and service providers who want to license and host applications and services for customers.
- **Select Plus**: Select Plus is a purchasing mechanism targeted at large organizations with a number of affiliates who want to purchase as one entity. It is no longer available to commercial customers but is available for public sector customers.

Many Microsoft cloud services are calculated based on the number of users (commonly referred to as *seats*) that will be subscribing to a particular service or plan. Several key characteristics should be assessed when deciding which model is right for your organization:

- Minimum number of seats
- When you can make changes to the number of seats (either additions or removals)
- The cadence of the billing (annual, pay as you go, or some other contract mechanism)
- Which products or services are available under the licensing model
- Duration of the agreement

For the MS-900 exam, we'll highlight the structure and requirements of the **Cloud Solution Provider (CSP)** model.

The CSP program is designed for Microsoft Partners and **Value-Added Resellers (VARs)** as a way to develop long-lasting, holistic partnerships with customers. The CSP program has a wealth of tools available to help partners and VARs provide value to their customers.

When evaluating the CSP program against the aforementioned criteria, we're able to determine the following characteristics:

- Minimum of one seat.
- The number of seats that can be changed on a monthly basis.
- Billing cadence is "pay as you go."
- All Microsoft Online Services products are available.
- The agreement has a minimum duration of one year.

 You can find more information about the CSP program licensing models by following this link: https://partner.microsoft.com/en-us/licensing. You can also learn more about the other licensing programs, such as EA and Open, at https://www.microsoft.com/en-us/licensing/licensing-programs/licensing-programs. It's also important to note that the Select Plus program is no longer accepting new commercial enrollments and is only available for public sector customers.

Licensing and acquisition costs are part of the **Total Cost of Ownership (TCO)** of any product or service (whether for on-premise or cloud services). In the next section, we'll examine more closely the case for cloud services by performing a cost-benefit analysis.

Cost-benefit analysis for on-premises versus the cloud

When deciding on a licensing model, many customers ask themselves several questions:

- How much would it cost to proceed with a comparable on-premise solution?
- What is the risk of not doing anything?
- How long will it take to achieve a **Return on Investment (ROI)**?

These types of questions highlight the importance of cost-benefit analysis in an online services solution acquisition.

Organizations should engage in a cost-benefit analysis or produce a business case to ensure they're making a wise business choice. When setting up the analysis, the organization should gather details surrounding the costs and capabilities of their current environment so that they can compare them to the Microsoft 365 solution.

When performing a cost-benefit analysis for a cloud solution, an organization should compare the following benefits of Microsoft 365 against their current infrastructure or any proposed on-premise infrastructure upgrades:

- Improved security
- Reduced TCO
- End-user productivity
- Increased availability and reduced downtime
- Employee savings with new or improved collaboration scenarios
- Employee savings with new or improved mobility scenarios
- Infrastructure maintainability
- Improved compliance
- Travel savings

The following table compares the capabilities of on-premise and cloud deployments:

CAPABILITY OR TASK	ON-PREMISES DEPLOYMENT	MICROSOFT 365 CLOUD SERVICE DEPLOYMENT
Infrastructure acquisition and maintenance	Customer-owned and customer-managed.	Microsoft-owned and Microsoft-managed.
Upgrades	Customer's responsibility.	Microsoft's responsibility.
Security	Customer's responsibility.	Microsoft implements security protocols and attestation for engineering and support resources. The customer is responsible for using the tools provided to further secure user identities, applications, and devices.
Compliance	The customer is responsible for developing, deploying, administering, and documenting controls.	Microsoft is responsible for some managed controls. Certification is performed and validated on a regular basis. Microsoft and the customer share responsibility for other controls. The customer is required to follow best practices to implement and document their portion of the controls.

End-user productivity	The customer is responsible for measuring productivity with the available tools implemented and maintained locally.	It's the customer's responsibility to manage and report on user adoption with reporting tools provided by Microsoft.
Mobility	Based on versions and applications deployed and managed by the customer and governed by customer networking configuration and capability. It requires the purchase, deployment, configuration, and management of a **Mobile Device Management** (**MDM**) platform.	Available for all apps included in the product suite. An MDM platform is included.

To help organizations and partners during the cost-benefit analysis process, Microsoft makes a number of tools and calculators available, including the following:

- **Microsoft OnRamp Resources**: This includes documents about the **Total Economic Impact** (**TEI**) of Microsoft 365 E3 and Microsoft 365 E5, as well as an analysis of improvements to end-user productivity. For more information, see `https://transform.microsoft.com/resources`.
- **Microsoft OnRamp Value Calculator**: This is a tool that provides you with calculations of cost and benefits achieved with Microsoft 365 for an organization, based on values from Forrester TEI studies for Microsoft 365. For more information, see `https://vc.transform.microsoft.com`.

Organizations should also take advantage of reviewing public case studies and, if possible, study how other companies measured the progress and benefits of a cloud solution. If an organization is engaging with a partner to purchase and deploy services, they may also be able to obtain customer references to get an understanding of a solution's real-world value.

Billing options

Billing or billing cadence has to do with the model with which a license payment is made as well as the frequency of payments. The billing cadence varies depending on the chosen license model.

In direct license models, such as when a customer acquires a solution directly via an online ordering portal, customers can choose to pay by credit card or bank account, by invoice, or by using a prepaid product key. The frequency of these payments can be monthly or annually, and customers can switch their payment methods and frequency over the course of a subscription.

Customers can choose payment servicing options during the checkout process:

 You can learn more about billing in Microsoft 365 here: `https://docs.` `microsoft.com/en-us/office365/admin/subscriptions-and-billing/` `subscriptions-and-billing?view=o365-worldwide`.

However, when using an indirect license model, such as CSP, EA, or the Microsoft Products and Services Agreement, purchasing and financing agreements are usually made through a partner or VAR and can have customized terms.

For example, in the CSP license model, the partner receives an invoice from Microsoft for the end customer organization's licenses, and the end customer organization signs a billing or payment agreement with the CSP.

You can learn more about billing with the CSP license model here: `https://docs.` `microsoft.com/en-us/partner-center/billing-basics`.

Summary

There are different options from which organizations can choose when deciding the license model for their agreement so that they can find the one that best suits their needs with regard to billing, duration, seat change requirements, and product availability. As we discussed, one of the main license models available is the CSP model, which is very flexible from both the provider (reseller) and customer perspectives in terms of billing. In addition, we also covered the importance of doing a cost-benefit analysis of the acquisition of a cloud solution, such as Microsoft 365, and we looked at the resources available to help you build it. You should be able to articulate the value and differences of the billing models available in Microsoft 365.

In the next chapter, we're going to look at the types of support and service offerings available with Microsoft 365.

Questions

Use the following questions to test the knowledge you gained in this chapter. You can find the answers in *Assessment Answers*:

1. Identify four licensing models used to acquire Microsoft licensing:
    1. CSP
    2. Commercial
    3. EA
    4. Enterprise Enrollment
    5. Microsoft Open
    6. Service Provider License Agreement

2. Identify four important factors when performing a cost-benefit analysis to acquire a cloud solution:
    1. Improved security
    2. Reduced security
    3. Reduced TCO
    4. Increased TCO
    5. Increased end-user productivity
    6. Improved availability

3. Identify four important factors when performing a cost-benefit analysis to acquire a cloud solution:
    1. Employee savings with new or improved mobility scenarios
    2. Improved compliance capability
    3. Reduced compliance capability
    4. Travel savings
    5. Reduced downtime
    6. Increase in physical equipment presence
4. Under a direct license model, which of the following is true of the customer organization?
    1. Pays Microsoft directly
    2. Pays a partner or VAR directly
    3. Is entitled to free licensing
    4. Has licensing included with hardware purchases
    5. Can apply for net 90 terms
5. Under an indirect license model, which of the following is true of the customer organization?
    1. Pays Microsoft directly
    2. Pays a partner or VAR directly
    3. Is entitled to free licensing
    4. Is not responsible for payment agreements

15
Support Offerings for Microsoft 365 Services

In this chapter, we're going to take a look at how and when to engage support for your Microsoft 365 environment. It's important to know the boundaries of a service, how to track and interrogate your environment's health, and how to get help when you need it.

There are a number of resources available to help you understand what is available to you. By the end of this chapter, you should be familiar with the performance and availability you can expect from Microsoft 365 as well as methods for obtaining support.

In this chapter, we'll cover the following topics:

- Understanding Microsoft 365 **Service-Level Agreements (SLAs)**
- How to determine the service health
- How to create a support request

Understanding Microsoft 365 SLAs

Like most service offerings, Microsoft 365 has an SLA attached to it. An SLA is the service provider's commitment to providing a defined level of availability and reliability. In the case of Microsoft 365, the SLA for operation includes 99.9% availability, excluding scheduled downtimes (typically, this is for service upgrades). Microsoft provides a mechanism to recuperate a portion of your bill as service credits should they fail to meet the SLA.

Microsoft's SLA identifies a few important notes about claims:

- Claims must be submitted to Microsoft's customer support and should include details of the service outage, such as the timeline and duration, the number of users and locations affected, and the steps you took to resolve the issue.
- Claims must be received by the end of the calendar month following the month where the incident occurred (for example, if the incident occurred on March 15, the claim must be received by April 30).

Microsoft also puts some boundaries and limitations around fulfilling their SLA, such as the failure on your organization to take necessary actions (for instance, neglecting to disable someone's access or unauthorized access resulting in your failure to follow good security practices), misuse of the services, your loss of network connectivity, or acts outside of your control (such as natural disasters or war).

The SLA guide provides a few key terms and definitions that are used throughout:

Term	Definition
Applicable Monthly Period	During a calendar month in which a Service Credit is owed, the number of days that you are a subscriber for a particular service.
Applicable Monthly Service Fees	Total fees actually paid by you for a service, which are applied to the month in which a Service Credit is owed.
Downtime	Defined for each service in the Service Specific Terms (in the SLA guide). Except for Microsoft Azure Services, Downtime does not include Scheduled Downtime. Downtime does not include the unavailability of a service due to the limitations described later and in the Service Specific Terms.
Error Code	An indication that an operation has failed, such as an HTTP status code in the 5xx range.
External Connectivity	This denotes bidirectional network traffic over supported protocols (such as HTTP and HTTPS) that can be and received from a public IP address.
Incident	Incidents refer to (i) any single event, or (ii) any set of events, that result in Downtime.
Management Portal	The web interface, provided by Microsoft, through which customers may manage the service.
Scheduled Downtime	Periods of Downtime related to network, hardware, or service maintenance or upgrades. Microsoft will publish a notice or notify you at least 5 days prior to the commencement of such Downtime.
Service Credit	The percentage of the Applicable Monthly Service Fees credited to you following Microsoft's claim approval.
Service Level	The performance metric(s) set forth in the SLA that Microsoft agrees to meet in the delivery of the services.
Service Resource	An individual resource available for use within a service.

Success Code	An indication that an operation has succeeded, such as an HTTP status code in the 2xx range.
Support Window	The period of time during which a service feature or compatibility with a separate product or service is supported.
User Minutes	The total number of minutes in a month, less all Scheduled Downtime, multiplied by the total number of users.

In addition to the general "99.9%" uptime that the Microsoft 365 service advertises, Microsoft also provides guidance for how service credits will be apportioned, given the amount of outage that occurs. This is done on a per-service basis, as shown here:

Monthly Uptime Percentage	Service Credit
< 99.9%	25%
< 99%	50%
< 95%	100%

The Microsoft 365 SLA guide is regularly reviewed and updated.

You can access the detailed SLA guide at `https://www.microsoftvolumelicensing.com/DocumentSearch.aspx?Mode=3 DocumentTypeId=37`.

Now that you have an understanding of how Microsoft 365 SLAs are structured and some of the terminology associated with them, we'll look at service health concepts.

How to determine the service health

Microsoft provides a number of ways in which to obtain information about the health of various Microsoft 365 services, including the following resources:

- The Service Health Dashboard
- The Service Status page
- The Microsoft 365 Status Twitter feed

The Service Health Dashboard will have the most comprehensive information regarding service health status and availability. However, it doesn't provide any text messaging or other alerting capabilities. The Microsoft 365 Status Twitter feed is a good resource for getting notifications.

You can learn more about these tools and methods next.

The Service Health Dashboard

As previously stated, the Service Health Dashboard should be the first step when determining whether your environment is experiencing issues. The Service Health Dashboard contains the current health status of all Microsoft 365 services. Normally, services will appear as "healthy", though, the status will be updated when a service is experiencing an issue. The Service Health Dashboard will display the most detailed and comprehensive information on any ongoing or resolved issues.

You can access the Service Health Dashboard using the following steps:

1. Log in to the Microsoft 365 admin center (`https://admin.microsoft.com`) with an account that has either the Global Admin or Service Admin role, expand **Health**, and then select **Service Health:**

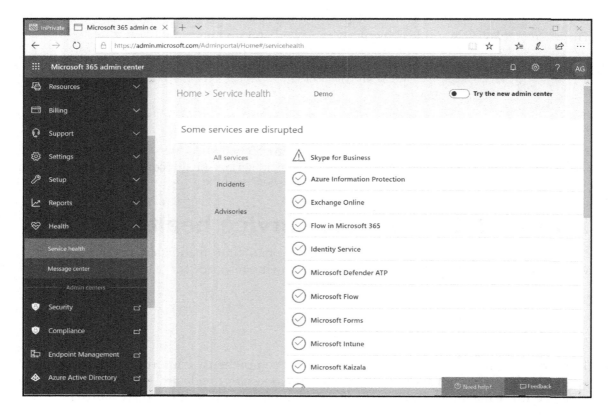

2. For services that display advisories or incidents, you can select the **Advisory** or **Incident** link next to the service, or expand the **Incidents** or **Advisories** menu option to display the relevant events:

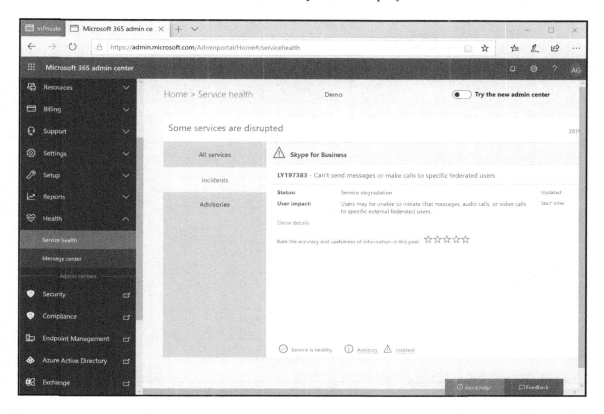

3. If an event has a **Show details** link, you can click on it to review more verbose details:

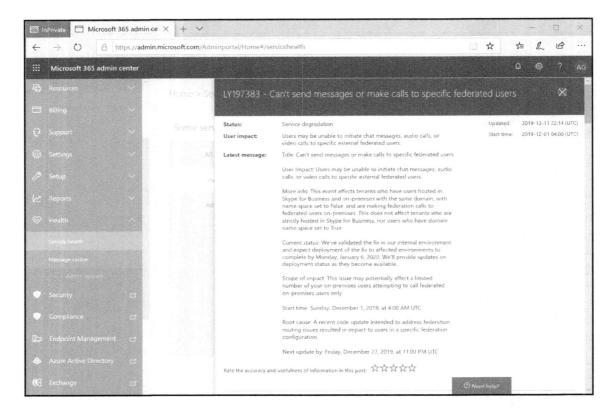

Periodically monitor the Service Health Dashboard for alerts so that you can inform your users should any issues arise before your users report them.

The Service Status page

If you are unable to log into the Microsoft 365 admin center, there may be an issue with the admin portal. Microsoft provides a second status page that allows you to check for errors when logging in to the Microsoft 365 admin center. You can access the Service Status page at https://status.office365.com:

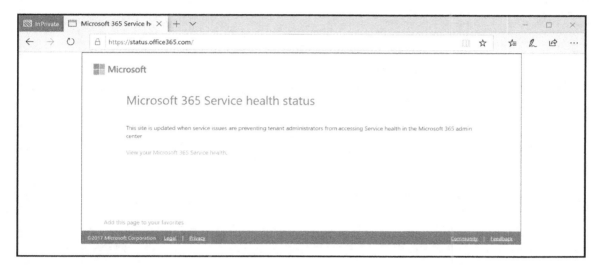

If the login services are working correctly, you'll typically see nothing except a link to the Service Health Dashboard, as shown in the preceding screenshot. If the login service or admin center portals themselves are experiencing errors, they will be displayed here.

The Microsoft 365 Health Status Twitter feed

Microsoft also maintains a Twitter feed for the Microsoft 365 service suite. The Microsoft 365 Health Status Twitter feed includes everything in the Office 365 suite and then adds on Windows, My Analytics, and Enterprise Mobility + Security products and services:

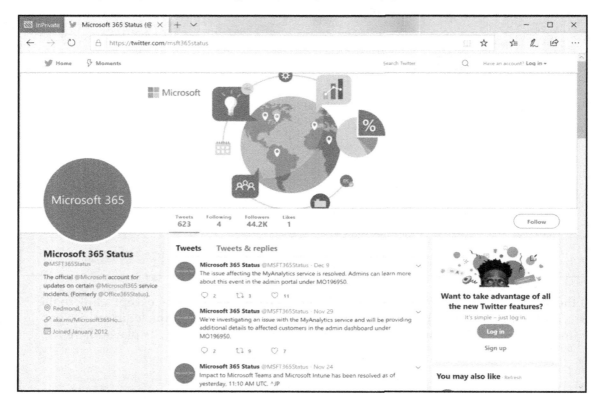

You can follow it on Twitter at @MSFT365status, or by navigating to https://twitter.com/msft365status.

If your organization is experiencing issues, you can use the next section on creating support requests to find help.

How to create a support request

Support requests for Microsoft 365 issues are typically raised through the Microsoft 365 admin center. You can create a support request using the following steps:

1. Log in to the Microsoft 365 admin center (`https://admin.microsoft.com`) and navigate to **Support** | **New service request:**

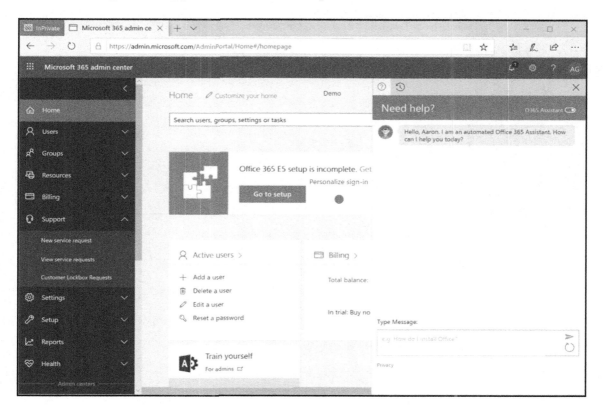

2. The **O365 Assistant** bot will likely display. You can choose to interact with it if your question is "how-to" related. You can also turn it off using the slider and start a normal support ticket. In this example, we'll turn it off and start a support request. Enter a few words and then click on **Get help:**

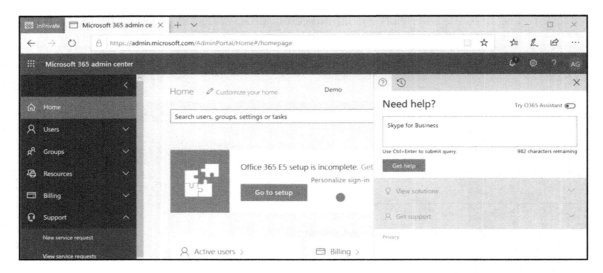

3. You can expand or collapse the **View solutions** menu to see common solutions matching your keywords:

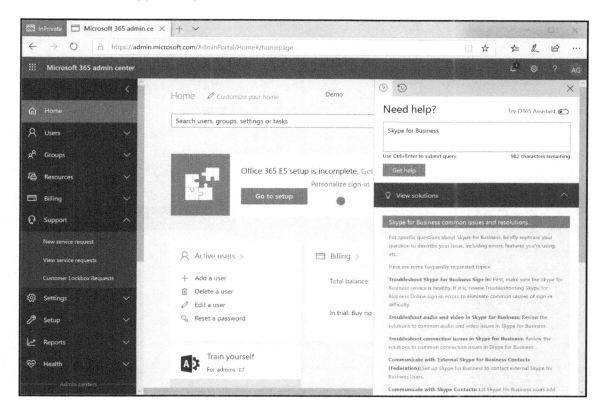

4. You can also scroll to the bottom, expand the **New service request by phone** option, and initiate a phone call with Microsoft support:

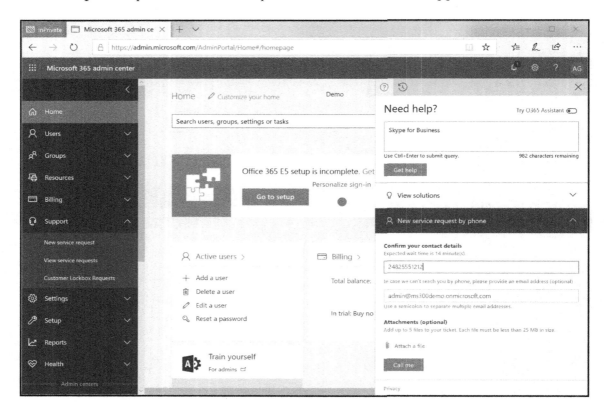

After a support request has been created, you can select the **Support | View service requests** option in the Microsoft 365 admin center to track the status of your service request or update it with new information. After opening your support ticket, the following Microsoft support matrix details how quickly support personnel will contact you:

Severity Rating	Impact Level	Initial Response Time	Customer Expectations and Notes
Severity A	**Critical business impact** Experiencing significant loss or degradation of services, requiring immediate attention.	Developer: N/A Standard: < 1 hr ProDirect: < 1 hr Premier: < 1 hr Azure Rapid Response: < 15 min 24x7 access	Severity A is reserved for issues that have a critical business impact, with severe loss and degradation of services for multiple users. Since you have designated that the issue demands an immediate response, you as a customer commit to continuous, 24 x 7 availability to work on the issue every day with the Microsoft team until resolution. Should you not be available, Microsoft may at its discretion decrease the issue to Severity B. You must also ensure that Microsoft has accurate contact information and that you are available.
Severity B	**Moderate business impact** Organization has moderate loss or degradation of services affecting multiple users, but work can continue in a somewhat impaired manner.	Developer: N/A Standard: < 4 hr ProDirect: < 2 hr Premier: < 2 hr Azure Rapid Response: < 2 hr Business hours access 4 (24x7 available)	Severity B issues have a moderate impact on your business with loss and degradation of services, but workarounds are available. If you've submitted an issue as Severity B, you have indicated that the issue demands an urgent response. If you choose 24 x 7 when you submit the support request, you commit to a continuous, 24 x 7 operation, every day with the Microsoft team until resolution, similar to Severity A issues. If you open the ticket with 24 x 7 expectation but are not available, Microsoft may at its discretion lower the issue to Severity C. If you choose business hours-only support when you submit a Severity B incident, Microsoft will contact you during business hours only. You must also ensure that Microsoft has accurate contact information and that you are available.
Severity C	**Minimum business impact** Customer is able to conduct business with minor disruptions or reduction of services.	Developer: < 8 hr Standard: < 8 hr ProDirect: < 4 hr Premier: < 4 hr Azure Rapid Response: < 4 hr Business hours access	Issues opened as Severity C indicate that the issue has a small impact on your business with the minor impediment of the service. For issues opened with Severity C, Microsoft will contact you during business hours only. You must also ensure that Microsoft has accurate contact information and that you are available.

Use the preceding matrix to help determine how to categorize the issues you are facing.

Summary

In this chapter, you learned about the Microsoft 365 SLA, including what it guarantees and what limitations have been put around it. Additionally, you learned how to monitor the various channels that Microsoft maintains for communicating service health: the Service Health Dashboard, the Service Status page, and the Microsoft 365 Service Status Twitter feed. Finally, you learned about opening and managing support requests from the Microsoft 365 admin center.

It is important to understand the support levels for release categories and the incident response matrix, both for the exam and for day-to-day operational requests.

In the next chapter, we'll cover the Microsoft 365 service life cycle.

Questions

Use the following questions to test your knowledge of this chapter. You can find the answers in *Assessment Answers*:

1. Which of these is *not* a way to view service status updates for Microsoft 365?
   1. Twitter
   2. Service Health Dashboard
   3. Security & Compliance Center
   4. Service Status page
2. The general SLA for Microsoft 365 availability is expressed as:
   1. 99%
   2. 99.9%
   3. 99.99%
   4. 99.999%

3. When opening a service ticket, which severity level is used to indicate a significant loss or degradation of services, requiring immediate attention?
    1. Severity A
    2. Severity B
    3. Severity C
    4. Severity 1
    5. Severity 2
    6. Severity 3

4. Which severity level indicates business hours-only support?
    1. Severity A
    2. Severity B
    3. Severity C
    4. Severity D

16

Service Life Cycle in Microsoft 365

Microsoft 365 is an evergreen product, meaning it's continuously under development and being updated. New features are constantly being developed, tested, and released. As such, Microsoft 365 a different life cycle than traditional software.

In a standard on-premises software life cycle, products typically go through pre-release stages where they're made available internally or to select customers for testing and then are eventually **Released To Manufacturing (RTM)**. After a product's release, it goes through a succession of product updates (typically, for 3 years) that can address features or security improvements. Each stage of a product's life cycle has defined support phases (standard support, extended support, and end-of-life), and each of these development and release milestones comes with different support terms.

With cloud products such as Microsoft 365, there are also several phases to the development process. Microsoft often seeks feedback from partners and customers on how well the features work during the stages prior to deployment.

In this chapter, we'll look at the release and support cycles, including the following:

- Release stages
- Support policies

Let's look at how the release stages of products and their support policies work together.

Release stages

In the Microsoft 365 and Azure clouds, Microsoft services generally go through three stages of availability:

- Private preview
- Public preview
- General availability

Let's look at each availability in more detail.

Private preview

Private preview is typically an invitation-only offering, though sometimes you can register to be part of a private preview. If you're an enterprise customer, you also may be nominated by your sales account team. Private previews are the very earliest stage of availability, where the capability and stability of a product may be fluid and undergoing a lot of change. Services that are in private preview should never be considered production-ready. If you are participating in a private preview, you may have the ability to give developer feedback directly. Products in private preview may not be fully compliant or suitable for users in highly regulated industries, such as the financial or public sectors. It is important to verify what controls and protections are in place to ensure that your use of a service in private preview doesn't introduce unnecessary risk to your organization.

Public preview

Public preview is typically open to any customer with valid qualifying subscriptions. Depending on the product, you may need to sign up for or accept certain licensing terms. For example, Office 365 Group-Based licensing was in public preview for several months before it was moved to the next stage (general availability). However, customers who had a valid Azure Active Directory Premium subscription were able to use the service immediately without signing up for additional services or features.

Products and services in public preview typically have some documentation, though it is not complete. Customers can frequently use products in public preview for little or no cost, and will then be offered a chance to purchase the service at standard pricing once the product is fully released.

Products in public preview may or may not have regulatory compliance capabilities, such as eDiscovery or litigation hold. It is important to verify what controls, capabilities, and protections are available to enable your organization to comply with any necessary regulations. While services in public preview typically work without major issues, like private previews they should not be considered production-ready.

Previews (both private and private) typically have their own terms of use and may be discontinued at any time without prior notification. Preview products, services, or features are not guaranteed to be brought forward into general availability. Previews are made available AS-IS and WITH ALL FAULTS, in line with the Microsoft's supplemental terms. Unless explicitly stated otherwise, this means preview products have no guarantees or warranties. Additionally, products in public or private preview may be subject to reduced or different security capabilities, compliance, or privacy commitments.

General availability

General availability (sometimes called *general release)* means a product has matured to the point where it can be released for all customers to purchase. Products in general availability can be considered production-ready. As with any new product, though, it's important to ensure the compliance and security controls available meet your organization's requirements.

Next, we'll look at how the stage of development and availability life cycle translates to support.

Support policies

Support policies govern how and when Microsoft will offer assistance for a particular product or service. From the support perspective, both public and private previews typically do not have to abide by the standard **Service Level Agreement (SLA)** terms for the service. Public and private previews may have their own limited SLAs, may have no SLA defined, or may explicitly inform you that there is no expectation of any particular responsiveness or availability. And, as stated earlier, previews can be ended or discontinued at any time with no or limited warning.

Unless the preview's specific terms and conditions stipulate differently, preview products are excluded from all SLAs and warranty claims, and the unavailability of products in preview will not constitute an SLA breach that would result in a service credit. An example set of preview terms is shown in the following screenshot:

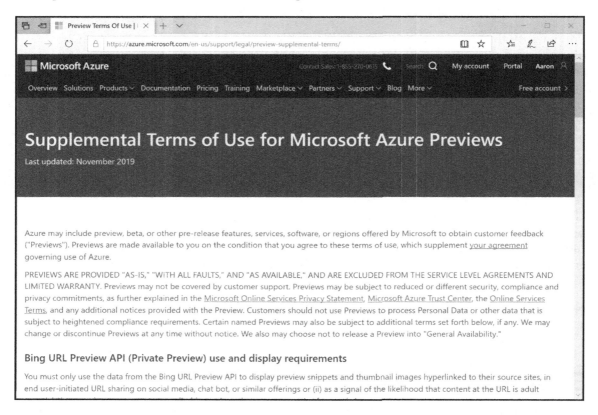

Products in general availability are fully supported in line with the product's individual SLA. Support for products in general availability can be obtained through support tickets via the Microsoft 365 support portal, Microsoft phone support, or through partners.

Summary

In this chapter, we covered the different development and release stages of Microsoft 365 products, including both private and public previews as well as general availability. Preview products are subject to change or cancelation and have no SLAs associated with them, whereas generally available products are fully supported for all customers with valid subscriptions.

This concludes the exam preparation guide for MS-900: Microsoft 365 Fundamentals. In the final chapter, you will find the answers to the end of chapter assessments scattered throughout the book.

Questions

Use the following questions to test your knowledge of this chapter. You can find the answers in *Assessment Answers*.

1. Identify the SLA that generally applies to preview services:
    1. No SLA unless otherwise specified
    2. Standard Microsoft Online Services Agreement for individual products
    3. Azure Services Agreement
    4. Supplemental Online Services Agreement

2. Identify the SLA that generally applies to products in general availability:
    1. No SLA unless otherwise specified
    2. Standard Microsoft Online Services Agreement for individual products
    3. Azure Services Agreement
    4. Supplemental Online Services Agreement

3. Which release stage of a product is generally invitation-only?
    1. Private preview
    2. Public preview
    3. General availability

4. At which release stage is a product fully documented and supported by a standard SLA?
    1. Private preview
    2. Public preview
    3. General availability

Assessment Answers

Here you'll find answers to the questions presented at the end of each of the chapters.

Chapter 1: Introduction to Cloud Computing

1. SaaS
2. Scalable; Current; Cost-effective
3. Desktop computer; Network cable
4. Microsoft 365 subscription; Storage maintenance fee
5. Capital Expenditure
6. Able to add or reduce service capacity on demand.
7. Redundant hardware; Multiple network paths; Data backups

Chapter 2: Cloud Deployment Models and Cloud Services

1. Private cloud; Hybrid cloud; Public cloud
2. Private cloud
3. Public cloud
4. IaaS; SaaS; Serverless
5. SaaS; PaaS; Serverless
6. Serverless computing
7. SaaS
8. IaaS
9. SaaS
10. Hybrid cloud
11. The cloud solution provider is responsible for managing applications and software updates.; The customer only pays for what they use.
12. Disaster recovery; High-performance compute clusters

Chapter 3: Core Microsoft 365 Components

1. Enterprise Mobility + Security; Windows 10 Enterprise Edition; Office 365
2. Windows Hello for Business
3. Email and calendaring tasks
4. Compliance center
5. Hybrid cloud
6. Compliance center
7. Compliance center
8. Compliance center
9. Team site; Communication site
10. False
11. True
12. False
13. Android; iOS; Windows; Mac
14. Azure Information Protection
15. Cloud app security broker
16. Multi-factor authentication

Chapter 4: Comparing Core Services in Microsoft 365

1. Cloud app security broker
2. Discover and manage the use of shadow IT; Assess compliance of cloud apps
3. Conditional Access
4. Access reviews
5. Co-management
6. Allows cross-premises calendaring and free/busy; Move mailboxes easily between on-premises and cloud
7. Migrating document library content
8. It doesn't replace any product
9. Exchange Online license; SharePoint Online license; Microsoft Teams license
10. Factory reset; Remote control

Chapter 5: Understanding the Concepts of Modern Management

1. Deployment ring
2. Windows Insiders; Semi-Annual Channel; Long-Term Servicing Channel
3. Global admin
4. Anything new such as improvements in a specific built-in application, visual refresh, or user experience
5. Monthly release that contains both security and non-security maintenance fixes
6. True
7. False
8. Purchase licenses
9. Access to data privacy messages in the Message center
10. Create and manage service requests

Chapter 6: Understanding Office 365 ProPlus

1. Semi-annual channel; Semi-annual channel (targeted)
2. Monthly channel (targeted)
3. The user does not have a subscription for Office 365 ProPlus; The Office 365 ProPlus activation service has been unable to connect to the internet for 30 days.
4. It is a subscription; It is per-user based.
5. It is a perpetual license; It is per-user or per-device based.
6. False
7. Click-to-Run
8. Office Customization Tool
9. https://config.office.com
10. Azure Identity; Office 365 ProPlus subscription license

Chapter 7: Understanding Collaboration and Mobility

1. A business approach enabling users to accomplish their jobs from anywhere.
2. Planner
3. Forms
4. Stream
5. False
6. True
7. Platform
8. Identity
9. Signing in to the productivity applications using their Office 365 identity.
10. Yammer

Chapter 8: Microsoft 365 Analytics

1. Microsoft 365 Activity Reports; Microsoft 365 Usage Analytics
2. MyAnalytics
3. Focus; Wellbeing; Network; Collaboration
4. Power BI; Power BI Desktop
5. Tenant ID
6. Microsoft 365 Admin Center
7. Anonymization

Chapter 9: Understanding Security and Compliance Concepts

1. Recommend security configurations for Microsoft 365 services; Provide configuration steps for security recommendations or links to configuration controls
2. Define application-based security policies; Wipe managed application profile
3. Azure portal
4. Security & Compliance Center

5. Office 365 groups; Security groups; Mail-enabled security groups; Distribution List Groups
6. Only cases that they created or are assigned to them
7. All cases
8. Identity; Data; Device; Apps
9. New and existing external users
10. They can be the same level of permissiveness as SharePoint sharing controls; They can be less permissive than SharePoint sharing controls.
11. Two-stage recycle bin; Preservation Hold Library; Versioning
12. The on-premises Active Directory password control settings are synchronized to Azure AD
13. Azure Information Protection
14. At rest; In transit
15. Password write-back
16. True
17. Audit Log Search

Chapter 10: Understanding Identity Protection and Management

1. Access Reviews
2. Active Directory Federation Services
3. Pass-through authentication; Active Directory Federation Services
4. Password hash synchronization; Cloud Identity
5. SMS or text message; Phone call; One-time passcode
6. Something a user knows; Something a user has; Something a user is

Chapter 11: Endpoint and Security Management

1. Azure Active Directory Premium P1
2. Azure Active Directory Premium P2
3. True
4. Office 365 Advanced Threat Protection Plan 2

5. Privileged Identity Management
6. Access Reviews
7. Azure Application Proxy
8. Identify "shadow IT"
9. Custom banned password list
10. Self-service password reset

Chapter 12: Service Trust Portal and Compliance Manager

1. Compliance Manager
2. Bitlocker; Internet Protocol Security (IPSec); Transport Layer Security (TLS)
3. Where is my data stored?
4. Separation of organizational data in a multi-tenant environment
5. At rest; In transit
6. True
7. General Data Protection Regulation
8. NIST 800-53; NIST CSF; GDPR

Chapter 13: Licensing Options Available in Microsoft 365

1. Microsoft 365 Business
2. False
3. Microsoft 365 Government Community Cloud
4. Microsoft 365 Commercial
5. Plan for a baseline; Define user profiles or personas; Define service and feature requirements
6. Productivity; Compliance
7. Security; Collaboration
8. Per-user
9. Public sector
10. IRS Publication 1075 Compliance; Criminal Justice Information Services Compliance; United States Data Residency

Chapter 14: Planning, Predicting, and Comparing Pricing

1. CSP; EA; Microsoft Open; Service Provider License Agreement
2. Improved security; Reduced TCO; Increased end-user productivity; Improved availability
3. Employee savings with new or improved mobility scenarios; Improved compliance capability; Travel savings; Reduced downtime
4. Pays Microsoft directly
5. Pays a partner or VAR directly

Chapter 15: Support Offerings for Microsoft 365 Services

1. Security & Compliance Center
2. 99.9%
3. Severity A
4. Severity C

Chapter 16: Service Lifecycle in Microsoft 365

1. No SLA unless otherwise specified
2. Standard Microsoft Online Services Agreement for individual product
3. Private preview
4. General availability

Other Books You May Enjoy

If you enjoyed this book, you may be interested in these other books by Packt:

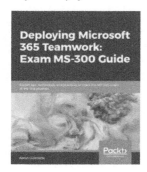

Deploying Microsoft 365 Teamwork: Exam MS-300 Guide
Aaron Guilmette

ISBN:978-1-83898-773-2

- Discover the different Microsoft services and features that make up Office 365
- Configure cloud services for your environment and extend your infrastructure's capabilities
- Understand site architecture, site settings, and hub settings in SharePoint Online
- Explore business connectivity services for view and access options in SharePoint Online
- Configure Yammer to integrate with Office 365 groups, SharePoint, and Teams
- Deploy SharePoint Online, OneDrive for Business, and Microsoft Teams successfully, including bots and connectors

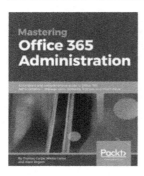

Mastering Office 365 Administration
Thomas Carpe, Nikkia Carter, Et al

ISBN: 978-1-78728-863-8

- Get an understanding of the vast Office 365 feature set
- Learn how workloads and applications interact and integrate with each other
- Connect PowerShell to various Office 365 services and perform tasks
- Learn to manage Skype for Business Online
- Get support and monitor Office 365 service health
- Manage and administer identities and groups efficiently

Leave a review - let other readers know what you think

Please share your thoughts on this book with others by leaving a review on the site that you bought it from. If you purchased the book from Amazon, please leave us an honest review on this book's Amazon page. This is vital so that other potential readers can see and use your unbiased opinion to make purchasing decisions, we can understand what our customers think about our products, and our authors can see your feedback on the title that they have worked with Packt to create. It will only take a few minutes of your time, but is valuable to other potential customers, our authors, and Packt. Thank you!

Index